WRITING

AND

MADNESS

WRITING AND MADNESS

(Literature/Philosophy/Psychoanalysis)

SHOSHANA FELMAN

TRANSLATED BY

MARTHA NOEL EVANS and the author

with the assistance of BRIAN MASSUMI

CORNELL UNIVERSITY PRESS

ITHACA, NEW YORK

The eight chapters in this book are the author's selection from the twelve chapters included in the original French edition, Shoshana Felman's *La folie et la chose littéraire*, © Editions du Seuil, 1978.

Essays 2 and 7 were first published in volumes 55 and 52 of *Yale French Studies* under the titles "Madness and Philosophy, or Literature's Reason" (© 1975 by *Yale French Studies*) and "Turning the Screw of Interpretation" (© 1977 by *Yale French Studies*).

Translation of essays 1, 3–6, and 8 copyright © 1985 by Cornell University

First published 1985 by Cornell University Press.
First published, Cornell Paperbacks, 1987.
Second printing 1989.

The publisher gratefully acknowledges the financial assistance of the French Ministry of Culture in defraying the cost of translation of essays 1, 3–6, and 8.

The paper in this book is acid-free and meets the guidelines for permanence and durability of the Committee on Production Guidelines for Book Longevity of the Council on Library Resources.

Library of Congress Cataloging in Publication Data

Felman, Shoshana.
  Writing and madness.

  Translation of: La folie et la chose littéraire. 1. Literature and mental illness. I. Title.
PN56.M45F413 1985   809'.93353   84-19845
ISBN 0-8014-1285-4 (alk. paper)
ISBN 0-8014-9394-3 (pbk. : alk. paper)

To the memory of my father
To my mother

CONTENTS

INTRODUCTION

1

Writing and Madness, or Why This Book?

> One of Blake's Proverbs states that *if others had not been mad,*
> *then we should be.* Madness cannot be thrust outside of
> human integrality which, without the madman, would not be
> complete. Nietzsche going mad—in our place—made this
> completeness possible: and those who lost their reason before
> him were not able to do it so spectacularly. But the gift a man
> makes of his madness to his fellow creatures, can it be
> accepted and then returned without interest? And if that
> interest is not the insanity of the one who receives the other's
> madness as a royal gift, what might its recompense be?
>
> Georges Bataille

I

Nietzsche going mad—in our place . . .

But what is *our place?* It can be neither in his madness nor out of
it: no more *inside* insanity than *outside* of it. For my part, I can
speak neither as mad nor as not mad.

"And if that interest is not the insanity of the one who receives
the other's madness as a royal gift, what might its recompense be?"
I have let the words of those who have made a gift of madness to us
in their writing come into this book: may they take my place,
think me. And let them reflect on this: "If others had not been
mad, then we should be."

Others *have* been mad. They have been mad, says Bataille, quite
spectacularly. This book, in dealing with them, hopes to reflect on

their place—in us. On their place, precisely where they have been mad *in our place.*

To construct the theory of that place: to assume, within the theory, this living relationship to a place which is not mine but which is in my place—such is my intent and desire in this book.

* * *

The significance of madness as a crucial question in the current cultural scene is well known. Not only has madness preoccupied many different disciplines but it has *caused them to converge*, thus *subverting their boundaries.* Sociology and philosophy, linguistics and literature, history and psychology, and of course psychoanalysis and psychiatry have all scrutinized madness and have themselves been put in question by this very scrutiny. While madness has today been recognized as one of the most subversive of all cultural questions, certain writers nonetheless deplore that it has been sensationalized to the point of banality.

> Psychiatric revolution. Psychoanalytic revolution. Anti-psychiatry. Madness or Unreason? The press has gotten into the fray, treating of it in endless debates. Writers of every stripe are meddling with it. One voice wants to "schizophrenize" society. Another calls for psychiatrists to be "punished and reconverted." Who "knows" and who doesn't "know"? Is it true that "psychiatrists and psychoanalysts are all dangerously insane"? . . . All this may be nothing more than the ironic and impatient reaction to a deluge of trite and worn-out commonplaces.[1]

The fact that madness has currently become a commonplace is, however, food for thought. And the fact that it has caused the verb "know" to be put in quotation marks is not the least of its consequences. In spite of its susceptibility to caricature, we begin to understand that if the issue of madness has been linked so insistently to the current upheaval in the status of knowledge, it is because madness poses in more than one way a question whose significance and meaning have not yet been fully assessed and whose self-evidence is no longer clear: not so much the question of

---

[1]M. Thuilleux, *Connaissance de la folie* (Paris: Presses Universitaires Françaises, 1973). Except where otherwise indicated, all translations of French quotations are by the general translators.

"who 'knows' and who doesn't 'know,' " but *What does it mean to "know"?*

＊　＊　＊

Admittedly, we are experiencing today an inflation in discourses on madness. In our wish to protect madness from the mystifying effects of the marketplace of fashion, we could deplore this phenomenon and take our distance from it. Or we could rejoice and join our voices to the general chorus, promoting our own "madness" goods as the latest thing in order to publicize our avant-gardism or, as Mallarmé would say, "proclaim ourselves to be our own contemporaries." Of course, "not all who would go mad, do go mad";[2] but the word "madness" is nonetheless available to all who wish to utter it.

Is it not paradoxical that in the midst of an era pervaded by discourses on madness, no one has yet addressed the question of the significance of this discursive inflation itself *for* madness—or for our time? Why this massive investment in the phenomenon of madness? While everyone today meddles with "madness," no one is asking: Why is everyone today meddling with madness? What does it mean to talk about madness? How can madness thus become a *commonplace?* As enticing and mystifying as this inflation in discourse may be, does it not in fact suggest that in the very solitude of madmen there is something at stake for all of us?

The fact that madness has currently become a *common* discursive *place* is not the least of its paradoxes. Madness usually occupies a position of *exclusion;* it is the *outside* of a culture. But madness that is a *common* place occupies a position of *inclusion* and becomes the *inside* of a culture.

It is perhaps precisely this which marks the specificity of "madness" in our time, as what can designate at once the outside and the inside: the inside, paradoxically, to the extent that it is supposed to "be" the outside. To say that madness has indeed become our commonplace is thus to say that madness in the contemporary world points to the radical ambiguity of the inside and the outside, insofar as this ambiguity escapes the speaking subjects (who speak only to have it escape them). A madness that has become a *common place* can no longer be thought of as a simple place (*topos*)

---

[2]As Jacques Lacan has ironically put it.

inside our era; it is rather our entire era that has become subsumed within the space of madness. No discourse about madness can now know whether it is inside or outside of the madness it discusses.

To be sure, as a commonplace, madness has ceased to seem strange to us. But isn't this very loss of the sense of the strangeness of madness precisely what is most strange, most *mad* in contemporary discourse?

*   *   *

What does it mean, then, to *talk about madness?* Since the publication of Michel Foucault's provocative *History of Madness,*[3] many French intellectuals have repeated Foucault's claim: madness is, primarily, a lack of language, an "absence of production," the silence of a stifled, repressed language. Accordingly, our historic task would be to give madness a voice, to restore its language: a language *of* madness and not *about* it. Now, our present cultural predicament, in Foucault's view, derives precisely from our incapacity to articulate this language: while intending to "say madness," one is necessarily constrained to speak *about* it.

These statements have been made over and over again, as if we had already understood what it means to talk *about* madness and all that remained for us to do was to comprehend the incomprehensible—to listen to the inaudible speech of madness, in itself.

This book, in contrast, does not seek to "say madness itself" but rather to ask the question: Do we really know what *talking about madness* means? Do we really understand the significance of writing *about* madness (as opposed to writing madness)? Since there is no metalanguage, could it not be that writing madness and writing *about* it, speaking madness and speaking *of* it, would eventually converge—somewhere where they least expect to meet? And might it not be at that meeting place that one could situate, precisely, *writing?*

*   *   *

However sensitive our contemporary cultural history has become to the significance of madness, I think we still have not

[3]Michel Foucault, *Folie et déraison: Histoire de la folie à l'âge classique* (Paris: Plon, 1961). (*Madness and Civilization: A History of Insanity in the Age of Reason.* Translated by Richard Howard, New York: Vintage Books [Random House], 1973.) (For a detailed discussion of Foucault's book, see next chapter.)

begun to appreciate the share that literature has had in producing that historical receptiveness. One hears altogether too often nowadays that literature is a thing of the past, that it is no longer "in" to talk about it. In a pinch, one can still speak of "texts" and "writing"—but not of "literature." Just as madmen were locked up and madness confined within the reductionist limits of the concept "mental illness," so literature is about to be confined within the reductionist limits of the concept of "belles lettres," that offspring of middle-class liberalism. There are those who claim that the demystification of this liberalism necessarily does away with the very notion of literature as well, as if it were not perfectly obvious that what we call the literary goes quite beyond the issues of bourgeois ideology, that literature not only surpasses, but in fact totally subverts the reductionist definition in which some have sought, and still seek, to imprison it. While it was through literature that madness became the order of the day, now it seems that literature itself has been dropped from the agenda. While madness has finally been recognized as a burning contemporary question, it is as though the question of literature has become anachronistic and irrelevant; it is spurned by all those who are exclusively interested in political passions and issues. Yet, a book like Foucault's reminds us that throughout our cultural history, the madness that has been socially, politically, and philosophically repressed has nonetheless made itself heard, has survived as a speaking *subject* only in and through literary texts.

The fascination madness presently exerts on contemporary theory thus rests on a paradox: while, on the one hand, it is said that the madness silenced by society has been given voice by literature, while experiences like those of Sade and Artaud are glorified (and literary texts are brought to witness—in their political and ethical capacity—before the tribunal of history), it is also commonly asserted, on the other hand, that literature itself is obsolete. The contemporary scene is thus structured by a contradiction: at the very moment some claim to be "liberating" madness—or, at the very least, to be undoing the cultural codes responsible for its repression—they are in fact denying and *repressing* literature, the sole channel by which madness has been able throughout history to speak in its own name, or at least with relative freedom. Now it is precisely its repression that makes of literature today a topical question whose stakes—like those of madness—are political.

This historical paradox of a confinement of literature concomitant with the freeing of madness, this contradiction prevailing in current ideology between its project of liberation and its policy of taboo, cannot be the result of pure coincidence. Might not literature's repression serve to counterbalance the contemporary project of liberating madness? Might not the present *non-recognition* of literature be the inevitable *counterpart* to the *recognition* of madness—and the fear it provokes? Indeed, the very ambiguity of the contemporary scene seems to me revelatory of some crucial truth, of which it is but a historical symptom: by virtue of their very historical opaqueness, madness and literature have been made partners throughout history, as objects of misapprehension and denial, as gravitational poles for the very energy of repression as it is activated within a shifting but ultimately irreducible field. Between literature and madness there exists an obscure but essential kinship: a kinship entailed, precisely, by *whatever blocks them off*, by that which destines them alike to repression and disavowal.

* * *

My intention is to explore this relation, to examine in what way literature and madness are informed *by* each other, in the process of informing us each *about* the other.

What is madness? My concern here will be less to find an answer than to undertake an analysis—and a problematization—of the question. What, indeed, are the cultural implications of the very act of raising madness as a question? When a text refers to "madness" "literarily" or "philosophically," rhetorically or theoretically—what is it actually doing? What does this maneuver mean? What is the economy, the strategy, the movement, the question involved in such a text?

Since madness and literature are precisely linked by what attempts to shut them out, the question "How does a text talk about madness?" is incomplete without the concomitant question: How, within the text itself, is madness *denied?* How does it confront what blocks it? I will therefore give particular attention to the modes and structures of *repression* within literary language so as to analyze the following: How does the denial that affects both literature and madness function? How does it function not only outside, but also inside, a text? What are the structures of misapprehension within the text? And how does the text misconstrue itself?

While studying madness through literature, and literature

through madness, I will strive to address the specificity of each text (its irreducible singularity), but also, at the same time, to examine the very status of the thing called literature. If, like madness, literature were constituted by a space of misapprehension and repression, would it be possible to say, or at least to suggest, what the object of this repression might be? Might not literature indeed be defined as that which speaks, precisely, out of what reduces it to silence? That which speaks by virtue of its own muffling? Could such a definition stand the test of practical criticism, of specific textual readings? This is what the following studies will examine.

If I thus propose to open up the literary field to the question posed by madness and its current implications for philosophy, psychoanalysis, sociology, and linguistics, I do so with the aim of rethinking, ultimately, the very specificity of the literary field as such. While using the information provided by these related disciplines, I will try to show how literature sheds light on madness in a specifically literary way, a way that is not merely a reflection of the theoretical pronouncements of psychoanalysis, sociology, or philosophy, but, while resembling those pronouncements, is also different from them: embodying a difference that, moreover, brings to light the way in which those theoretical pronouncements are, indeed, already different from themselves—tinged with a shade of the madness they examine. Reckoning with the historical awareness of the question posed by madness in contemporary culture, as well as with the theoretical renewal of this question, this book would like to constitute an opening toward a renewal of literary studies and to explore, by listening to the speech of madness in the literary text, new modes of reading and new modes of apprehending what is fundamentally at stake in the peculiar thing called literature.

II

To speak of madness—in what language?
The majority of the texts included in this volume were originally written in French (for French publications),[4] while others are writ-

[4]"Gérard de Nerval: Writing Living, or Madness as Autobiography," first appeared as "Aurélia ou le livre infaisable," *Romantisme*, no.3 (1972); "Honoré de Balzac: Madness, Ideology, and the Economy of Discourse" first appeared with the

ten in English (for an American public).[5] The authors studied in this book are, in turn, divided between two languages: French—Nerval, Balzac, Flaubert; and English—Henry James—who, incidentally, also happened to speak French, and who, traveling frequently between America and Europe, sought precisely to define the very tenor of his writing as a product of this travel back and forth, as the decision to speak *from* the vantage point of this shuttle experience so as to communicate its meaning, to convey its *undecidability:* "I aspire to write," he said, "in such a way that it would be impossible to an outsider to say whether I am at a given moment an American writing about England or an Englishman writing about America (dealing as I do with both countries)."[6] Borrowing James's words, I would say that I too aspire to write in such a way that it would be impossible to an outsider to say whether I am a French person writing about America or an American writing about France. (As it happens, I am neither French nor American.)

Whence the necessity for commuting between languages? Does this necessity have anything to do with madness? Or with literature? What is a foreign language? What is a native language? What constitutes a language, and what constitutes a grammar? In what language would it be possible to read the meaning of a grammar?

"There is often something radically strange in the language of others," writes an American critic.[7] But doesn't writing about madness involve, precisely, the necessity of encountering—in language—something radically strange? Taken by itself, each language is auto-familiar: it has its own concepts, its own system of thought which, within it, condition the thinkable. The way we think and speak arises out of decisions our language has already

---

title "Folie et discours chez Balzac: 'L'Illustre Gaudissart,'" *Littérature,* no. 11 (1973); "Gustave Flaubert: Living Writing, or Madness as Cliché" appeared as "Thématique et rhétorique, ou la folie du texte," *La Production du sens chez Flaubert; Actes du colloque de Cérisy,* 10/18 (Paris: U.G.E., 1975); "Jacques Lacan: Madness and the Risks of Theory (The Uses of Misprision)" first appeared in an abridged version as "La méprise et sa chance," *L'Arc,* no. 58 (1974).

[5] "Foucault/Derrida: The Madness of the Thinking/Speaking Subject" first appeared under the title "Madness and Philosophy, or Literature's Reason," *Yale French Studies,* no. 52 (1975); "Henry James: Madness and the Risks of Practice" appeared under the title "Turning the Screw of Interpretation," *Yale French Studies,* nos. 55/56 (1977).

[6] *Letters* to William James, 1898.

[7] G. Hartman, *Critical Inquiry,* 3, no. 2 (1976).

made for us: language discreetly dictates to its users—in an invisible manner—self-evident assumptions and proscriptions that are inscribed in its grammar (which is, by definition, imperceptible from inside the language). In order for grammar to appear as such, one must dislodge one's language from its self-presence, from its assumptions and proscriptions, by subjecting them to the otherness of a different grammar, by putting them in question through the medium of a foreign language.

The very essence of repression is defined by Freud as a "failure of translation," that is, precisely as the barrier which separates us from a foreign language. If madness and literature are both ruled by the very thing that represses them, by the very thing that censors them in language, if they both—each in its own way—proceed from a "failure of translation," the attempt to read them will necessitate a crossing of the border between languages. And while it is, no doubt, impossible—by passing from one language to another—to cancel out the "failure of translation," to suppress or lift the barrier of repression, it must be possible to displace that barrier, to *make it visible* in order to subject it to analysis. Wouldn't the attempt to "break out of metaphysics"[8] necessarily entail a break, first of all, with the *physics* of a mother tongue? "What constitutes meaning in the mother tongue of one's fatherland if not the private property of childhood speech?" writes Philippe Sollers. "A national, mother-tongue cannot be dreamt: it makes a subject dream in its own dream. *But the dreaming of one language may be the waking of another,* and when it is night in one zone, it may be day in another."[9] If the "failure of translation" between languages is in some sense radically irreducible, what is at stake in the passage from one language to another is less translation in itself than the translation *of oneself*—into the otherness of languages. To speak about madness is to speak about the difference between languages: to import into one language the strangeness of another; to unsettle the decisions language has prescribed to us so that, somewhere between languages, will emerge the freedom to speak.

* * *

[8]This formula, often repeated in the French intellectual scene, defines the stake of the contemporary European philosophical attempt: "to break out of metaphysics" is the philosophical injunction of Nietzsche, Heidegger, Derrida . . .

[9]"Joyce and Cie," *Tel Quel,* no. 64 (1975), 15.

If it were possible to know the place from which one speaks (and the place from which one is silent), I would say that this book speaks from a *plural* place and from a *dialogical* perspective constituted by an intellectual exchange between America and France, between French and English, between the Gallic and the Anglo-Saxon contexts. This exchange necessarily involves the confrontation of two different sets of cultural and ideological assumptions and of two different theoretical and literary fields.

While it is out of this confrontation that I write, this book does not, however, represent a synthesis of these two domains, nor is it a mere reflection of their peaceful coexistence: the cultural situation it implies in effect involves a *conflict* between codes; the confrontation of the different contexts is thus not a spectacle but a dynamic, an inter-*action* which displaces both domains and de-centers them with respect to each other. What is at stake is not simple exchange, but a movement of *ex-centering*.

To play out both the *encounter* and the *interval* between the French and the American cultural contexts, their ex-centricity with respect to each other, in order to elicit in the resultant interspace a movement of dialogical and differential meaning—such has been my way of experiencing, in yet another mode, the very question posed by madness.

*   *   *

The French theoretical context of this book is sufficiently marked out by the names of the theoreticians who are quoted or discussed—Lacan, Derrida, Foucault, etc.—as well as by the use of a certain critical and conceptual vocabulary. The reader must be careful, however, not to rush into a simple "recognition" of this double frame of reference—terminological and nominal—not to defuse these references by a label that would catalogue them in a code of familiar stereotypes. This book is written from a position ex-centric to those centered codes. From the outside, the *agonistic* scene of the French context can be read differently from the way in which, from the inside, it perceives itself. The texts referred to and the theoretical issues they raise burst the confines of the theater where they occupy center stage, where they themselves attend to the dramatic spectacle of the antagonisms that enmesh them. From a de-centered position, from a distance, or rather from the vantage point of a moving relation of changing distance and proximity, the lines of demarcation between self-proclaimed adversary theories seem much less decisive and discernible. Systems of thought are not necessarily opposed in the same way their authors are: it is always possible to have chosen the wrong adversary. To be sure, differences, sometimes radical ones, do exist: but these differences, being *asymmetrical,* often elude the simple structure of opposition. The references to French names in this book should not, therefore, be hastily interpreted as a simple index of theoretical codes—of *theoretical complicities.* These proper names are not meant to function, here, as banners; they do not mark the closure of positions staked out in advance or of preconceived answers, but the opening of questions whose answers are yet to come.

These French references, in other words, are here the marks not of a subscription to a code, but of a *relationship to a text*—to a number of crucial texts whose interpretation I by no means see as granted, whose implications remain to be discovered, formulated, and put to the test. When in the following studies I refer to these theoretical texts (Lacan, Derrida, Foucault) and to the debates in which they are involved, what I seek to read, explore, and analyze in them is not so much the dated stakes of their polemical vicissitudes, but rather the way these texts exceed the knowledge of their speaking (writing) subjects, the way the knowledge of the text eludes the scene the authors of the texts play for each other.[10] Linked as they are to well-known names, the theoretical issues represented by these names are here somewhat displaced.

The same is true of the terminology—the key concepts this book uses as pragmatic instruments of criticism. These terms are not used as identifying code words, but rather as theoretical *problems* whose consequences are still to be explored, whose possibilities are still to be articulated or put to the test by the singular challenge of a literary text. Each text studied will put into question the terminology and critical instruments used to approach it, giving them in the end a different, singular, and renewed meaning. As a result, it is not just the literary texts that will, in light of these theoretical problematics, be opened up to an entirely different reading; the critical terms and theoretical instruments themselves will be rediscovered and reinterpreted. In other words, the the-

---

[10]Cf. Chapter 6, "The Uses of Misprision," for further discussion of this point.

oretical tools will not function here as a new *meaning* to confer upon the text, but as a new way of *being affected* by the text. The critical terminology will thus enter in not as a new way of speaking, but as a new way of standing silent before the thing called literature.

*   *   *

As for the American context of this book, I would like, briefly, to explain its essential contours. They are summed up in the work of the people around me, a theoretical current which has been identified (so I have read in the American press) as "the Yale School." Significantly, this current has also been given (again in newspapers or journals) a number of disparate labels: "the new Franco-American School," "the Post-New-Critical Critics," "the Deconstructors," or "the Uncanny Critics." What, then, is this "Yale School," and what exactly is perceived to be "uncanny" about it?

Since I myself teach at Yale, I would first of all like to make it clear that the label created by the mass media actually refers to no homogeneous, unified current of thought. Though the *symptom* of the label is, no doubt, revealing in itself, like any of its kind (for example, the *Nouvelle critique* label in France), the label has been created only for polemical convenience. Nonetheless, for ease of exposition, I will partially, provisionally adopt it in an attempt to synthesize what there actually is in the work of my colleagues (despite the diversity of theoretical and pragmatic *answers*) in the way of a common set of *questions* or preoccupations. Since these questions have, in turn, left their mark on this book, they may clarify what lies behind it.

One could define the common focus of these questions as relating to the general—and central—problem of the place of rhetoric in a theory of literary language, or rather, of the place of literature in a theory of rhetoric, that is, of a general theory that would account, all at once, for *linguistic efficacy* (language as action) and for *linguistic intelligibility* (language as knowledge).

The dominant figure in the "Yale School" (and the one whose impact here is particularly felt), the originator and principal theoretician of this critical approach, is Paul de Man,[11] whose

---

[11]Cf. particularly his books, *Blindness and Insight: Essays in the Rhetoric of Contemporary Criticism* (New York: Oxford University Press, 1971) and *Allegories of Reading* (New Haven and London: Yale University Press, 1979).

thought, nourished by three cultural contexts (German, French, and Anglo-American), is based on four fields of research whose teachings on rhetoric it brings into resonance: philosophy, linguistics, logic, and literary theory. Thus, this approach to rhetoric, while marking a recent tendency in American criticism, has also arisen in a plural, non-centered context that is both international and interdisciplinary.

As part of the current revival of rhetorical research, the "Yale School" tendency goes hand in hand with the French "Neo-Rhetoric" movement. It differs from it, however, in its very conception of rhetoric, in the way in which it understands its own object of study. These differences are, perhaps, due to the fact that the French trend, an offspring of formalism and structural linguistics, aims for a *science* of literature, conceived above all as a brand of *semiology*, while the American tendency, on the other hand, links rhetoric and literary theory (which is not thought of as a science) in their relation to *logic* and *philosophy*.

In what way is this philosophy of rhetoric distinguished from a pure semiology of rhetoric? In a semiology of rhetoric, figures and tropes have the same status as linguistic signs; their properties are thus studied with an eye to establishing a kind of exhaustive descriptive inventory, a kind of *code* of figures and tropes. In the philosophy of rhetoric I am attempting to sketch out, however, what is studied, rather, is the *epistemological functioning* of rhetorical tropes and figures, *insofar as this functioning precisely differs from the epistemology of signs*—insofar as it participates in the *subversion* of the univocal model of the code and the semiological principle of consistency in the relation between sign and sense.

In de Man's terms, French semiologists employ rhetorical categories along with grammatical ones, and sometimes equate rhetorical transformations with syntagmatic transformations—as if the logic of rhetoric were *continuous* with that of grammar, as if the study of tropes and figures were a simple extension of the study of grammatical models. "One can ask," writes de Man, "whether this reduction of figures to grammar is legitimate. The existence of grammatical structures, within and beyond the unit of the sentence, in literary texts is understandable, and their description and classification are indispensable. The question remains if and how many figures of rhetoric can be included in such a taxonomy."[12] In contrast, American theorists such as Kenneth Burke and logicians such as Peirce emphasize the distinctiveness and heterogeneity of grammar and rhetoric. "In his definition of the sign," argues de Man, "Peirce insists, as is well known, on the necessary presence of a third element, called the interpretant, within any relationship that the sign entertains with its object. The sign is to be interpreted if we are to understand the idea it is to convey. . . . The interpretation of the sign is not, for Peirce, a meaning, but another sign: it is reading, not a decodage, and this reading has, in its turn, to be interpreted into another sign, and so on *ad infinitum*."[13] Peirce calls the laws of the infinite process by which "one sign gives birth to another" a *pure rhetoric*, as opposed to the two other branches of semiotics: "pure grammar," which studies the formal conditions signs must meet to incorporate a meaning, whatever it may be, and "pure logic," which studies the formal conditions of truth for signs.[14]

In contrast to the theories of the French semiologists, de Man's rhetorical theory thus operates within the tension, the discontinuity, between grammar and rhetoric. De Man replaces "pure grammar" (dependent, in his view, on the postulate of dyadic, non-problematical meaning) with theories of the performative based on the work of J. L. Austin, which distinguish "constative" language (descriptive, cognitive, and informative) from "performative" language (the enunciation of which completes a *speech act*, and thus is independent of the cognitive criterion of truth or falsehood). Its introduction into de Man's theory of rhetoric does not, however, leave the concept of the "performative" intact; the "performative" itself is, in some fundamental ways, modified, displaced, rethought, particularly in the light of the philosophy of Nietzsche. While Nietzsche's own move from a constative conception to a performative conception of language is, in de Man's view, irreversible, the differentiation between constative and performative language remains cognitively undecidable. Since the *speech act*, in its status as an act, puts in question language as simple *cognition*

---

[12]P. de Man, "Semiology and Rhetoric," *Diacritics*, no. 3 (1973), 28. (Reprinted in *Allegories of Reading* [New Haven: Yale University Press, 1979].)

[13]*Ibid.*, p. 29.

[14]C. S. Peirce, "Logic as Semiotic: The Theory of Signs," *Collected Papers*, vol. V (Cambridge: Harvard University Press, 1960).

(knowledge), the speech act in itself cannot *know what it is doing* any more than it can *know what it doesn't know.* "Every speech act," writes de Man, "produces an excess of cognition, but it can never hope to know or understand the process of its own production. . . . There is never enough knowledge to account adequately for the illusion of knowing."[15] If the Nietzschean critique of metaphysics is, according to de Man, structured as an *aporia* between constative language and performative language, it is because Nietzsche's supreme discovery may well be that of the *aporetic nature of rhetoric itself:* "the discovery of what is called 'rhetoric' is precisely the *gap* that becomes apparent in the pedagogical and philosophical history of the term. Considered as a persuasion, rhetoric is performative, but when considered as a system of tropes, it deconstructs its own performance. Rhetoric is a *text* in that it allows for two incompatible, mutually self-destructive points of view."[16] Rhetoric, in this conception, is thus nothing other than that very structure of aporia which, actively *crosses* every reading effort, systematically undoing understanding.

*   *   *

Developed in conjunction with the work of the "Yale School," this book articulates, however, and rethinks in its own way— through its encounter with specific texts—the conception of rhetoric underlying it. This conception is distinguished from the one predominant in France (the so-called "Neo-Rhetoric") by the following features, which define it:

1) It conceives of rhetoric as having a performative function that is not simply co-extensive with its cognitive function; rhetorical research, whether it wants to or not, necessarily participates in the action of the language it explores, and cannot be considered purely a constative or descriptive inquiry.

2) Consequently, figures are to be read as speech *acts,* that is, as *forces* rather than as forms. The study of rhetoric thus becomes less a kind of geometry than a kind of physics: it consists in the study of *movements* produced by the *interaction* of forces in language. The figure is not simply a *topos* (the identification of a

---

[15]P. de Man, "The Purloined Ribbon," *Glyph,* no. 1 (1977), 45. (Reprinted in *Allegories of Reading.*)

[16]P. de Man, "Action and Identity in Nietzsche," *Yale French Studies,* no. 52 (1975), 29. (Reprinted in *Allegories of Reading.*)

place), since the dynamic constantly displaces the topological, since the performative endlessly modifies the constative demarcations. Neither is it simply a *pathos* (the blind displacement of affective or psychic intensities), since the repetitive opacity of the movement of forces endlessly produces a cognitive excess. Nor is it simply a *logos* (the transparency of a meaning), since the cognitive excess produced by speech acts cannot know itself, and therefore has no meaning, and since the repetition of forces, which is inconsistent or non-totalizable, is not subsumed by any code. Neither the fixity of a *topos*, nor the opacity of a *pathos*, nor the transparency of a *logos:* the figure produces simultaneously a topos-effect, a pathos-effect, and a logos-effect, which reciprocally deconstruct one another, and between which the figure constitutes precisely the very movement of *inadequation,* and the very *work of difference.*

3) Rhetoric is not, therefore, a system of transformations governed by a *single generative model* (a system of deviations controlled by the consistency of a code), but rather the subversion of one logical model by another one entirely foreign to it; rhetoric has to do with the discontinuity, the *interference* between *two* codes, between *two* or more totally heterogeneous systems.

4) Such a theory of rhetoric cannot claim the status of a *science* of literature, because its own definition of rhetoric excludes the possibility of its being logically adequate to its object of study. For however rigorous and developed the (constative) study of figures might become, it could never enable one to *predict* their performative functioning. Because rhetorical study itself cannot help but participate in the rhetorical performance it explores, and can therefore never perfectly control the epistemological rigor of its own rhetoric, a perfect knowledge of rhetoric (albeit a scientific one) is theoretically inconceivable.

5) This conception of rhetoric avoids the symmetrical opposition, set up in the French polemic, between a "general rhetoric" and a "restricted rhetoric," since it functions simultaneously as a general rhetoric *and* as a restricted rhetoric, deriving *from* the aporetic structure—from the tension—between the two. Like "restricted rhetoric," it does not believe rhetoric can be subsumed under a single, unique figure, under a single figural mode that would function as the archetype of all of the others. It does recognize the necessity and usefulness of rhetorical treatises, the rele-

vance of the distinctions between different kinds of figure, between figures and tropes, metonymy and metaphor, literal and figural meaning. But it asserts that rhetoric takes these distinctions as its *point of departure* only to *depart* from them in the end, that rhetoric only constructs these classifications in order, in the final analysis, to displace or subvert them. To the extent that, as Peirce says, "conservatism" consists in the "fear of consequences," while "radicalism" is defined by "the desire to push consequences to their furthest limits,"[17] what we are dealing with here is a radical theorization: a *radicalization* of the theory of rhetoric. But if the logic of rhetoric is not simply one of construction, but one of deconstruction—specifically of *self-deconstruction*—then this radicality is not dependent on a choice made by the theorist: it is co-extensive with any use of language, *inherent* in the very functioning of rhetoric. Rhetorical constructions function, accomplish acts of language, in such a way that they end up unhinging the very epistemological foundations which they presuppose and postulate, and upon which they are built. It is in the nature of rhetorical performance to pull the rug out from under its own feet.

Rhetoric is thus neither simply general nor simply restricted. The system of tropes and figures is not a simple system of classifications, of distinctions and oppositions: it is also the *movement* that displaces the very *factors of stability* supporting the classification system. It is the system of substitution, shift, and perturbation of the foundations upon which that system rests.

6) This rhetorical theory looks specifically for the *uncanny moment in the theory:* it uses logic and the instruments of logic in the aim of finding the aporetic moment at which logic itself falters. It uses concepts in a paradoxical attempt to point out precisely what conceptualization cannot integrate, the residue of its own operation, its point of articulation with what it (necessarily) leaves out. And it is this uncanny moment—which the theory uncovers yet by which the theory itself is placed in check—it is this moment that subverts, in rigor, its own rigor, this vanishing point of understanding, which, in this rhetorical conception, is felt to be the most forceful, the most probing and most fundamental to the very nature of the *rhetorical act* as it generates the specificity of the thing called literature.

[17]C. S. Peirce, "The Scientific Attitude and Fallibilism," *Philosophical Writings of Peirce* (New York: Dover, 1955), p. 58.

III

In this book, the above conception will be *put to the test;* its possibilities will be investigated and its implications questioned. For this reason, I would now like, in summarizing briefly what is theoretically at play in the studies that will follow, to point out, specifically, the way in which each of them relates to this rhetorical problematic. If, *a priori,* the reader finds these comments obscure, he or she can consult them *a posteriori,* or read them concurrently with the respective texts they both summarize and clarify.

While the Contents organizes the different studies according to different *types of discourse* (philosophy, literature, psychoanalysis) in their relation to madness, the analysis I will presently outline elucidates the interrelations among the chapters from a different point of view (that of rhetoric). I thus hope to set forth yet another structure, and other possible trajectories of reading.

Chapter 5, "Honoré de Balzac: Madness, Ideology, and the Economy of Discourse," is a textual exploration, on the one hand, of the *rhetorical epistemology* of metonymy and metaphor, and, on the other hand, of the *rhetorical performance* of the shifting (the substitution and subversion) of its own epistemological foundations.

Chapter 3, "Gérard de Nerval: Writing Living, or Madness as Autobiography," reconsiders the historical notions of Realism and Romanticism, analyzing them as two different relations, and two ways of narrating the relation, between rhetoric and madness.

Chapter 4, "Gustave Flaubert: Writing Living, or Madness as Cliché," is an analysis of the methodological and theoretical implications of the radicalization of the concept of rhetoric. Through a concrete analysis of the way in which in Flaubert's *Memoirs of a Madman* the text's performance (its speech act, its rhetorical action) differs radically from its *meaning,* or its statement, this study will rethink the *figure as that through which the theme escapes,* that which causes the text's statement to misfire, subverting and alienating its meaning. The text as a whole is thus interpreted not in its literal sense, but as a figure of its own performance.

Chapter 2, "Foucault/Derrida: The Madness of the Thinking/Speaking Subject," explores, through the debate between Foucault and Derrida on the idea of madness and its relation to philosophy, the way in which the question of the status of literature remains *unthought,* though always in some way present, in both their thinkings. It is this dynamic, unthought element that structures the relationship between their theories, displacing both the *structure* and the *purport* of their opposition. Insofar as these two theories—however different from one another—can be rhetorically considered as *figures of each other,* they allow a figure of madness to emerge out of the very space between them: the figures of, precisely, an *a-topos*—the non-place, the inadequation and the incongruence of the very work of difference between the two systems of thought (and within their own rhetoric).

Chapter 6, "Jacque Lacan: Madness and the Risks of Theory (The Uses of Misprision)," articulates the theory of rhetoric with the teachings and issues of Lacanian psychoanalysis, as well as with the difficulties and contradictions inherent in it. For Lacan, rhetorical figures are homologous to the mechanisms of the unconscious, in other words, to the rhetoric of a *"Real"* that provokes its own misapprehension, and in which *logical time* can only mark "the moment of understanding precisely (by) the effect produced by the failure of understanding."[18] If psychoanalysis, like rhetoric, *uses logic* to look for the precise moment of *aporia,* of *the faltering of logic*—if it wrings logic in an attempt to link knowledge back to what it cannot assimilate—it is because psychoanalysis, like rhetoric, is not only a theoretical statement of radical misunderstanding, but also a theoretical performance of the uses of misprision. The uses of misprision are, on the one hand, the use of the error of transference (a rhetorical error *par excellece*) in the practice of the cure, and, on the other hand, the theoretical possibilities created by the use of rhetorical *aporia* in Lacan's writings. I maintain that Lacan's uniqueness (the uncanniness of the *wager* he lays in making psychoanalysis confront its own madness by pushing its logical consequences to their limits) resides as much in what he brings through rhetoric as in what he brings to theory—and in the openings forged by the interaction between the two. It is perhaps not by chance that *rhétorique,* as Michel Deguy has pointed out, is (in French) an anagram of *théorique:* in the Lacanian *performance* (something altogether different from the conceptual whole that is taken to be "Lacan's theory"), misprision produces its effects precisely by *anagrammatizing* the *theoretical* through the *rhetorical.*

[18]J. Lacan, *Scilicet,* no. 1 (Paris: Seuil, 1968), p. 25.

But psychoanalysis is itself trapped by rhetoric. Although Lacan—by the *way* he states more than by *what* he states—has *opened* psychoanalysis to the operations of literature and its non-totalizable, unmasterable splicing action between the articulated and the unarticulated, literature still functions as a *trap for psychoanalysis* when psychoanalysis tries to "explain" or master it, to catch the unconscious in the (literary) act. Chapter 7, "Henry James: Madness and the Risks of Practice (Turning the Screw of Interpretation)," brings to light what distinguishes a rhetorical reading from an analytic reading (in particular, from the kind that passes for a "Freudian reading" in the United States). Whenever it "explains" literature, particularly when it locates *madness* in literature, psychoanalysis is in danger of revealing nothing more than its own madness: the madness of the interpreter. Through a reading of Henry James's *The Turn of the Screw;* through a reading of the readings of that text (an analysis of the critical debate the book has given rise to); and on the basis of certain rhetorical and theoretical *consequences* of the *encounter* between Lacanian psychoanalysis, the theory of rhetoric elaborated by the "Yale School," and James's own remarkable rhetorical *performance,* this chapter sets forth a theory of the *reading effect* as a *transference effect.* It is a theory of reading centered on a rhetorical analysis and a theoretical examination of the occurrences of transference in both the text and its critical readings.

Charles Mauron, in his theory of "psycho-criticism," distinguishes literary analysis inspired by psychoanalysis from psychoanalysis proper by the absence, in the former, of the crucial element of transference. Transference, as a real-life drama in which the analyst and analysand actively participate, is traditionally thought of as inherent to psychoanalysis, as what constitutes the specificity of the analytic situation as distinct from the literary experience. I will maintain, however, that transference (rethought in a new way) actually does define, but in a different way, the specificity of the literary experience; that transference, of all the concepts of psychoanalysis that have relevance to literature and literary criticism, is at once the most important and suggestive, and, paradoxically, the least explored. I will hold (and attempt to demonstrate) that we enter the literary text only *through* transference: through the lure of rhetoric. I suggest, then, that in literature (but perhaps in psychoanalysis as well), the notion of transference must be rethought in terms of a theory of rhetoric. But at the same time rhetoric must itself be rethought, reinterpreted, in terms of the analytic conception of transference.

I will endeavor here to undertake this task and to articulate this question in the light of Henry James's *The Turn of the Screw*. The remarkable *power* of that text (borne out in the critical literature by the violence of the critical passions and quarrels it has provoked) can be explained only by the existence of a transferential structure: I will set out to study at once the incidence of rhetoric, the incidence of transference, and the incidence of rhetoric *as transference*, in the relationships among the characters and narrators, as well as in the relationships between the text and its readers.

What emerges from this study is a theory of the *reading effect* (and of the transference effect) as the *dynamic interpretant* of the text (*interpretant* in Peirce's sense: not a person, but an *effect*—of the signifier, or of meaning). This theory, in other words, demonstrates the *transference effect* as the interpretant of the dynamic *place* of the addressee—*the reader*—insofar as the reader is himself "sign of a sign," sign of the text. The theory of rhetoric thus finds itself transformed and renewed, opening onto a general theory of the reader and of reading: a theory of the reader as a participant in a living transferential drama, as an unconscious textual *actor* caught without knowing it in the lines of force of the text's "pure rhetoric,"of the *addressing power* of its signs, and of their reference to interpretants. Reading, in this way, is here rethought, reformulated as the blind *repetition*, the performative enactment of the *rhetoric* of the text (and not of its meaning).

* * *

In accordance with its own conceptions, the conception of this book is itself, of course, nothing other than a reading effect. As such, it is, in its turn, nothing other than a sign of the sign "madness," the dynamic interpretant and the semi-conscious performer of the rhetorical action of that sign.

This book is, then, itself an effect of the signifier "madness." It inquires not so much into the meaning of that signifier as into its power: it asks not what it *is* (or what it signifies), but what it *does*—what are the textual acts and speech events it activates and sets in motion.

If the analysis endeavored in this book in the end reflects the very madness of the interpreter, it is because somewhere, in some way—at the vanishing point of the uninterpretable toward which the effort of interpretation heads, but where it falls apart—the rhetoric of madness meets, and merges with, the very madness of rhetoric as such.

SHOSHANA FELMAN

New Haven, Connecticut

PART ONE

MADNESS AND

PHILOSOPHY

"Man" signifies "thinker":
There lies the madness.
                    Nietzsche

2

Foucault/Derrida: The Madness of the Thinking/Speaking Subject

—Madness/Philosophy/Literature
—The History of Madness
—The Philosophy of Madness
—The Madness of Philosophy
—Philosophy and Literature
—Literature and Madness
—Literature's Reason

Madness/Philosophy/Literature

> The belief in truth is precisely madness.
> (Nietzsche, *Das Philosophenbuch*)

"Blindness,"* says the entry of the *Encyclopédie* under the word "Folie," "blindness is the distinctive characteristic of madness":

To deviate from reason knowingly, in the grip of a violent passion, is to be weak; but to deviate from it confidently and with the firm conviction that one is following it, is to be what we call *mad*.[1]

---

*This chapter is not translated; it is the author's original English version.
[1]Author's translation. All passages quoted in this chapter have been translated by the author, either from the French original or from the French edition cited in the footnotes.

What characterizes madness is thus not simply blindness, but a blindness *blind to itself*, to the point of necessarily entailing an *illusion of reason*. But if this is the case, how can we know where reason stops and madness begins, since both involve the pursuit of some form of reason? If madness as such is defined as an *act of faith* in reason, no reasonable conviction can indeed be exempt from the suspicion of madness. Reason and madness are thereby inextricably linked; madness is essentially a phenomenon of thought, of thought which claims to denounce, in another's thought, the Other of thought: that which thought is not. Madness can only occur within a world in conflict, within a conflict of thoughts. The question of madness is nothing less than the question of thought itself: the question of madness, in other words, is that which turns the essence of thought, precisely, *into a question*. "The capacity for self-reflection is given to man alone," writes Hegel: "that is why he has, so to speak, the privilege of madness."[2] Nietzsche goes still further:

> There is one thing that will forever be impossible: to be reasonable!
> A bit of reason though, a grain of wisdom (. . .)—that leaven is mixed in with everything: for the love of madness wisdom is mixed with all things![3]

Whereas Hegel places madness inside thought, Nietzsche places thought inside madness. In Pascal's conception, these contradictory positions could amount to the same. "Men," says Pascal, "are so necessarily mad that not to be mad would only be another form of madness." Rousseau, it seems, would agree: "Nothing resembles me less than myself";

> I am subject to two principal dispositions which change quite regularly (. . .) and which I call my weekly souls, one finds me wisely mad and the other madly wise, but in such a way that madness wins out over wisdom in both cases . . .[4]

One could indeed go on reciting a whole series of aphoristic statements issued by philosophers on madness. A question could

[2]Hegel, "Philosophie de l'esprit," in *Encyclopédie* (Paris: Germer Baillère, 1867), p. 383.
[3]Nietzsche, *Ainsi parlait Zarathustra* (Paris: Le Livre de Poche, 1968), p. 193.
[4]J.-J. Rousseau, "Le Persifleur," in *Œuvres complètes*, t. I (Paris: Pléiade, 1959), p. 1110.

36

be raised: Are these pronouncements *philosophical,* or *literary?* Is their effect as aphorisms ascribable to a rhetorical device, or to the rigor of a concept? Do they belong in literature, or in philosophy? If madness so remarkably lends itself to aphoristic statements, to plays of language and effects of style, it could be said that, even in philosophy, its function is rhetorical or literary. But on the other hand, if one turns now to literature in order to examine the role of madness there (in Shakespeare's works, for instance), one realizes that the literary madman is most often a disguised philosopher: in literature, the role of madness, then, is eminently philosophical. This paradox of madness, of being literary in philosophy and philosophical in literature, could be significant. The notions of philosophy, of literature, of madness, seem to be inherently related. And madness, in some unexpected way, could thus elucidate the problematical relationship between philosophy and literature.

Previously confined almost exclusively to the domain of literature, or to the brevity of aphoristic thought, madness, in the modern world, has become a major philosophical preoccupation. It is doubtless no coincidence that in a figure such as Nietzsche, madness invades not only the philosophy, but also the philosopher himself. The impact of Nietzsche, as a figure in which poet, philosopher, and madman coincide, is crucial in the intensification of the interest in madness, as well as in the recently increased proximity between philosophy and literature. Nietzsche's madness stands before the modern world as both an invitation and a warning, as the danger on which the condition of its very possibility is built. To reflect on the significance of "Nietzsche's madness"[5] is thus to open up and to interrogate the entire history of Western culture. Nothing less, indeed, is undertaken by Michel Foucault's important study, *Folie et déraison. Histoire de la folie à l'âge classique.*[6]

---

[5]Cf. Heidegger, *Nietzsche* (Paris: Gallimard, 1971) and Georges Bataille, "Sur Nietzsche" and "La Folie de Nietzsche," in *Œuvres complètes,* t. I, III (Paris: Gallimard, 1973).

[6]The work has so far appeared in three French editions: Plon, Paris, 1961 (original edition); 10/18 (abridged edition), Paris, 1964; Gallimard, "Bibliothèque des histoires," Paris, 1972—a new unabridged edition from which, however, the original Preface has been eliminated, and to which two formerly unpublished Appendices have been added. Unless otherwise indicated, my references to Foucault's work are to the recent Gallimard edition, hereafter cited as *HF* in the text. (Quoted passages are my translation.) The English edition of Foucault's book, entitled *Madness and Civilization* (Vintage), is a translation of the abridged edition of 10/18.

The History of Madness

Ils ont enfermé Sade; ils ont enfermé Nietzsche; ils ont enfermé Baudelaire.

Breton, *Nadja*

It is not just the wisdom of the ages but also their madness that bursts out in us. It is dangerous to be an heir.

Nietzsche, *Thus Spoke Zarathustra*

Foucault's main object—and the challenge of his study—is to contend that anthropology, philosophy, psychology, psychiatry, are built upon a radical misunderstanding of the phenomenon of madness and a deliberate *misapprehension* of its language. The entire history of Western culture is revealed to be the story of Reason's progressive conquest and consequent repression of that which it calls madness. The turning point occurs, as Foucault sees it, in the Cartesian *Cogito:* in his first *Méditation,* Descartes expels madness from the confines of culture and robs it of its language, condemning it to silence. Descartes encounters the phenomenon, the possibility of madness, right at the beginning of his quest for truth, through his methodical pursuit of doubt. The doubt strikes first the senses as a foundation of knowledge. At this elementary stage of the method, the closest and most evident certainties communicated by the senses are not, however, submitted to doubt: to cast doubt on the obvious, one would indeed have to be mad. How, writes Descartes, can I doubt "that I am here, sitting beside the fire, in my dressing-gown, holding this paper in my hands, and other things of that sort?"

And how shall I deny that these hands and this body are mine? unless perhaps I were to compare myself to those lunatics whose brains are so disturbed and blurred by their black bilious vapors that they go around calling themselves kings, while they are very poor, and saying that they are clothed in gold and crimson, while they are completely naked, or imagining that they are jugs or have a body of glass. . . . But then, they are madmen, and I would hardly be less demented if I followed their example.

38

This, as Foucault sees it, is the decisive sentence: the statement of a break with madness, a gesture of exclusion which expels it from the very possibility of thought. Indeed, Descartes does not treat madness in the same way as he treats other illusions, dreams, or errors of the senses: in contrast to mistakes in sense perception and to dream illusions, madness is not even allowed to serve as an instrument of doubt; if even dreams, even perceptual errors contain some elements of truth, the same cannot be said of madness: "If its perils do not compromise the method nor the essence of truth, it is not because such and such a thing, even in the thought of a madman, cannot be false, but because *I who am thinking cannot be mad* (. . .) It is an impossibility of being mad inherent not in the object of thought, but in the subject who thinks (. . .) Dreams or illusions are overcome in the very structure of truth; but madness is excluded by the subject who doubts. Just as it will soon be excluded that he does not think, that he does not exist" (*HF*, p. 57). A man can still be mad; but thought cannot. Thought is, by definition, the accomplishment of reason, an exercise of sovereignty of a subject capable of truth. I think, therefore I am not mad; I am not mad, therefore I am. The being of philosophy is thenceforth located in non-madness, whereas madness is relegated to the status of non-being.

The Cartesian gesture is symptomatic of the oppressive order, of the monarchic and bourgeois regime which was at that time being organized in France. The philosophical decree of exclusion anticipates the political decree of the "great internment" (*le grand renfermement*), by which, one morning in Paris, 6000 people were taken—fools, madmen, loiterers, drunks, tramps, paupers, and profaners—to be confined: that is how, in 1657, the General Hospital was created. This General Hospital, however, was not a medical institution: it was "the third force of repression" (*HF*, p. 61), a semi-judiciary structure which, working alongside the law and the police, had the power to try, to convict, and to execute—outside of court. Internment is thus an invention of Classicism, an invention which assigns to madmen the status of outcasts which had, in the Middle Ages, been reserved to lepers. The medieval conception of madness as something cosmic, dramatic, and tragic loses, in the Classical age, its quasi-religious mystery: madness is now desacralized, and through its exclusion takes on a political, social, and ethical status.

In 1794 begins a new era: the enchained madmen of Bicêtre are liberated by Pinel; psychiatry is constituted, madness is released from its physical chains. But this liberation, in Foucault's eyes, masks a new form of confinement: madness is now reduced to the diminished status of "mental illness," to be caught in the positivistic net of erudite determinism. The binary, metaphysical structure of the Classical age: Being and Non-being, Error and Truth, is now replaced by a three-term anthropological structure: Man, his madness, and *his* truth. Madness sheds the negative foreignness by which, for the Classical mind, it eluded any objective grasp, so as to become an object among others, submitted to the process of knowledge and rational understanding. Science thereby takes up where the Cartesian *ratio* left off: in the very acquisition of its specificity, madness, according to Foucault, is still excluded, still a prisoner, bound now by the chains of its objectification, still forbidden the possibility of appearing in its own right, still prevented from speaking for itself, in a language of its own.[7]

The Philosophy of Madness

> Comment Dieu ne deviendrait-il pas malade à découvrir devant lui sa raisonnable impuissance à connaître la folie?
>
> Bataille, *La Folie de Nietzsche*

> Tâche doublement impossible.
>
> Foucault, *Histoire de la folie*

[7]A similar conception of the Western world's attitude toward madness is outlined in the works of the American psychiatrist Thomas Szasz. Cf., for instance, this sharp passage from *Ideology and Insanity* (Garden City, New York: Doubleday Anchor, 1969): "Modern psychiatric ideology is an adaptation—to a scientific age—of the traditional ideology of Christian Theology. Instead of being born into sin man is born into sickness. (. . .) And, as in his journey from the cradle to the grave man was formerly guided by the priest, so now he is guided by the physician. In short, whereas in the Age of Faith the ideology was Christian, the technology clerical, and the expert priestly; in the Age of Madness the ideology is medical, the technology clinical, and the expert psychiatric (. . .) Indeed, when the justificatory rhetoric with which the oppressor conceals and misinterprets his true aims and methods is most effective—as had been the case formerly with tyranny justified by theology, and is the case now with tyranny justified by therapy—the oppressor succeeds not only in subduing his victim but also in robbing him of a vocabulary for articulating his victimization, thus making him a captive deprived of all means of escape" (p. 5).

For historians whose task it is to narrate—and denounce—the way in which the history of culture has throughout excluded madness, the problem is how to avoid repeating, in their own historical accounts, the very gesture of excluding madness which is constitutive of history as such. In other words, the historian's problem is that of finding a language: a language other than that of reason, which masters and represses madness, and other than that of science, which transforms it into an object with which no dialogue can be engaged, *about* which monologues are vacantly expounded—without ever disclosing the experience and the voice of madness in itself and for itself. The aim, the challenge, the ambitious wager of Foucault's endeavor is thus to say madness itself, to open our ears to "all those words deprived of language"—forgotten words on whose omission the Western world is founded: "all those words deprived of language whose muffled rumbling, for an attentive ear, rises up from the depths of history, the obstinate murmur of a language which speaks by itself, uttered by no one and answered by no one, a language which stifles itself, sticks in the throat, collapses before having attained formulation and returns, without incident, to the silence from which it had never been freed. The charred root of meaning."[8]

> The language of psychiatry, which is a monologue of reason *about* madness, could only be founded on such a silence. I did not want to write the history of that language, but rather the archeology of that silence.
> . . . The object, that is, is to write not a history of knowledge, but the rudimentary movements of an experience. A history, not of psychiatry, but of madness itself, before it has been captured by knowledge.[9]

In a sense, the study of Foucault involves, but at the same time puts in question, the very nature of discursive thought and philosophical inquiry. The fundamental question which, though not enunciated, is implicitly at stake, is: What does understanding mean? What is comprehension? If to comprehend is, on the one hand, to grasp, to apprehend an object, to objectify, Foucault's implicit question is: how can we comprehend *without* objectifying, without *excluding?* But if to comprehend is, on the other hand

[8]*Histoire de la folie*, Preface of the original edition (Plon, 1961).
[9]*Ibid.*

(taken in its metaphorical and spatial sense), to enclose in oneself, to embrace, to *include,* i.e., to contain within certain limits, the question then becomes: how can we comprehend *without* enclosing in ourselves, without *confining?* How can we understand the Subject, without transforming him (or her) into an object? Can the Subject comprehend itself? Is the Subject *thinkable,* as such? To put the question differently: is the *Other* thinkable? Is it possible to think the Other, not as an object, but as a subject, a subject who would not, however, amount to the same?

For the historian and the philosopher of madness the problem then is how, while analyzing History's essential structure of muffling madness, to give it voice, restore to madness both its language and its right to speak; how to say madness itself, both as Other and as Subject; how to speak from the place of the Other, while avoiding the philosophical trap of dialectic *Aufhebung,* which shrewdly reduces the Other into a symmetrical same; while rejecting all discourses *about* madness, how to pronounce the discourse *of* madness. Is such a discourse possible? Precisely how can one *formulate* a "language which sticks in the throat, collapsing before having attained any formulation"? How can one *utter* a "language that speaks by itself, uttered by no one and answered by no one"? How can madness as such break through the universe of discourse?

It can now be seen that what is at stake, in Foucault's historical study, is in fact the philosophical search for a *new status of discourse,* a discourse which would undo both exclusion and inclusion, which would obliterate the line of demarcation and the opposition between Subject and Object, Inside and Outside, Reason and Madness. To enounce Difference as language and language as Difference; to say inside language the outside of language; to speak, in a philosophical way, from within what is outside philosophy; this is what Foucault conceives of as a *problem of elocution,* in which he sees the major difficulty of his enterprise: the elocutionary difficulty of what he calls a "relativity without recourse," of a language deprived of the foundation of any absolute truth.

. . . it was necessary to maintain a kind of relativity without recourse (. . .)

An ungrounded language was thus required: a language which played the game, but which authorized exchanges. It was essential at all costs to preserve the *relative,* and to be *absolutely* understood.

There, hidden and expressed in a simple problem of elocution, lay the major difficulty of the enterprise.[10]

This "simple problem of elocution" becomes at times for Foucault an impossibility inherent in the very terms of his project.

> *But the task is no doubt doubly impossible:* since it would have us reconstitute the dust of actual suffering, of senseless words anchored by nothing in time; and especially since that suffering and those words can only exist and be offered to themselves and to others in an act of division which already denounces and masters them (. . .) The perception which seeks to seize them in their natural state belongs necessarily to a world which has already captured them. The freedom of madness can only be heard from the top of the fortress which holds it prisoner.[11]

The Madness of Philosophy

> Ce qui m'oblige d'écrire, j'imagine, est la crainte de devenir fou.
> Bataille, *Sur Nietzsche*

> Though this be madness, yet there is method in't.
> Shakespeare, *Hamlet*

That any *translation* of madness is already a form of its repression, a form of violence against it, that the praise of folly can only be made in the language of reason, this fundamental insight is in turn developed by Jacques Derrida in his critique of Foucault.[12] Not only, remarks Derrida, does madness remain necessarily confined in the fortress which holds it prisoner, but Foucault's own enterprise is itself imprisoned by the conceptual economy it claims to denounce:

> Can an archeology, even of silence, be anything but a form of logic, that is, an organized language, (. . .) an order (. . .)? Would not the

[10]*Ibid.*
[11]*Ibid.*
[12]Jacques Derrida, "Cogito et histoire de la folie," in *L'Ecriture et la différence* (Paris: Le Seuil, 1967). Hereafter cited as *ED* in the text.

archeology of silence end up being the most effective, the most subtle renewal, the *repetition* (. . .) of all that has been perpetrated against madness, in the very act of denouncing it?

It is perhaps not enough to do without the conceptual tools of psychiatry in order to disculpate our own language. The whole of European language (. . .) has participated (. . .) in the adventure of Occidental reason. *Nothing* in that language and *no one* among those who speak it can escape the historical guilt which Foucault seems to want to put on trial. But this is perhaps an impossible trial, since the hearing and the verdict are an endless reiteration of the crime by the simple act of their elocution. (*ED*, pp. 57–58)

Foucault, of course, was fully aware of the impossibility of his task. Derrida however would like to go beyond that awareness, by reflecting on the significance of the impossibility itself. How can the very *possibility* of Foucault's book be situated with respect to its impossible aim? For Derrida, the relationship of mutual exclusion between language and madness, exclusion which Foucault's own discourse cannot avoid perpetuating, is not *historical*, but *economical*, essential to the economy of language as such: the very status of language is that of a break with madness, of a protective strategy, of a difference by which madness is deferred, put off. With respect to "madness itself," language is always *somewhere else.* The difficulty of Foucault's task is thus not contingent, but fundamental. Far from being a historical accident, the exclusion of madness is the general condition and the constitutive foundation of the very enterprise of speech.

Sentences are normal by nature. They are impregnated with normality, that is, with meaning. (. . .) They contain normality and meaning, no matter what the state of health or madness of their utterer may be (. . .)

So that . . . any philosopher or any speaking subject (and the philosopher is merely the epitome of the speaking subject) who is trying to evoke madness *inside* of thought (. . .) can only do so in the dimension of *possibility* and in the language of fiction or in the fiction of language. In doing so, his own language reassures him against the threat of actual madness. (*ED*, pp. 84–85)

But this is not a failing or a search for security belonging to any one particular historical language (. . .), it is inherent in the essence and intent of all language in general. (*ED*, p. 84)

Descartes's exclusion of madness proceeds then not from the *Cogito* but from his very intention to *speak*. Derrida in fact proposes a somewhat different interpretation of the first *Méditation:* in *his* reading, the disqualification of delirium is quoted in the text ironically, as the objection of the non-philosopher, which is temporarily accepted by Descartes, only to be surpassed by the hypothesis of universal sleep and constant dream. Far from excluding madness, Descartes fully accepts it in assuming, at a later stage, the possibility of absolute delusion through the hyperbole of the *malin génie*, a demon who distorts and twists not only sense perceptions but intelligible truth itself. Whereby Descartes's proceeding does not imply, as Foucault would have it, "I who am thinking cannot be mad," but rather: "Whether or not I am mad, *cogito, sum*" (*ED*, p. 86); "even if the whole of what I am thinking is tainted with falsehood or madness (. . .) I think, I am *while* I am thinking" (*ED*, p. 87). By straining toward the undetermined, toward the sense of nonsense, the Cartesian Cogito is itself a "crazy project" (*ED*, p. 87) strangely similar to Foucault's (impossible) undertaking. Of course, the discourse of Descartes insures itself through its own language, through the production of a "work," against the kind of "madness" from which it springs; as does the discourse of Foucault. In this sense indeed Foucault's book, itself "a powerful gesture of protection and confinement," is nothing less than "a Cartesian gesture for the twentieth century" (*ED*, p. 85). And the History of Madness would thus peculiarly resemble the History of Philosophy.

> To define philosophy as wanting-to-say-hyperbole is to admit—and philosophy is perhaps that gigantic admission—that within the pronouncements of history, in which philosophy recovers its equanimity and excludes madness, philosophy betrays itself (. . .); it breaks down, forgets itself and enters into a phase of crisis which is essential to its movement. I can only philosophize in *terror*, but in the *avowed* terror, of going mad. The avowal is there, present as both an unveiling and a forgetting, a protection and an exposition: an economy. (*ED*, p. 96)

By thus reformulating Foucault's thought, but with a change of emphasis and with a different punctuation, Derrida elaborates a textual chiasmus, which he does not articulate as such but which sums up the scheme of his argumentation: any Philosophy of Madness can only bear witness to the Reason of Philosophy; philosophical reason itself, however, is but the *economy* of its own madness. The impossible *philosophy of madness* becomes, in Derrida's reading, the inverted and irrefutable sign of the constitutive *madness of philosophy.*

Philosophy and Literature

> Language is a sweet madness. While speaking man dances over all things.
>
> Nietzsche, *Thus Spoke Zarathustra*

In this theoretical confrontation between Derrida and Foucault, the problem, of course, is not that of deciding which way of reasoning is "correct." The question "whose reasoning does justice to madness" is in any case an absurd question, a contradiction in terms. It is clear, at the same time, that the thoughts on both sides, although no doubt governed by different desires, in fact enrich, reinforce, and illuminate each other. I do not intend, for that reason, to side with one or the other of the two respective positions, but rather to seek to examine what is the *issue* of the debate, what is *at stake* in the argumentation.

Even while attesting to the madness of philosophy, Derrida then judges contradictory and logically impossible any philosophy of madness (of "madness in itself"), since the phenomenon of madness, being in its essence *silence,* cannot be rendered, *said* through logos. This impossibility is twice enounced by Derrida, articulated in two different contexts, which I would here like to juxtapose:

1) Speaking of Descartes;

> So that, to come back to Descartes, any philosopher or any speaking subject (and the philosopher is merely the epitome of the *speaking subject*), who is trying to evoke madness *inside of* thought (and not just in the body or in some extrinsic form), can only do so in the dimension of *possibility* and in the language of fiction or in the fiction of language. (*ED*, p. 84)

46

2) Speaking of Foucault;

> What I mean is that the silence of madness is not *said*, cannot be said
> in the logos of this book, but is indirectly made present, meta-
> phorically, if I may say so, in the *pathos*—I take the word in its best
> sense—of this book. (*ED*, p. 60)

In both cases, madness escapes philosophy (philosophy in the strict
sense of the word), but in both cases madness by no means disappears, it takes refuge in something else: in the first case, it is the
principle of *fiction*, "the language of fiction or the fiction of language," which harbors madness; in the second case, it is the *pathos*
of its *metaphoric* evocation. Metaphor, pathos, fiction: without
being named, it is *literature* which surreptitiously has entered the
debate. The discussion about madness and its relation to philosophy has thus indirectly led us to the significant question of literature; and the way in which madness displaces, blocks, and opens
up questions seems to point to the particular nature of the relationship between literature and philosophy.

In Derrida's discourse, an opposition, then, is sketched out between *logos* and *pathos*. The silence of madness, he writes, is not
said in the *logos* of the book but *rendered present* by its *pathos*, in a
metaphorical manner, in the same way that madness, *inside of
thought*, can only be evoked through *fiction*. What then is the
meaning of this opposition between *logos* and *pathos?* Does it
amount to the opposition between metaphor and literal meaning, or
between figure and concept? How does the pathos of figurative
language relate to the *silence* of madness? In what way can silence
be conveyed by literature? Why is it to literature that the task of
"saying madness" is entrusted? What kind of relationship intercon-
nects madness with "the language of fiction"? In what way can
madness "inside of thought" be evoked by "the fiction of language"? What is, precisely, the status of fiction "inside of thought"?
In what way does literature attest to the intercourse between
thought and madness? In what way, "in the language of fiction or in
the fiction of language," and to what extent can thought maintain
itself in Difference? Can thought maintain itself as thought within
the difference that pertains to madness?—All these questions assail
the debate: questions Derrida does not ask, but that are suggested by

47

his objections, in his response to Foucault; questions that Foucault does not raise, but that nevertheless underlie his book.

Literature and Madness

> Dans la folie (. . .) il nous faut reconnaître (. . .) un discours où le sujet, peut-on dire, est parlé plutôt qu'il ne parle.
>
> Jacques Lacan, *Ecrits*

On the idea that literature, fiction, is the only possible meeting-place between madness and philosophy, between delirium and thought, Foucault would doubtless agree with Derrida. It is in fact to *literature* that Foucault turns in his search for the authentic voice of madness—to the *texts* of Sade, Artaud, Nerval or Hölderlin. The essential connection between madness and literature in Foucault's study presents itself from two different perspectives: 1) *in a metonymic manner,* by the constant reference to the theme of madness *inside* literature; 2) *in a metaphoric manner,* as Derrida suggests, by the "literarity" of Foucault's book itself, its pathos: the intensity and the emotion that pervade its style. It thus seems that literature is there to *re-place* madness: metaphorically (substitutively) and metonymically (contiguously).

Derrida and Foucault thereby agree on the existence of a literary buffer zone between madness and thought. This literary zone does not, however, play for each the same role, in relation to philosophy. For Foucault, literature gives evidence *against* philosophy; this is not the case for Derrida. For Foucault, the fictions of madness undermine, *disorient* thought. For Derrida, on the contrary, at least in the case of Descartes, the fiction of madness has as its end to *orient* philosophy. As we have seen, Descartes, attempting to "evoke madness *inside of* thought (and not just in the body or in some extrinsic form), can only do so in the dimension (. . .) of fiction,″ by inventing a *malin génie,* a mysterious demon who may perhaps deceive us in all things, imbue with errors and illusions not only the perception of the senses but also the truths of mathematics, distorting intelligibility itself. Through this fiction of the *malin génie* Descartes, in Derrida's account, assumes the hypothetic possibility of his own madness, but continues nonetheless to *think,* to *speak,* to live. Fiction being thus the means by which the philosophic subject takes on madness—in order to protect himself against it, to exclude it (or to put it off) in the act of speaking—literature for Derrida, or rather intra-philosophic fiction, itself becomes a metaphor of the madness of philosophy.

Foucault maintains a different view, and contests in turn Derrida's account of Descartes. For Foucault indeed, the fiction of the *malin génie* is "anything but madness":

> All is, perhaps, illusion, but with no credulity. The *malin génie* is doubtless much more deceitful than an obstructed mind; he can conjure up all the illusory trappings of madness; he is anything but madness. One could even say that he is just the opposite: since madness makes me *believe* that my nudity and my misery are robed in illusory crimson, whereas the hypothesis of the *malin génie* enables me *not to believe* that these hands and this body exist. As far as the extent of the delusion is concerned, the *malin génie* indeed is not less powerful than madness; but as for the position of the subject with respect to the delusion, *malin génie* and madness are rigorously opposed. (. . .)
>
> The difference is clear: when confronted with the shrewd deceiver, the meditating mind behaves, not like a madman panic-stricken in the face of universal error, but like an equally shrewd adversary always on the alert, constantly reasonable, and never ceasing to be the master of his fiction.[13]

The philosopher ends up getting his bearings, *orienting himself* in his fiction: he only enters it in order to abandon it. The madman, on the other hand, is engulfed by his own fiction. As opposed to the subject of logos, the subject of pathos is a subject whose position with respect to fiction (even when he is the author) is not one of mastery, of control, of sovereign affirmation of meaning, but of *vertige,* of *loss of meaning.* It could then be said that madness (as well as pathos and, perhaps, literature itself) is *the non-mastery of its own fiction;* it is a blindness to meaning. In contrast, the discourse of philosophy (for example, in the figure of Descartes) is precisely distinguished by its control, its position of mastery, of domination with respect to its own fiction.

By thus acknowledging that the relationship between philosophy and madness cannot be separated from literature's essential

---

[13]*Histoire de la folie* (Paris: Gallimard, 1972), Appendix II: "Mon corps, ce papier, ce feu," p. 601. Foucault's italics.

questions, that the communication between thought and madness cannot be direct, but necessarily must pass through fiction, the focus of the debate has shifted, the accent falling now on the specific nature of the relationship between madness and fiction, and on the *status of fiction* in relation to philosophy. The question here emerges: if "the language of fiction," in Derrida's terms, is thus distinguished from the language of philosophy *per se*, determined therefore as its Other, as its *outside*, how can it at the same time be "confined," enclosed *within* philosophy? Is the literature *within* philosophy inside or out? To state, as does Foucault, that the mad subject cannot situate himself within his fiction; that, *inside* literature, he knows no longer *where* he is, is to imply indeed that fiction may not exactly be located *"inside of* thought," that literature cannot be properly enclosed *within* philosophy, that fiction, in other words, is not simply *present* in philosophy, present, that is, to itself and at the same time present *to* philosophy: that the fiction is not always where we think, or where it thinks it is; that if, excluded from philosophy, madness is indeed to some extent *contained* in literature, it by no means constitutes its *content*. All this can be summed up by saying that the role of fiction in philosophy is comparable to that of madness inside literature; and that the status, both of fiction in philosophy and of madness inside literature, is not *thematic*. Literature and madness by no means reside in theme, in the content of a statement. In the play of forces underlying the relationship between philosophy and fiction, literature and madness, the crucial problem is that of the subject's *place*, of his *position* with respect to the delusion. And the position of the subject is not defined by *what* he says, nor by what he talks *about*, but by the place—unknown to him—*from which* he speaks.

Literature's Reason

> We work in the dark—we do what we can—we give what we have. (. . .) The rest is the madness of art.
> Henry James, *The Middle Years*

The question now is to examine whether, with respect to the delusion, the position of the subject and the content of his statement can coincide, whether the subject and the theme of madness can become present to each other, establish a synonymous, symmetrical relationship. Literature could very simply serve as a transparent intermediary between madness and philosophy, it could indeed succeed in *saying* madness *inside* of philosophy, if it could have with madness on the one hand and with philosophy on the other, a pure relationship of symmetry and of homologous equivalence. But for Foucault the History of Madness is, on the contrary, the story of a radical *dissymmetry:* of something which occurs, precisely, in the gap, in the discrepancy between the history of philosophy and that of literature. Foucault's own discourse tries to situate itself within this very gap that history has opened up between philosophy and literature, logos and pathos. In relation to philosophy, literature is, for Foucault, in a position of excess, since it includes that which philosophy excludes by definition: madness. Madness thus becomes an overflow, that which remains of literature after philosophy has been subtracted from it. The History of Madness is the story of this surplus, the story of a literary residue.

In the beginning of the Classical period, it is true, literature itself is silent: "Classical madness belonged to the realm of silence (. . .): there is no literature of madness in the Classical period" (*HF*, p. 535). Descartes's decree succeeded then in silencing—along with madness—a certain type of literature as well. This is not the last on Foucault's list of grievances against Descartes: "Descartes, in the very movement of proceeding toward truth, *renders impossible the lyricism* of unreason" (*HF*, p. 535; my italics). Madness, however, starts to reappear in the domain of literary language with Diderot's *Neveu de Rameau,* and continues to gain strength and ground in Romanticism. As a "lyrical explosion" (*HF*, p. 537), insanity, in nineteenth-century literature, is given as a "theme for recognition" (*HF*, p. 538), a theme in which the reader is called upon to recognize himself; but philosophical cognition still continues to exclude this literary recognition: "embraced by lyrical experience, this recognition is still rejected by philosophical reflection" (*HF*, p. 538). If Foucault denounces, then, "the modern world's effort to speak of madness only in the serene, objective terms of mental illness and *to obliterate its pathos*" (*HF*, p. 182; my italics), what he most decries, indeed, is this *obliteration of the pathetic resonance,* this suppression, by philosophy and science, of the literary overflow. The History of Madness, for Foucault, is nothing but the story of this obliteration: "Madness, *the lyric glow of illness,* is ceaselessly snuffed out."[14]

This is a crucial point. Madness, for Foucault, is nothing but that which the history of madness has *made possible precisely by suppressing it:* the "lyric glow of illness." Madness, which is *not* simply mental illness, *not* an object, is nothing other than the excess of its pathos, a "lyrical explosion" (*HF,* p. 537), a "torn presence"; it is precisely this capacity for suffering, for emotion, for *vertige,* for *literary* fascination. Madness, in other words, is for Foucault pathos itself, a *metaphor of pathos,* of the unthought residue of thought. And if, as Derrida asserts, madness can only be made present "metaphorically," through the very pathos of Foucault's book—then the pathos of the book is a metaphor of pathos. Pathos thus turns out to be a metaphor of itself, caught in the movement of its own metaphoric repetition. Madness, in other words, is for Foucault (like pathos) a notion which does not *elucidate* what it connotes, but rather, *participates* in it: the term madness is itself pathos,[15] not logos; literature, and not philosophy. And if pathos can refer us only to itself, is its own metaphor, then madness, in Foucault's book, like literature itself, becomes a metaphor whose referent is a metaphor: *the figure of a figure.*

How is this possible? Foucault's reference to Nietzsche can perhaps enlighten us:

> The study which follows would be but the first (. . .) in that long inquiry, which, under the sun of the great Nietzschean search, would try to confront the dialectics of history with the immobile structures of tragedy.
>
> (. . .) At the center of these borderline-experiences of the Western world bursts out (. . .) that of tragedy itself,—Nietzsche having shown that the tragic structure from which the history of the Western world proceeds is nothing other than the refusal, the forgetting, and the silent fall of tragedy through history.[16]

[14]*Ibid.,* Appendice I: "La Folie, l'absence d'œuvre," p. 582. My italics.

[15]It should be noted that the French word "folie" is both more inclusive and more common than the English word "madness": "folie" covers a vast range of meaning going from slight eccentricity to clinical insanity, including thus the connotations both of "madness" and of "folly," and in addition, appearing as an indication of excess, almost in the role of a superlative, in clichés such as "amoureux fou," "aimer à la folie," etc. It is perhaps not insignificant as well that "folie" in French is feminine: its grammatical gender confers upon it a kind of elusive femininity which is lost, along with its varied connotations, in an English translation.

[16]Preface of the original edition (Plon, 1961).

The tragic structure of history proceeds from the obliteration of tragedy by history. The pathetic resonance of madness proceeds from history's obliteration of the pathetic resonance of madness. Madness as pathos is, in other words, the metaphor of the erasing of a metaphor; the history of madness is the story of the metaphor of history's forgetting of a metaphor.

Placing Foucault's failure (not the failure of his enterprise but that of his declared ambition to say "madness itself") in his necessary and unavoidable recourse to metaphor, Derrida objects to the absence of a guiding definition in Foucault's book, the lack of a clear concept delimitating madness:

> . . . the concept of madness is never submitted to a thematic examination on the part of Foucault; but isn't this concept—outside of everyday popular language which always drags on longer than it should after being put in question by science and philosophy—isn't this concept today a *false concept,* a concept so disintegrated that Foucault, by refusing psychiatric or philosophic tools, which have done nothing but imprison madmen, ends up making use—and he has no alternative—of a *common, equivocal notion,* borrowed from a *fund beyond control.*[17]

The very rigor of the objection begs the question: for what Foucault intends in fact to put in question is the way in which philosophy and science precisely do *put into question* "everyday popular language"; and particularly the *control* that they claim to exert over this "fund beyond control." Madness cannot constitute a concept, being a metaphor of metaphor. The requirement of Derrida (that of the madness of philosophy) is the philosophical requirement *par excellence:* that of a concept, of a maximum of *meaning.* But the requirement of Foucault (that of the impossible philosophy of madness: of pathos) is the requirement of literarity *par excellence*—the search for metaphor and for a maximum of *resonance.* It goes without saying that both Derrida and Foucault are powerful writers, and as such, inhabited by language: they both find themselves, in one way or another, *up against* literature. But in this theoretical debate over the status of the term "madness," it turns out that one is clearly enouncing the demand for a *concept* of metaphor, whereas the other solicits and pleads for a *metaphor* of concept.

[17]Derrida, "Cogito et historie de la folie," p. 66. My italics.

A double paradox, then, two philosophically untenable philosophical positions; indeed not one but *two* "*tâches doublement impossibles,*" two "doubly impossible tasks," both contradicted by their own language, in which the *content* of the statement can never coincide with the *position* of a subject who, in both cases, oversteps himself, passes out into the other. Perhaps the madness of philosophy and the philosophy of madness are, after all, each but the figure of the other? Which in no way implies that they are coextensive, that they amount to the same thing; but rather, that if each is eccentric to the other, both of them are, in addition, eccentric to the very framework of their opposition, rebellious to the very structure of their alternative.

That madness is at once a "common notion" and a "false concept," Foucault would but agree; in order to repeat it, differently. For in Foucault's conception, the proper meaning of the notion "madness" is precisely that it has no proper meaning, that it is, and rigorously, "a false concept," a metaphor indeed—of the radical metaphoricity which corrodes concepts in their essence, a metaphor of literature, from whose obliteration philosophy proceeds. Madness—or literature: this "equivocal and common notion," to use the terms of Derrida, this "false concept," is necessarily, inevitably "borrowed from a fund beyond control," fund unfounded and whose sole foundation is indeed the loss, the absence of control: loss of the relation to the mastery of meaning, of achievement, of production. "What then is madness?" asks Foucault; "Nothing, doubtless, but the absence of production (*l'absence d'œuvre*)."[18] Unaccomplishment *at work:* active incompletion of a meaning which ceaselessly transforms itself, offers itself but to be misunderstood, misapprehended. It becomes thus clear that this unfounded fund can by no means be *thematic,* that it is "beyond control" precisely since, eluding a thematic apprehension, it is *rhetorical,* that is, consisting in the very principle of *movement,* in an endless, metamorphic transformation. It was then inevitable that Foucault would not submit this fund, as Derrida suggests, to "a thematical examination": any examination of its theme can but reveal its fusion with another, its energetic alteration, its endless metamorphosis; any examination of its *place,* of its conceptual center, encounters only the decentralizing energy of its *displacement.* The answer here can but disseminate the question.

[18]Preface of the original edition (Plon, 1961).

If it is true then that the question underlying madness *cannot be asked*, that language is not *capable* of asking it; that through the very formulation of the question the *interrogation* is in fact excluded, being necessarily a confirmation, an *affirmation*, on the contrary, of reason: an affirmation in which madness does not question, is not *in question*; it is, however, not less true that, in the fabric of a text and through the very act of writing, the question is *at work*, stirring, changing place, and wandering away: the question underlying madness *writes*, and writes itself. And if we are unable to locate it, read it, except where it already has escaped, where it has moved—moved *us*—*away*—it is not because the question relative to madness does not question, but because it questions *somewhere else:* somewhere at that point of silence where it is no longer we who speak, but where, in our absence, we are *spoken*.

PART TWO

MADNESS AND

LITERATURE

The last madness which will remain with me
will probably be that of believing myself to be
a poet.

Nerval

3

Gérard de Nerval: Writing Living, or Madness as Autobiography

—"The Doubly Impossible Task"
—"The Unwritable Book"
—The Plural of "I": The Tensions of the Narrative
—"I Is an Other": The Double
—Loss: The Name of the Other
—"The Outpouring of Dream"
—The Magic Alphabet
—The Sphinx
—Ariadne's Thread

Nerval:

> I am *madde.*[1]

> I agree officially that I was ill. I cannot agree that I was mad or even hallucinating.[2]

> I am afraid I am in a house of wise men and the madmen are on the outside.[3]

Rimbaud:

> My turn now. The story of one of my insanities . . . I began it as an investigation. I turned silences and nights into words. What was unutterable, I wrote down. I made the whirling world stand still. . . .

[1]Letter to Arsène Houssaye, October 20, 1854, in *Oeuvres*, Bibliothèque de la Pléiade (Paris: Gallimard, 1952), vol. I, p. 1174.
[2]Letter to Anthony Deschamps, October 24, 1854, *Oeuvres*, I, 1175.
[3]Letter to Mme Emile de Girardin, April 27, 1841, *Oeuvres*, I, 904.

Not a single one of the brilliant arguments of madness—the madness that gets locked up—did I forget: I could go through them all again, I've got the system down by heart.[4]

Breton:

Where does the mind's stability cease? For the mind, is the possibility of erring not rather the contingency of good? There remains madness, "the madness that gets locked up," as has been aptly described. That madness or another . . .[5]

They came to tell me that Nadja was mad, confined in the Vaucluse asylum. . . . But to my mind, all confinements are arbitrary. I still don't see why a human being should be deprived of his freedom. They locked up Sade, they locked up Nietzsche, they locked up Baudelaire.[6]

Artaud:

But all the same, too many signs show us that what kept us alive isn't working anymore, that we are all madmen, desperate and sick. And I invite *us* to react.[7]

I am suffering from a terrible illness of the mind. . . . I am a man whose mind has made him suffer greatly, and by virtue of that, I have the right to speak. . . . I have accepted once and for all to submit to my inferiority.[8]

I would like to write a book that would disturb people, that would be like an open door leading them where they never would have agreed to go, a door opening quite simply onto reality.[9]

Foucault:

One could write a history of *limits*—of those obscure gestures, forgotten as soon as they take place, by which a culture rejects some-

[4]"Second Delirium: The Alchemy of Words," *Complete Works*, trans. P. Schmidt (New York: Harper & Row, 1967), pp. 203, 204, 208.
[5] *Manifestoes of Surrealism*, trans. R. Seaver and H. R. Lane (Ann Arbor: University of Michigan Press, 1969), p. 5.
[6]*Nadja* (Paris: Le Livre de Poche), pp. 157, 163–164.
[7]*Le Théâtre et son double*, Collection "Idées" (Paris: Gallimard), p. 118.
[8]"Correspondance avec Jacques Rivière," *Oeuvres complètes* (Paris: Gallimard, 1970), I, 30, 38.
[9]*Ibid.*, I, 62.

thing that henceforth will be outside it. . . . Western man's perception of space and time reveals a structure of rejection by which a word can be denounced as not belonging to language, a gesture as not being a meaningful act, and a figure as having no right to take a place in history. This structure is constitutive of both sense and non-sense, or rather, of the reciprocity which links them to each other; it alone can account for the general fact that in our culture there can be no reason without madness, even when the rational knowledge one has of madness subjugates and disarms it by according it the fragile status of a pathological anomaly.[10]

Rimbaud: the story of one of my insanities; Nerval: the story of *my* madness; Breton: the madness of *our* history; Artaud: the history of *our* madness; Foucault: the history of *madness*.

In grouping these authors together, I intend neither to map out an itinerary nor to trace a chronology, but rather to suggest a circuit of texts, the possible trajectory of a reading, and to establish—in texts as disparate as they are diverse and across clearly irreducible historic differences—the permanence of a certain discourse: a Romantic discourse, if ever there was one. The word "Romantic" is here used in a sense that still seeks us out, to the extent that it is not so much an answer as a question, not so much an object of knowledge as a sign; to the extent that it remains, indeed, to be defined through the singular adventure of the text.

"The Doubly Impossible Task"

If Michel Foucault appears today to be something like the "last" Romantic, it is because he marks, in modern discourse, the moment of emergence of a new awareness, whereby a philosophic enterprise complements and takes the place of a poetic one. *Madness and Civilization: A History of Insanity in the Age of Reason* is, in fact, the theoretical outcome of a certain praxis of Romantic language.

Foucault's aim, as we have seen, is to define the relationship between reason and madness at a point prior to their separation.

[10]Préface, *Folie et déraison, histoire de la folie à l'Age Classique* (Paris: Plon, 1961). (This Preface is not included in the English edition.)

But since the language of psychiatry is based precisely *on* that separation, since it is a unilateral monologue of reason *about* madness, Foucault must avoid that language to be able to listen to the silence to which madness has been reduced, and to make that silence speak.

Aware, however, of the contradictory tensions involved in the task of *saying a silence,* Foucault himself recognizes that his project of saying madness by circumventing reason is, in fact, an impossible undertaking:

> But the task is no doubt doubly impossible. . . . It was essential at all costs to preserve the *relative,* and to be *absolutely* understood.
> There, hidden and expressed in a simple *problem of elocution,* lay the major difficulty of the enterprise: I had to bring to the surface of the language of reason a division and a debate which of necessity remain below it, since this language becomes intelligible only well beyond that division.[11]

"But the task is no doubt doubly impossible." All the same, that impossible book had somehow to be written. And the question can be asked whether every great book is not fundamentally impossible (and as such, all the more necessary).

"The Unwritable Book"

Isn't it remarkable that Gérard de Nerval's *Aurélia* was likewise pronounced by its author to be an impossible book?

In the eyes of Nerval's friends, moreover, *any* book had become impossible for him after his second attack of madness. Alexandre Dumas wrote on that occasion a sort of funeral oration for Nerval's mind:

> It is a charming mind . . . in which, from time to time, a certain phenomenon occurs. . . . Imagination, that resident lunatic, momentarily evicts reason . . . and impels him toward *impossible theories* and *unwritable books.*[12]

[11]*Ibid.* Hereafter in this chapter, all italics in quoted material are mine unless otherwise stated.

[12]Dumas's text is quoted by Nerval in his Preface to *Les Filles de feu* (Paris: Le Livre de Poche, 1961), pp. 13–14. My italics.

Nerval responds to Dumas in his preface to *Les Filles du feu:*

> I dedicate this book to you, *cher maître,* as I dedicated *Lorely* to Jules Janin. Several days ago everyone thought I was mad, and you devoted some of your most charming lines to the epitaph of my mind. . . . Now that I have recovered what is vulgarly called reason, let us reason together . . .
>
> I am going to try to explain to you, my dear Dumas, the phenomenon about which you spoke.[13]

Nerval's request to Dumas is the same Artaud will make to Rivière a century later: *"Deign to accept me,"* implores Nerval pathetically, "at least in the capacity of a monster."[14] "For I cannot hope"—Artaud will echo later—"that time or work will remedy these absurdities or these failings, and so much disquiet. . . . Nothing less is at stake for me than knowing whether or not I will have the right to think, in poetry or in prose."[15] The issue is just as serious for Nerval, and involves nothing less than the very meaning of his existence. For behind the apparent sympathy in Dumas's discourse, as later in Rivière's, there lies a gesture of rejection and exclusion:

> The letter I have just gotten from the Cavern . . . advises me to give up "an art which doesn't suit me and for which I have no need . . ." Alas! This is a bitter joke, for I have never had more need, if not for producing art, at least for its brilliant products. This is what you haven't understood.[16]

Nerval's intention is henceforth to annul—by means of writing— this verdict of exclusion and, without rejecting any part of himself, to make the other acknowledge him. That is why, without *disavowing* his madness, Nerval nonetheless undertakes to *deny* it, to contest the reductionist definition given it by the language of reason. I am no more *mad* today, says Nerval, than I was *dead* several years ago. Your language, he implies to Dumas, cancels me out as a subject, reduces me to silence. Now listen to me, because, contrary to what you may think, I have some things to say, to say *to you.* "Now that I have recovered what is vulgarly called reason, let us

[13]*Ibid.*
[14]*Ibid.,* p. 23.
[15]"Correspondance avec Jacques Rivière," *Oeuvres,* pp. 31–32.
[16]Nerval, Préface, *Les Filles du feu,* p. 22.

reason together." Let us reason, that is to say, let us communicate, even if I must, in order to do that (to make myself heard, to be acknowledged, to continue to talk, to live), pass back through your norms: articulate a "reasonable" discourse. Nerval's dedication to Dumas thus becomes an appeal, an entreaty, a recourse to the other, and its irony barely hides the vehemence, the violence, and the urgency through which Nerval desperately poses as one who is at once mad and not mad, one whose only truth is to be found in the enigma of the madman he is—and is not.[17]

> I am going to try to explain to you, my dear Dumas, the phenomenon about which you spoke. . . . There are, as you know, certain story-tellers who cannot make up a story without identifying themselves with the characters of their imagination. . . . Well now, can you believe that a story could sweep one so entirely away that one becomes incarnate, as it were, in the hero of one's imagination. . . ! What could have been only a game for you, *maître,* had become for me an obsession, an intoxication.[18]

Every reading, says Nerval, is a kind of madness since it is based on illusion and induces us to identify with imaginary heroes. Madness is nothing other than an intoxicating reading: a madman is one who is drawn into the dizzying whirl of his own reading.[19] Dementia is, above all, the madness of books; delirium, an adventure of the text.

The role of madness in books will be a direct consequence of the role of books in life:

> The chain was broken and the hours were marked as minutes. It would have been the Dream of Scipio, the Vision of Tasso, the *Divine Comedy* if I had succeeded in concentrating my memories in a masterpiece. Resigning henceforth the renown of the inspired, the illumined, and the prophetic, I have to offer you only what you so justly call impossible theories, *an unwritable book.*[20]

---

[17]Cf. Foucault, *Folie et déraison,* p. 633: "Modern man's only truth is in the enigma of the madman that he is and isn't."

[18]Préface, *Les Filles du feu,* pp. 14–15.

[19]For a treatment of the troubling—but fundamental—relationship between madness and reading, cf. below, Chapter 7, "Turning the Screw of Interpretation."

[20]Préface, *Les Filles du feu,* p. 15. Nerval's italics.

In point of fact, Nerval's poetic enterprise resembles to an astonishing degree the philosophic enterprise of Foucault. In much the same way as Foucault, Nerval attempts to *say* madness *itself*, to write a history of madness while trying to avoid the trap of "what is vulgarly called reason." Is it a triumph of Unreason or the refusal to believe that "unreason" exists, that there can exist, even in madness, something radically foreign to the reasonableness of things? Like Foucault, Nerval seeks to return to that zero point where Madness and Reason have not yet become mutually exclusive, but are rather conjoined in an enigmatic union:

> Someday I will write the story of this descent to the underworld, and you will see that *it was not entirely deprived of reasoning even though it always lacked reason.*[21]
> I cannot agree that I was mad or even hallucinating. If I am insulting Medicine, I will be at her feet when she acquires the features of a deity.[22]

Like Foucault, Nerval wishes above all to escape clinical diagnostics, that monologue of reason *about* madness. Like Foucault, he makes every effort to remain outside of the health-sickness opposition in order to reach a truth which lies beyond their contradiction.

Let it be well understood: this reading of one text as it echoes in another, this referring of one text to another is meant here to imply neither an historical relationship nor a literary influence. Foucault has been cited only to provide a modern reference point, allowing us to locate our own discourse in that of Nerval. My aim is not to show in what way Foucault may have read Nerval, but rather, in what way Nerval's text understands—rejoins—Foucault. I read Nerval in an attempt to understand how, in Nerval, today, we are *already read.*

To read *Aurélia* would mean then, here, to follow the trace of the impossible task as it is accomplished in the text: to see in what respect the impossible is necessary and the necessary is impossible; to see how this relationship of the impossible and the neces-

---

[21]*Ibid.*, p. 24. My italics.
[22]Letter to A. Deschamps, *Oeuvres*, I, 1175.

sary is transmuted into a line of force in Romantic discourse—and writing—and why it still continues to challenge us even today.

The problem here again is one of *elocution:* Who speaks in the narrative of *Aurélia* and from what place, from what discursive position does he speak? Since Nerval rejects the medical language and point of view, how can his own mode of discourse be defined? How does he succeed in saying madness? How can madness, in itself, survive translation into language? "What then, in its most general but most concrete form, is madness," writes Foucault, "for those who from the outset reject any sort of mastery knowledge might have over it? Nothing else, doubtless, than the *absence of production* [*l'absence d'oeuvre*]."[23]

How then can Nerval hope to *produce* a literary work out of this very *absence of production?*

The Plural of "I": The Tensions of the Narrative

On the very first page of *Aurélia*, the narrator makes the following statement:

> I am going to attempt to transcribe the impressions of a long illness which took place entirely within the confines of my mind; and I do not know why I use the term "illness," for as far as I myself was concerned, I had never felt better in my life.[24]

This *myself* who *never felt better* does not coincide exactly with the one who says *I* at the beginning of the sentence: "I am going to attempt to transcribe the impression of a long *illness . . .*" It is through this uneasiness of feeling double, through this very division of the self, that the speaker here affirms the (impossible) necessity of overcoming, by the very practice of his discourse, the linguistic separation between health and illness, between reason

[23]Préface, *Folie et déraison.*
[24]*Aurélia, Selected Writings of Gérard de Nerval,* trans. G. Wagner (New York: Grove Press, 1957), p. 115. All references to *Aurélia* will be to this edition.

and madness. The use of the pronoun *I* consequently becomes very complex in the narrative of *Aurélia:* in a process of constant splitting, the *I* stands for two distinct characters: the hero—and the narrator. The hero is a "madman"; the narrator, a man who has recovered his "reason." The hero is given over to sleep and its apparitions; the narrator is wide awake and alert. The hero lives madness in the present; the narrator reports it after the fact: he is out of synchrony with the hero. The hero often describes himself as possessing a supernatural power, a super-strength: "I thought my strength and energy were doubled" (p. 115). "Possessed of electrical forces, I was going to overthrow all who approached me" (p. 120). The narrator's mode of being is defined, on the contrary, as impotence: "*I cannot* give here anything but a rather odd idea of the result of this strife in my mind" (p. 140).

The hero believes he has absolute knowledge: "I seemed to know everything, understand everything" (p. 115). The narrator professes ignorance and doubt: "It was one of those strange relationships which I do not understand myself, and which it is easier to hint at than define" (p. 141); "These were approximately the words which were either spoken to me or whose meaning I thought I could feel" (p. 121). The hero introduces a visionary, dream-like mode of discourse which constantly moves toward hyperbole or overstatement: "My friend . . . grew larger in my eyes and took on the aspect of an Apostle" (p. 119); "Immediately one of the stars I could see in the sky began to grow larger" (p. 172). By contrast, the narrator initiates a *critical* mode of discourse which constantly tends toward litotes, understatement, reduction, reserve: "if I had not in view to be useful, *I would stop here,* and make no attempt to describe my later experiences in a series of visions which were either insane, or, vulgarly, diseased" (p. 121).

The structure of *Aurélia* is based, then, upon an unresolvable tension between these two contradictory discursive tendencies in the narrative: the mode of hallucinatory inflation and the mode of critical deflation.[25]

[25]Cf. R. Dragonetti, "Portes d'ivoire ou de corne dans 'Aurélia' de Gérard de Nerval; Tradition et modernité": "The double possibility of the Dream, the horned and ivory gates of poetic language, sets in motion the critical movement of the text, which then flows back over its dream substratum" (*Mélanges offerts à Rita Lejeune* [Paris: J. Duculot, Gembloux,] II, 1554). More than one idea in this chapter was inspired by this admirable study, to which I can but refer the reader.

"I is an Other": The Double

The split inherent in the "I" in *Aurélia* determines not just the formal structure of the narrative, but its subject-matter as well. Not only is the narrator distinct from the hero, the hero himself is split and is unable to rejoin himself. This internal division takes concrete form in the hallucination of the *double.* Within the dream discourse, the hero's "I" is constantly dispossessed by the so-called *other:*

> Someone of my build, whose face I could not see, went with my friends. . . . "But there's some mistake!" I cried. "They came for *me* and *another* has gone out!" (p. 122)

> To my terror and fury—it was my own face, my whole form magnified and idealized. . . . I thought I heard talk of a mystical marriage—my own—in which the *other* was to profit from the mistakes of my friends and of Aurélia herself. (pp. 138, 139)

> I imagined that the man they were waiting for was my *double,* and that he was going to marry Aurélia. (p. 142)

> The Beloved Bridegroom, the King of Glory, it is He who has judged and condemned me, and taken to His own Heaven the woman He gave me and of whom I am now forever unworthy! (p. 150)

On the one hand, the double is the materialization of the subject's narcissistic preoccupations; on the other, this projected image of likeness dramatizes the impossible, incarnates the sign of a prohibition. For it is precisely as other, as not-I, that the double *can*—and *may*—marry Aurélia; it is by virtue of his otherness that he succeeds in removing the prohibition, in making himself recognized so as to penetrate the space of love. As the "King of Glory," the "Beloved Bridegroom," he usurps the place of the "I" and castrates him. What this means is that the "I" is excluded, exiled from the kingdom of pleasure; and that he realizes that he is and will always be secondary, ex-centric to himself. If his place—as he envisions it—is forever missing, it is because his movements are inscribed within a radical dimension of castration.[26]

[26]On the uncanniness of the experience of the double and its relationship to castration, cf. Sigmund Freud, "The Uncanny," *Standard Edition* (London: Hogarth Press, 1955), XVII, 217–256.

Loss: The Name of the Other

Castration is, in fact, the constituent, constitutive experience of
Aurélia. If Nerval examines himself and his madness under a femi-
nized title, it is because "woman" symbolizes that locus of lack
around which his delirium crystallizes. "Aurélia" is not, in reality,
a female character in the narrative, but the nominal force of an
absence, a signifier of loss. From the outset, and at the very sources
of the story, she is *named* precisely as what is *lost:*

> A woman whom I had loved for a long while and whom I shall call
> Aurélia, was *lost* to me. (p. 115)
> *Eurydice! Eurydice!* Lost once more!
> All is *finished,* all is *past.* Now I must die and die without hope.
> What then is death? Nothingness? . . . Would to God it were! But God
> himself cannot make death a nothingness. (p. 147)[27]

Our past is not what is past. It is something that never stops
coming to pass, and to pass us by; it is what never ceases to be
repeated as a vanished Present. Time lost is time endlessly recap-
tured as lost, found once again in the image of loss. Death, then, is
not nothingness, but the death-in-life that one must *live.* Loss is
the repetition of loss: "twice lost"; "the chain was broken and the
hours were marked as minutes."[28]

> The Thirteenth returns. . . . Once more she is the first;
> And she is still the only one, or is this the only moment;
> For you are surely queen, first and last?
> For you are surely king, o first and last lover? . . .
>
> Love the one who loved you from cradle to the grave;
> The one alone I love loves me dearly still:
> She is death—or the dead one. . . . Delight or torment![29]

She is death—or the dead one: this is the supreme image, ultimately anonymous, of woman. That is why Aurélia, *named* as one
lost at the outset, in the end *loses her name* as well:

---

[27]The italics are mine unless otherwise indicated.
[28]Préface, *Les Filles du feu,* p. 15.
[29]"Artemis," *Chimeras, Selected Works,* p. 223.

> Oh, how beautiful is my dear friend. . . . That night Saturnius came
> to my assistance and my dear friend took her place at his side. . . . I
> recognized the beloved features of * * *. (pp. 173–174)

At the height of her femininity, in her final apparition, Aurélia
returns to anonymity. Or rather, the text, for the last time, designates her as a blank: at the dream's moment of fulfillment, absence
itself is named by a name that is only a gap.

Nameless, her only name the name of absence, woman is no
more than the trace of a passing, the illusion of an identity:

> I am the same as Mary, the same as your mother, the same being also
> whom you have always loved under every form. At each of your
> ordeals I have dropped one of the masks with which I hide my fea-
> tures and soon you shall see me as I really am. (p. 162)

You shall see me: in the future. For in the present I am precisely
what is invisible. "I am the same" means, therefore: I am she who
is not; death—or the dead one.

It is in this way that desire is transformed, by a chain of infinite
substitutions, into a frantic metonymy: Aurélia's death repeats
and consecrates the lovers' separation, which was itself grafted
upon the original loss of the mother:

> I never knew my mother, who had insisted on following my father on
> one of his campaigns. . . . She died of fever and exhaustion in a cold
> province of Germany. (p. 135)

Repeated frustration becomes the dizzying contemplation of an
eternal death, a sickness unto death: "Everywhere the suffering
image of the eternal Mother was dying, weeping or languishing" (p.
136).

"The Outpouring of Dream"

"Madness," said Schopenhauer before Freud, "is nature's last
resort against anxiety." It is because "real life" is nothing other
than a gaping hole that Dream, little by little, pours into it. Loss

becomes a doorway opening onto the "invisible world." In the hollow of the real grows a compensatory delirium, made through a reversal of signs; born of loss and separation, hallucination endlessly strives to reunite the lovers, to recapture the lost object, to re-establish a cosmic harmony.

My own role seemed to be to re-establish universal harmony. (p. 163)

One evening, at about midnight . . . I noticed the number on a house, lit by a street-lamp. The number was that of my own age. As I looked down I saw in front of me a woman with hollow eyes, whose features seemed to me like Aurélia's. I said to myself: "I am being warned either of *her death* or of mine!" . . . I began searching the sky for a star I thought I knew . . . , walking, as it were, toward my destiny, anxious to see the star up to the moment when death would strike me down. . . . It seemed to me that my friend was employing superhuman strength to make me move. . . . "No," I cried, "I don't belong to your Heaven. Those in that star are waiting for me. . . . Let me go to them, for the one I love belongs to them, and it is there we are to meet again." (pp. 118, 119, 120)

The number on a house, a figure illuminated by chance, sets off a whole scene of delirium. Hallucination begins by a reading of signs. Madness is, before all else, an intuition about the functioning of the symbol, a blind and total faith in the revelation of a sign which, although spawned by chance, harkens to a necessity, a fatality: "But what if this grotesque symbol were something else, what if it were . . . the fatal truth under the mask of madness?" (p. 139).

The symbol simultaneously conceals and reveals. That is, the symbolic revelation solicits the interpreter, but also resists him; truth only travels under a mask. It takes on its full significance only by being *unreadable*:

Then I saw plastic images of antiquity vaguely take form before me . . . they seemed to represent symbols whose meaning I grasped only with difficulty. Yet I think what it meant was: "All this was to teach you the secret of life and you have not understood it. Religions and legends, saints and poets, all concurred in explaining the fatal enigma, and you have interpreted it wrongly . . ." (pp. 154–155)

71

The Magic Alphabet

The entire world is from then on a symbolic discourse, which the hero interprets according to his desires and fears. His delirious faith in the sign has as its only goal to conjure away—by magic—the curse of castration, to regain a lost potency, a potency seen as fundamentally erotic, which will allow the hero to affirm himself and vanquish the other:

> I shouted out: "I know he has struck me once with his weapon, but I am not afraid and await him, knowing *the sign* with which to defeat." . . . I stepped back to the throne then, my soul filled with unutterable pride, and raised my arm to *make a sign* which to me appeared to have *magical potency*. A woman's cry, vibrant and clear, and filled with excruciating agony, woke me with a start. The syllables of the *unknown word* I had been about to utter died on my lips . . . (p. 142)

The sign clearly becomes here the symbol of phallic power. That is why madness is conceived all along as a mode of transgressive knowledge; transgression, a breaching of the mystery beyond the limits of what is known or allowed, is also expressed by an erotic metaphor:

> I have never been able to *penetrate* without a *shudder* those ivory or horned *gates* which separate us from the invisible world. (p. 115)

> I used all my willpower to *penetrate further* that mystery whose veils I had partly lifted. (p. 140)

Transgression, however, is only possible through the medium of the symbol: the phallic omnipotence invoked by the magic sign mimics "the syllables of an *unknown world*" which, when the hero awakens, "*die* on his lips." Madness will then set off in quest of this unknown language, this mysterious code of potency—a code which would have no place for lack, a language in which plenitude would become possible:

> The *magic alphabet*, the mysterious hieroglyphs have only come down to us incomplete and falsified, either by time or by men who have an interest in remaining ignorant. *Let us rediscover the lost*

letter, the effaced sign, let us recompose the dissonant scale, and *we shall gain power* in the world of the spirits. (pp. 148–149)

The delirious quest for the magic language, however, leads in reality only to the abandonment of human language. The madman no longer uses speech to communicate with those around him. In order to communicate with the spirits, Nerval renounces the world of men. To reach for the star, he takes leave of his friend. Though its goal is to rejoin the other, his delirium in fact only widens the gap that separates him from others. Nerval's tragedy is precisely this loss of the other: this vicious circle of the imaginary—a narcissistic entrapment—is what constitutes the core of his madness.

The Sphinx

It is in the insane asylum that the circle of narcissism is broken for the first time.

> At last I was torn from these macabre reflections. . . . Among the patients was a young man, once a soldier in Africa, who had refused to take food for six weeks. . . . Moreover, he could neither see nor speak.
> This sight made a deep impression on me. Until then I had been given up to the monotonous circle of my own sensations or moral sufferings, and here I met an unaccountable creature, patient and *taciturn*, seated *like a sphinx* at the last gates of existence. I began to love him because of his misfortune and abandonment, and I felt uplifted by this sympathy and pity. (pp. 171–172)

"This figure in distress," notes Roger Dragonetti, "is again the *double*, but one that reveals to Nerval the image of his own impoverishment: the true likeness of a peer."[30] *I* is no longer so much an *other*, since the other has become an other *self*. "I spent hours examining myself mentally, my head bowed over his, and holding his hands" (p. 172). Recovery thus begins with the discovery of the other.

[30]Dragonetti, "Portes d'ivoire . . . ," *Mélanges*, II, 1563.

His mirror image, this living dead man, reveals to Nerval not only the spectacle of his own madness, but also an image of destiny: destiny is silence. "Seated like a *sphinx* at the last gates of existence," this mute creature poses for Nerval the *question of silence,* and reveals at the same time the price of human language—the place of encounter with the other. We then witness an initiation into speech: an initiation that takes the form of a teaching process. The hero himself relearns speech while teaching his pathetic companion to talk:

> I was delighted the first time a word came from his mouth. No one would believe me, but I attributed this commencement of cure in him to my ardent will-power. (p. 172)

> I spent whole hours singing him old village songs. . . . I had the happiness of seeing that he heard them, and he opened his eyes for a second, and I saw that they were blue. . . . Then he began to speak . . . and he recognized me and addressed me in a familiar way, calling me brother. (p. 177)

From the muteness of the poor madman, Nerval derives not only the power to recommence speaking himself, but also the power to become a donor, a dispenser of speech. The communication involved is the reciprocal gift of what one does not have: "Saturnus" restores to Nerval what he himself has lost, what he is deprived of—speech.[31] In the void of mutual privation, there is established in this way an exchange that leads to a double miracle, a double recovery: for Nerval, and for the soldier from Africa, a rebirth into language, and into the Other.

Ariadne's Thread

This rebirth into human language necessarily entails, for Nerval, the abandonment of the magic language:

> I was overjoyed to rediscover these humble relics of those years alternating in fortune and misery. . . . My books, an odd assortment of the

[31]Cf. Jacques Lacan, *Ecrits: A Selection,* trans. A. Sheridan (New York: Norton, 1977), p. 286: "This privilege of the Other thus designates the radical form of a gift of what he does not have, namely his love."

knowledge of all ages . . . —they had left me all that! *Those books were enough to drive a wise man mad. Let me try to see to it that they will also be enough to drive a madman wise.* With what delight have I been able to file away in my drawers the mass of my notes and letters . . . ! Oh joy! Oh mortal sorrow! These yellowed characters, these faded drafts, half-crumpled letters, these are the treasures of my only love. . . . Let me read them again. . . . Many of them are missing, others torn or crossed out; here is what I re-discover. (pp. 169–170)

Madness swings over into a kind of wisdom we now see dawning. If insanity is best described as an intoxication of reading, that which is written in books, then "wisdom" is precisely what has *yet to be written.* Filing one's notes is already a move in the direction of textual production (*l'oeuvre*): it is a rediscovery of the cache of "faded drafts." "Many letters are missing," it is true, and "others torn or crossed out." But human language, in contrast to the "magic alphabet," necessarily implies an acceptance of rupture, of tearing. "These yellowed characters" speak out of the very lack that founds them.

It is noteworthy that at this point the narrative, up to here written in the past tense, suddenly switches to the present tense.[32] "Let me read them again. . . . Many of them are missing . . . here is what I re-discover." Recovery is also a discovery of the present. And the present is a re-reading: a new attitude toward the past.

Writing, the inheritance of the disinherited, now becomes the only consolation for the "disconsolate":

The divinity of my dreams appeared smiling. . . . She said to me: "The ordeal you have undergone is coming to an end. . . ." I wanted some *material sign* of the vision which had consoled me, so *I wrote* these words on the wall: "This night you came to me."

In this sublime night, Nerval stakes claim—on the basis of a doubt—to a drop of ink: "Some sort of duty to recreate everything with recollections."[33] But here recollection turns toward the fu-

---

[32]The first sentence in the present tense occurs several lines earlier, and introduces the passage just quoted; in it, the breach of the present is marked—in both form and content—by a kind of promise of admirable poetic simplicity: "My room lies at the end of the corridor, on the one side of which live the insane, and on the other the asylum servants. It has only the privilege of one window, opening toward the courtyard . . ." (p. 168).

[33]Mallarmé, "Conférence sur Villiers de l'Isle-Adam," *Oeuvres complètes,* Bibliothèque de la Pléiade (Paris: Gallimard, 1945), p. 481.

ture, not the past; it is the promise of an end, which is in fact a re-beginning: "The ordeal you have undergone is coming to an end." The written sign commemorates a meaning. But the memory kept is a memory of language, the trace of a nocturnal visit whose illumination makes *sense* only in that it makes one *wait*. The letter at once promises and defers. The "material sign" marks therefore the juncture at which the past meets the future: at which the past is *yet to be*. Whereas the past is the impossible, that which *did not come to pass*—the impossible love for an "apparition," for a Star—the future, paradoxically enough, is this memory—belonging to no one—of desire, a memory which transforms recollection into waiting: the impossible becomes a hope.[34]

Once again, it is recourse to the symbol that allows one to live, to bear and transcend the real frustration. Writing will, however, bring about a reversal of Nerval's relationship to signs. While the hallucination had been a reading of signs, a deciphering of one's reality, writing will attempt, in contrast, to decipher one's own *dream*. The writer thus becomes the reader, the interpreter, of his own madness:[35]

> I resolved to *fix* my dream-state and learn its secrets. "Why should I not," I asked myself, "at last force those mystic gates, armed with all my will-power, and *dominate* my sensations instead of being *subject* to them? Is it not possible to *control* this fascinating, dread chimera, to *rule* the spirits of the night which play with our reason?" (p. 176)

It is thus that the hero is transformed into a narrator. The critical movement of the narrative has succeeded in fixing, dominating, controlling the movement of the dream. At least for a moment, Nerval rules over those spirits of the night that were playing with his reason; he *dominates* the sign instead of being *subject* to it:

> Surrounded by monsters against which I struggled obscurely, I seized *Ariadne's thread*. . . . One day I will write the story of this descent to the underworld, and you will see that it was not entirely deprived of reasoning even though it always lacked reason.[36]

[34]"To create," says Nerval, "is to remember" (Préface, *Les Filles du feu*, p. 15). But to remember is also to create: to create the memory of the letter.

[35]Cf. Dragonetti, for whom *Aurélia* constitutes "an interpretive discourse which transforms the dreamer by turns into the reader and into the witness of his own visions" ("Portes d'ivoire . . . ," *Mélanges*, II,554).

[36]Préface, *Les Filles du feu*, p. 24.

To *produce a work* out of the very *"absence of production"* [*l'absence d'oeuvre*] meant, thus, to produce a work in which speech is not an already acquired knowledge, but an initiation; to write a book in which writing is, precisely, its own search and its own rite of passage. "To seize Ariadne's thread" was, for Nerval, to recognize that the lost letter will never be refound. It was to be content with a "dissonant scale," an incomplete, deficient alphabet with which to say the unsayable, and nevertheless to attempt to inscribe silence, to arrest the intoxicating swirl of madness. It was to write *Aurélia*.

4

Gustave Flaubert: Living Writing, or Madness as Cliché

—The Thematics of "Madness"
—The Ironic Function of "Madness"
—The Irony of Irony: The Rhetoricity of "Madness"
—Thematics and Rhetoric

Seen as the first draft of what Flaubert will three versions later finally call the definitive, publishable text of his *Sentimental Education*, the *Memoirs of a Madman* has long been considered as merely the "preface to a writer's life." But can a writer's life really be said to have prefaces? Can the well-known oeuvre be clearly set off from the rest, which would serve as its hors d'oeuvre? Can one locate the point at which the author's real works begin? And can one, indeed, restrict those works to what are customarily and somewhat arbitrarily known as *master*works? It is perhaps time to attempt to read, among the texts of an author like Flaubert, those rafts of drafts that lie in the margins of the official oeuvre, in which writing can still be seen as a process of struggle and work. For doesn't "the production of meaning in Flaubert"[1] take place precisely in those folds where the text is actively sketching and scrapping itself, marking its boundaries only to bound over them?

The Flaubert that wrote *Memoirs of a Madman*, then, was a sixteen-year-old boy. The text is "romantic" to the hilt, but nev-

[1]Title of the colloquium for which this piece was originally written.

ertheless sets out to attack the values and illusions of Romanticism: at once naïve and sophisticated, talky and declamatory, buzzing with awkwardness and intelligence, it disconcerts and ensnares readers, provoking them into becoming, in imitation or in reaction, either too ironic or too naïve. How can such a text be read? How is one to account for *both* its simplification *and* its sophistication, *both* its irony *and* its faith?

I shall propose here, successively, three directions for reading: 1) a "thematic" reading of "madness"; 2) a reading of the *ironic function* of "madness," of the irony the text directs toward the naïveté of Romantic "madness"; and 3) an *ironic* reading of the text's irony, which will bring out that irony's own naïveté: a reading generated by the irony that the text *writes*, so to speak, in its strata of silence, over and against the irony it *speaks*.

These three interpretations, all of which seem to me to be both suggested and authorized by Flaubert, will, however, prove contradictory, successively subverting each other to reveal the dynamics of the production of meaning in the text as inseparable from such questions of approach and from a general problematic of reading.

The Thematics of "Madness"

Let us then follow the Ariadne's thread of the *theme* of "madness," which instead of leading us out of the labyrinth, will lead us straight into it. We are warned at the beginning of the book: "it is a madman who has written these pages."[2] A madman in what sense? We read further: "I was in boarding school from the age of ten, and I soon developed there a profound loathing for my fellow man. . . . All my inclinations were found offensive: in class, it was my ideas; at recess, my uncivilized preference for solitude. From then on, I was a madman" (III, p. 232). Madness, then, is an uncivilized solitude, an "eccentricity," the difference that separates the young romantic from those around him. It is also a grand and unique love, the impossible desire for a woman one will never see again: "O, Maria . . . precious angel of my youth . . . adieu! And yet, how I

[2]Gustave Flaubert, *Mémoires d'un fou*, in *Oeuvres complètes*, "L'Intégrale" edition (Paris: Seuil, 1964), I, 30.

would have loved you! . . . Oh, my soul melts with delight at every *madness* that my love invents" (XXII, p. 247). "No, I could never express to you what sweet sensations, what heartfelt intoxications, what bliss and *madness* there is in love" (X, p. 237).[3] Madness is thus the dream of an imagination overwrought in solitude. And it is sometimes terrifying: "I had frightening visions, enough to drive one *mad* with terror" (IV, p. 233). "It was just barely, if at all, that they granted me imagination, which was, according to them, a fever in the brain akin to madness" (V, p. 234).

According to them. Hence the term madness is borrowed from the language of others, in which it implies a judgment, a condemnation: "Youth! The age of *madness* and dreams, of poetry and foolishness, all synonyms on the lips of those who judge the world *sanely*" (III, p. 232; Flaubert's emphasis). The fact that the narrator calls himself "mad" suggests that he accepts the division such a judgment implies, that he judges himself to be different from the norm, to stand outside the values of bourgeois society: "They laughed at me . . . who would never have a positive idea, who would never display a propensity for any profession" (III, pp. 232–233). "Oh, how full of dreams my childhood was! What a poor *madman* I was, without set ideas or positive opinions!" (II, p. 230). Madness, then, in a positivistic world, is the rejection of positivity.

Here, in sum, is the essence of the narrative project of the *Memoirs of a Madman:* "I am therefore going to write the story of my life. . . . But have I lived? . . . My life is not a collection of facts; my life is my thought. . . . You will learn of the adventures of that life . . . so rich in feeling, so poor in facts" (II, pp. 230, 232). The lexical distribution of the term "madness" reflects this narrative project quite remarkably: the twenty-five occurrences of the term (or the related terms, "mad," "follies," etc.) found in the space of twenty-three chapters (eighteen pages in the "Intégrale" edition) are unevenly distributed; as if by chance, the term "madness" happens to be absent from three consecutive chapters, precisely the ones that relate the *facts* of the story—the encounter with the great love (chapters XI, XII, XIII). In the middle of the work, we find a kind of hole in this "madness." The term reappears when the woman departs. Madness, then, is not an event, it is not the *fact* of love, but rather what comes before—and after. "I put myself back

---

[3]Here, as elsewhere, the italics are mine unless otherwise indicated.

in a past that would never return. . . . There was chaos in my heart, an immense buzzing, a madness. Everything had gone like a dream" (XIV, p. 239).

"Madness" is also an excess of remembrance. The *Memoirs of a Madman* is then perhaps the madness of memories, or of memory itself: a memory wihout a referent, a memory not of what is external, some event or fact, but of what is internal, a desire, a reminiscence—a memory not so much of the object of desire as of the desiring subject himself. We recognize here what is at stake in any Romantic project of "confession": the possibility of unveiling a subjective "identity," a project that entails both "sincerity" ("I made a vow to tell all," XV, p. 239) and expressivity ("these pages . . . contain an entire soul," Dedication, p. 230). This undertaking is, however, felt to be impossible; it is experienced as an unresolvable tension between an interior and anterior subject and a language whose exteriority renders it incapable of expressing that subject's real meaning or fundamental origins.

> I would tell you many other things, much more beautiful and sweet, if I could say all that I felt of love, of ecstasy, of regret. Can one say in words the beating of one's heart? (XXI, p. 247)

> How can one express in words those things for which there is no language, those things imprinted on the heart, those mysteries of soul unknown to the soul itself? (XIII, p. 238)

To "ex-press" oneself is thus an impossible task; one could never "press" words hard enough to "ex"-tract from their exteriority the nectar of the inner heart or mind.

> How high my mind flew in its delirium, high in those regions unknown to man where there are neither worlds, nor planets, nor sun! I possessed an infinity more immense, if that is possible, than God's, where poetry was cradled and tried its wings in an atmosphere of love and ecstasy; then came the inevitable descent back down from such sublimity to words,—and how can words express the harmony arising in the poet's heart, those Titan thoughts that make phrases bend beneath them . . . ? By what rungs climb down from the infinite to the empirical? . . . Then I had moments of sadness and despair, I felt my own force breaking me and my frailty bringing me shame, for language is only a feeble and distinct echo of thought. (II, p. 231)

To one who rejects all positivism, language itself seems too "finite," too empirical. And that is perhaps another, the ultimate, madness of the *Memoirs:* the desire to ex-press a "soul," an interiority that can never be externalized—the desire to de-limit the limitless. Madness is at once what is ineffable and the desire to *name* the ineffable.

The Ironic Function of "Madness"

While language is judged inadequate as the "expression" of the subject, it nonetheless retains one power: that of naming and, through naming, mastering the object. They name *me:* they judge me, they *categorize* me as *mad.* But *I* can claim the power of mastery inherent in words as well; I can name, I can categorize them:

> Them, laugh at *me!* They who are so weak, so common, so narrow-minded! . . . At me, who felt as big as the world, who could have been reduced to dust by a single one of my grand thoughts, poor *madman!* (III, p. 232)

> A *madman!* That strikes horror. What then are you, reader? What category do you place yourself in? In the category of *fools* or of *madmen!*—Given a choice, your vanity would yet prefer the latter condition. (I, 230)

Is the narrator himself a madman, or a fool? The answer is not self-evident, nor is the question simply rhetorical: it will be raised quite seriously at another level of the text.

In any case, "madness" here turns into irony: it no longer adheres entirely to its meaning; it stands at a certain distance from itself, takes a strategic step back from the condemnation it suffers. Madness is no longer quite the image of a "soul," the profound essence or fundamental nature of the narrator's subjectivity, but a social mask, a *role to be played.* Beneath the mask of accusation, the accused becomes the accuser, pointing his finger at the exposed faces of the "fools": madness designates as its opposite not sanity, but stupidity. It is as though reason did not exist at all, or existed only as a term of negative comparison. What enters into *opposition* are two ways of *being opposed* to reason: either through pettiness, which characterizes the "category of fools" (what is commonly called reason—bourgeois good sense, the logic of self-interest); or through greatness, in the case of the "category of madmen." There is obviously in "madness" more than a touch of complacency and pride. Saying "I am a *madman*," in this context, boils down to saying "I am not a fool." Madness thus constitutes the negation effected by the stigmatizing term "madness," and is expressed by a reversal of signs:

> You would be mistaken to see in this anything other than the diver-
> sions of a poor *madman!* A *madman!*

> And you, dear reader, perhaps you just got married or paid your debts?
> (I, p. 230)

The lexical choice has thus become a strategic operation.[4] "Madness" invokes the stigmatizing power of language, but that power, since it is based on the structure of *opposition*, is *reversible*. Flaubert's text will ceaselessly mobilize the ironic power of *antith-esis* and chiasmus: first seen as a purely negative state, madness becomes an active force of negativity, merging with the dynamic of reversal inherent in language, with the very principle of negativity constitutive of language as such. Thus the king's fool, in a play by Flaubert from the same period as the *Memoirs of a Madman*, says to Louis XI:

> Isn't it true, uncle, that you are very pleased when you have called
> someone a *madman?* A convincing argument! A *madman!* Well now,
> a *madman* is a *wise man* and a *wise man* a *madman*, for what is a
> *madman?* . . . A *madman* is the cleverest invention of *wisdom*.[5]

So language, while incapable of externalizing the interiority of the subject, is able to reverse the very opposition between exterior and interior, to invert their power relations. The Flaubertian usage of the term "madness" demonstrates not only that the *outside* is, in reality, *inside*—that what society rejects under the name of

---

[4]Cf. a longer analysis of this same operation in Stendhal in S. Felman, *La Folie dans l'oeuvre romanesque de Stendhal* (Paris: Corti, 1971), chaps. V, VI.

[5]Flaubert, *Louis XI*, in *Oeuvres complètes*, I, 132.

"madness" as its *exterior,* in fact constitutes the very *interior* of subjectivity—but also that the non-mad are fools, that those who believe themselves to be *inside,* inside society and inside reason, are actually "out of it," in the realm of stupidity. Therefore, "a madman is a wise man and a wise man a madman." Though outside of society, the narrator nonetheless considers himself "in the know." In this inverted world, is he then inside or outside? Who's in and who's out? Who's mad? Who's not?

> What good, I ask myself in all sincerity, is a book that is neither instructive nor amusing . . . but tells of a madman, that is, the world, that strapping idiot, which has been spinning in space for centuries without ever taking one step forward? (I, p. 230)

"Madness" becomes generalized, but at the same time relativized: it is now nothing more than an effect of *perspective.* And the perspectives are many. "What a strange thing is this diversity of opinions, of systems, of beliefs and follies!" (XX, p. 244).

Here again, lexical frequency follows the ironic movement of the text: as the text progresses, "madman" disappears in favor of "follies": the essence of the substantive is subverted by the *plural,* which fragments and deconstructs it:

> There are in life so many loves for man! At four, he loves horses, the sun, flowers . . . at ten, he loves girls . . . at thirteen, a big, buxom woman, for I remember that what adolescents adore *madly* is a woman's bosom. . . . At sixty, he loves a prostitute . . . and casts her an impotent look, a regret for the past. . . . How many *follies* there are in a man! Oh! there is no question about it, a harlequin's suit is not more varied in its colors than the human spirit in its *follies.* (XV, p. 241)

Madness is the illusion of being able to salvage something from time, the belief in the possibility of eternity, of the absolute: in love, or in God. Madness, then, is *illusion* as such, *belief* inasmuch as it is always credulous; it is the loss of perspective, the relative mistaken for the absolute. Madness is not simply love, but *the belief in love.* If the thematics of madness say "I suffer" ("madness!"), then the irony of the narrator says "I don't believe it" ("follies!"): I *doubt* what I am suffering from.

Doubt is the death of the soul: it is a leprosy that attacks enfeebled races, a sickness caused by science and leading to *madness*. *Madness* is the doubt of reason; it is perhaps reason itself! (XIX, p. 244)

In a strange synthesis, the text tries simultaneously to write Rousseau, Voltaire, and Descartes: I suffer; I don't believe in what I suffer from; I doubt it; I doubt, therefore I think. "Madness is the doubt of reason," "my life is my thought":

Oh! How long my thought went on! Like a hydra, each of its headings devoured me. Thoughts of mourning and bitterness, thoughts of a weeping buffoon, thoughts of a philosopher in meditation. . . . Oh, yes! How many hours of my life have flowed past . . . *in thought, in doubt!* (II, p. 230)

The narrator himself indeed becomes the very image of the mad buffoon he describes:

There is thus nothing but darkness around man; everything is empty, and he yearns for something solid; he himself tumbles through the formless vastness in which he would find rest; he clutches at everything, but everything slips away; homeland, liberty, belief, God, virtue, he has grasped at all these things and they have all fallen from his hands; he is like a *madman* who drops a crystal glass and laughs at all the fragments he has made. (XX, p. 244)

The Irony of Irony: The Rhetoricity of "Madness"

Flaubert's irony, as we have just seen, mobilizes the *rhetorical* power of language. The narrator is well aware of the rhetorical play of his writing, but sees it only as an exercise in eloquence:

I am going to put down on paper . . . all that takes place in my mind and in my soul; laughter and tears . . . sobs that come *first from the heart* and then spread out like dough into *sonorous periods,* tears thinned in *romantic metaphor.* (I, p. 230)

In the narrator's view, the rhetorical figure is exterior and posterior to what it talks about, to the signified, the *theme* that precedes and founds it, just as language was external to the soul. The *theme* would thus be the soul of the text, the original meaning of the figure. And the text would be a figure whose truth is named by the theme. Since the play of signs is thus subordinated to the signified content, rhetoric seems to be *subordinate* to the theme, doubling it, reinforcing its effect in a flow of eloquent continuity.

This esthetics of emphasis, of eloquence and plenitude, tends naturally toward a kind of verbal delirium: toward the excesses of hyperbole. But the author denies the fact that his style is exaggerated: if he uses hyperbole, it is because the feeling itself (the theme) is hyperbolic, beyond the reach of language. If a word seems exaggerated, if the rhetorical figure seems to "surpass" the theme, it is because the theme is, in effect, much greater than the figure.

> But you will perhaps think that in many places the expression is *forced* and the picture is darkened at will; remember that it is a *madman* who has written these pages, and, if the *word* often seems to *surpass the feeling* it expresses, it is because, elsewhere, it has *bent* under *the weight of the heart.* (Dedication, p. 230)

This passage merits close reading: "remember that it is a *madman* who has written these pages, and if the word often seems to *surpass the feeling* it expresses . . ." The "word": What word? Wouldn't it be possible to read the clause, "a madman . . . has written these pages" not only as causal or explanatory, but as the *antecedent* of what follows: "and if the word surpasses the feeling"? To read, in other words: "remember that it is a madman who has written these pages, and if the word (the word I have just written: 'madman') often seems to surpass the sentiment it expresses, it is because, elsewhere, it has bent under the weight of the heart"? Nothing in the syntax rules out such a reading. "Madness," or "madman," would from the start be hyperbolic: a hyperbole that tries, of course, to justify or credit itself by invoking the pressure behind it, "the weight of the heart." But what if "the weight of the heart" were also, as it well might be, *already* a hyperbole, nothing but another "word" that often "surpasses the feeling"? Since it is the "word" that is in question—since it is a question *only* of words—how can we know what is word and what is feeling? Where is the feeling if not in the word? How can we separate the heart from the hyperbole, the theme from the *figure?*

Things are not as simple as they seem. Once rhetoric comes into play, it snowballs, never stopping where we want it to, within the limits we try to assign it.

Rhetoric is a strange game: its only rule is to bend the rules, to surpass the code of the game. "If the word often seems to surpass the feeling it expresses, it is because, elsewhere, it has bent under the weight of the heart." If hyperbole is visible, it is because, *elsewhere*, there is a weight on the heart. *Here*, we have hyperbole. The weight of the heart is not here, but elsewhere. Elsewhere, but where? We will never know, except by drifting with the sign toward the figure of another sign, by agreeing to rediscover meaning within the hyperbole, "the weight of the heart." If the "weight of the heart" and the excessive word thus relate to each other through the reversals of a chiasmus, then it is impossible to *stop* the movement of reversal, to fix their places once and for all, to know which comes first, which founds the other. We will never know which it is, the "weight of the heart" or the word "madman," that often "surpasses the feeling"; we will never know which of the two is not a word, which one is not rhetorical, that is, at once excessive and external. The rhetoricity of "madness" makes the difference between inside and outside *undecidable:* it deconstructs the very system of their opposition. What we have here is clearly no longer a "rhetoric of madness" in the sense of an eloquent *expression* of "madness," but rather a madness of rhetoric itself: the madness of its unceasing and uncontrollable movement, of its infinite, indefinite relay from one sign to another.

It is a movement of *displacement* which breaks the continuity between theme and figure, interposing a gap, a pause. "There is a gap in the story, a verse missing in the elegy" (XV, p. 241).

Rhetoric is the relation of the infinite to the finite. But this relation is not the "impossible" relation of expression that the narrator imagines it to be: the "Titan thoughts that make phrases bend beneath them," and which oblige the poet to "climb down from the infinite to the empirical," to "shrink the giant who embraces the infinite" (II, p. 231). The infinite is not a thematic excess: It is, on the contrary, the rhetorical *lack* that makes the discourse function. The infinite is composed not of an excess of signified, but rather of a *missing signified*, of an *excess of signifier* that is constantly being displaced, replaced by another signifier.

The rhetorical figure is not a "phrase bent by a Titan's thought," a rhetorical wisp bent by the mass of the theme, but a mass of language through which the theme escapes the reader, a linguistic mass through which my thought, displaced, escapes me.

Meaning, then, can only be inscribed in the gap left by its own disappearance, by its own *castration*.

> At night I would listen for hours to the wind sighing dolefully through the long, empty corridors. . . . I had frightful visions, enough to drive one *mad* with terror. I was in bed in my father's house. . . . The door opened by itself, and they came in. There were many of them. . . . They were covered with rough, black beards, unarmed except for steel blades between their teeth, and, as they circled my bed, their teeth began to chatter, and it was horrible. . . . At other times, I was in a green countryside dotted with flowers, beside a river; I was with my mother who walked along the riverbank; she fell. I saw the water foam up, circles spreading and suddenly disappearing. . . . I lay down on my stomach in the grass to look, I saw nothing . . . and I heard the cry: "I'm drowning! I'm drowning! Help me!" The water flowed by, flowed by, transparent . . . (III, IV, p. 233)

Inscription is possible only because there is erasure. The castration of meaning, the drowning of the signified, determines the flow, the substitution and displacement of signifiers. The erasure of the mother determines the inscription of Maria, who is in effect found, by metonymy, under water, beside the sea (*mer*)—beside the mother (*mère*)?—and whose coat is "saved" in the beginning when the narrator retrieves it from the water.

> Each morning I went to watch her swim; I watched her from afar under the water. . . . I stared long at her footprints, and would have wept to see the waves slowly erase them. (X, p. 237)

Maria: a rhetorical inscription, an inscription in the signifier both of desire and of the law, because the name Maria encompasses both the mother—Mary, the Virgin Mother—and the name-of-the-father—*mari* [husband], *mariée* [married], the forbidden.

Hence, thought is first an unconscious rhetoric, an ordered blindness, a play of signifiers over which one has no mastery:

> You call yourself free, and each day your acts are determined by a thousand things. You see a woman, and you love her, you are dying of

love for her; are you free . . . to calm the ardor that consumes you? Are you free from your thoughts? A thousand chains restrain you, a thousand goads drive you on, a thousand shackles stop you. (XX, p. 244)

But if one is so well aware and asserts so clearly that thought is determined—without knowing it, and under the illusion of freedom—by these goads, by these shackles and chains, by this rhetoric that functions through it and that it misapprehends and overlooks, how then can one in the same breath propose the meaning of one's own thought? How can one propose, in the same text, this project, this certitude: "I am going to tell the story of my life"; "My life is my thought"?

The narrator's discourse is clearly a contradictory one: the *theme* of thought is not transparent to itself; no more transparent, indeed, than the theme of madness. To say "I am mad" is already, logically, a contradiction in terms: either the speaker is "mad" and what he says (the theme) is non-sense, or else he is saying something meaningful, and is therefore sane (at least at the moment he says it). The act of enunciation contradicts and problematizes the statement it issues. The question then arises: *Who* is mad in the text? *Who* is thinking in the text? But the very formulation of this question, springing out of the contradiction within the theme, disqualifies a thematic answer; it disqualifies the theme *as* answer. In the logic of the theme, contradiction is inadmissable. But the rhetoric of the text *suspends* that logic: it *resides in* thematic contradiction, functioning according to a different logic, that of the unconscious, which, as we know, knows nothing of contradiction. Rhetoric is nothing other than a mode of contradiction in the text. The "theme" is never simple, never simply reversible in a dialectic with two terms. Rhetoric is precisely the non-simplicity, the non-self-transparency, of the theme. Or to put it another way, rhetoric is never external to the theme: it resides in it, pervades it, but in so doing decenters it, articulates it otherwise. Within the theme, rhetoric is a discourse that is radically other.

* * *

In order to attempt to isolate this other discourse—this discourse that the text articulates otherwise than in the theme—in order to bring out the irony of the writing, as opposed to that of the

narrator—the silent irony and not the irony that speaks—one possible strategy would be to turn the text back upon itself. We can, as
we have just done, turn the rhetorical categories (such as hyperbole) back on the theme; or we can turn the theme itself over to
reveal its own gaps, to discover in what way it fails to coincide,
precisely, with itself.

We can, for example, ask the following question: if the narrator's
irony is the *madness of doubt,* what does this madness of doubt
forget to doubt? There are several possible answers, of which the
most obvious is: the narrator forgets to doubt . . . precisely *his own
madness*—his madness as it constitutes his self-definition. For it
does not suffice to call oneself a "madman" to *be* one. As Jacques
Lacan suggests aphoristically: "Not all who would go mad, do go
mad."[6] It is thus precisely the hero's "madness" that the reader
must rigorously place in doubt. If there is "madness" in the text—
and that can be maintained—it is not where the narrator thinks he
sees it. It does not lie in the thematic meaning, but somewhere
else.

The madness of the narrator is first of all negatively defined: it is
a name for his being-other, his *difference* from the world. But since
the narrator turns the accusation around and calls the world
around him "mad," offering us a book that "tells of a madman,
that is, the world" (I, p. 230), what the text underscores is not at all
the would-be difference of the "I," but rather its *resemblance* to
the world it denounces—a resemblance that the narrator, of
course, fails to recognize, even though his own vocabulary, the
lexicon of "madness," brings it to the fore. The narrator does not
perceive that the world, like a mirror, sends back his own driving
principle: what Hegel analyzed as the "law of the heart," self-
affirmation as a resistance to others and an assertion of individual
uniqueness. The narrator fails to recognize that the principle governing the "category of fools," for example, is not in fact a contingency foreign to his own nature, but indeed the same principle
of narcissistic egoism that constitutes the "category of madmen"
as well. Self-interest is the equivalent of pride: in the order of
narcissism, "fools" and "madmen" are perhaps the same. As a
result of this governing misapprehension, as a result of this thematic (but not thematized) blindness, the narrator is caught in the

[6]*Ecrits* (Paris: Seuil, 1966), p. 176.

trap of his own self-image: the image of the "beautiful soul," auto-seductive and auto-destructive. He illustrates perfectly Hegel's definition of madness:

> The heart-throb for the welfare of mankind passes therefore into the rage of frantic self-conceit . . . by projecting outside of itself the perversion which it really is, and by straining to regard and to express that perversion as an other.[7]

The narrator, then, misapprehends the true nature of his madness, which is precisely *not to doubt*, thus *to believe in*, his madness as his mode of being different—*being other*—as his negative self-definition. But he also forgets to doubt his madness as his mode of *being-himself*, as his positive self-definition. It is the height of irony that his "poor madman without set ideas, without positive opinions" (II, p. 230), who would never display "a propensity for any profession" (III, p. 233), assumes the role of the Romantic "madman" as a positive attribute, as a trade, a vocation and indeed a career. "All Romanticism achieved," writes Georges Bataille, "was to make unhappiness a new form of career."[8] This also brings to mind an admirable passage in *Notes from the Underground*, where Dostoevski analyzes and demystifies the subtle workings of this Romantic "vocation":

> Oh, if I had done nothing simply from laziness! Heavens, how I should have respected myself because I should at least have been capable of being lazy; there would at least have been one quality, as it were, positive in me, in which I could have believed myself. Question: what is he? Answer: A sluggard; how very pleasant it would have been to hear that of oneself! It would mean that I was positively defined, it would mean that there was something to say about me. "Sluggard"—why, it is a calling and a vocation, it is a career. Do not jest, it is so. I should then be a member of the best club by right, and should find my occupation in continually respecting myself. . . . Then I should have chosen a career for myself, I should have been a sluggard and a glutton, not a simple one, but, for instance, one with sympathies for everything good and beautiful.[9]

---

[7]*The Phenomenology of Mind*, trans. J. B. Baillie (New York: Harper & Row, 1967), p. 397. Translation modified.

[8]*Oeuvres complètes*, I, 526.

[9]*Notes from the Underground*, trans. C. Garnett (New York: Dell, 1959), pt. I, chap. 6, pp. 39–40.

Once more, the dialectic of madmen and fools boils down to the same: the negation of a negation is but a *denial* [dénégation], that is, in effect, a confirmation of the system. The refusal to choose an occupation is replaced by the analogous need to be "somebody," to assume a specific role. Whether it is in the category of "madman" or the category of "fools," the naming game is the same, and simply confirms the *rule* of "categories": the search for the security of being *categorized*, of having a *positive identity*. What is unbearable in either case is to remain uncategorized.

The *Memoirs of a Madman*, read from this angle, is the story of the illusion of an adjective made into a noun: *"mad* man" changed into *"madman,"* an attribute turned into an essence, a characteristic turned into a *character*. The narrator's mistake lay in putting madness *in the title*, believing he held *title* to madness. If there is one thing madness is not, it's a title: no one can ever be appointed to it. Contrary to what the narrator says, the text thus tells the story not of a man entitled to madness, but of a man mad about titles.

The title of madness gets its authority only from dreams and fantasy. "Madness" is not the assertion of a fact, but the locus of an aspiration: "madness" is the *desire* for madness, a blind rush toward meaning, a dream of excess and hyperbole, of plenitude and potency which, once again, seeks only to forget, to deny castration—the castration of meaning.

> I filled my lungs with that cool, salt ocean air which so fills the soul with energy. . . . I gazed upon the deep, upon space, the infinite . . .
> Oh! But that isn't where you will find the boundless horizon, the immense abyss. No, a wider, deeper abyss opened before me. *That abyss contains no tempests;* if it had a tempest, it would be *full*— and it is *empty!* (II, p. 231)

But to create the tempest of a madness, or the madness of a tempest, through a riot of writing, an intoxication with hyperbole, an orgy of language—isn't that precisely to create the illusion of a plenitude in the void?

"I was drunk," the narrator of *November* will later say:

> I was *mad*, I imagined myself a great man . . . I carried in my loins the very life of a god. . . . I made myself a temple to hold something divine, and the temple remained empty.[10]

[10]Flaubert, *Novembre*, in *Oeuvres complètes*, I, 252.

"Madness" is a hyperbole of the self produced through an intox-ication of language; it is the illusion of drunkenness which, in fact, masks an incapacity to be drunk, to "be mad." The narrator of the *Memoirs* may be fooling himself, but the fool in *Louis XI* does not:

> For what is a madman? It is he who sleeps in the wind and thinks it's hot, *drinks water and believes he is drinking wine.*[11]

Thus, while he dismantles the theme of illusion, the narrator himself falls victim to the supreme, ironic illusion of his own "madness": the illusion of a difference (a negative self-definition); the illusion of identity (a positive self-definition); the illusion of plenitude and intoxication. Madness is, once again, belief: the be-lief that one is identical to oneself and differs from others; the belief that one is dizzy with wine when one has only drunk water; the belief that one is mad, when one is not, or only ever so slightly. But this leads to a paradox: whoever believes himself mad when he is not, is mad by virtue of that very belief. Mad not because he believes himself mad, but because he *believes himself* at all— because he identifies with the shadow of an image in a lake or a mirror: because he *alienates himself* in the madness of a specular identification.[12]

Thus, in the very act of defusing illusion, the narrator's irony only reinforces the structure and effect of illusion, since it adds to the others the illusion of having no more illusions: the belief that one no longer believes. While the narrator's irony consisted in his madness of doubt, the naïveté of that irony—the irony of the text—consists in the fact that the narrator's true madness in effect escapes him.

In the same way, through what the narrator calls his "thought," he tells the story of that in him which is *not* thought: he narrates *himself* as *un*thought. "Desire," writes Emmanuel Levinas, "is only the fact of thinking more than you think."[13] Desire, and maybe madness, too. In this strange relation—constitutive of rhet-oric—between thought and desire, between writing and madness, the text actively *unthinks* the narrator's thought. In his thematic

---

[11]Flaubert, *Louis XI*, p. 132.

[12]Cf. the Lacanian aphorism which here takes on all its significance: "If a man who believes himself to be king is mad, a king who believes himself to be king is no less mad" (*Ecrits*, p. 170).

[13]*Totalité et infini. Essai sur l'extériorité* (The Hague: M. Nijhoff, 1961).

"message," "I think that I doubt," the narrator still forgets to doubt the "I think." But the text thinks it for him, rhetorically turning what it *says*—"I think that I doubt"—into what it *writes*—"I doubt that I think." Paradoxically, the theme of madness is articulated in the text by the Cartesian formula: "I think, therefore I am." But the text's irony—not the way it speaks of "madness" but the way it is rhetorically traversed by it—is articulated on the contrary by a Lacanian formula: "I think where I am not, therefore, I am where I do not think . . . I am not wherever I am the plaything of my thought; I think of what I am, where I do not think to think."[14]

Thematics and Rhetoric

I have thus proposed three different readings of the *Memoirs of a Madman*. In this plurality of interpretations, it was not a matter of a simple "peaceful-co-existence" of various aspects of a text but, rather, a strategic confrontation of different *positions* of meaning. The text was treated as a field of forces and shifting intensities, and any one of the three readings was necessarily an intervention in the conflict; each successive reading indeed subverted the authority of the one that came before. Of these three readings, none can be considered exclusive or privileged, since all three are fundamentally interdependent: the more complex a reading becomes, the more it relies on another, which it must deconstruct by analyzing its specific mode of error or illusion. Although they were presented successively, the three interpretations do not constitute a chronology, or an evolution in the development of the text. They all exist side by side, simultaneously cohabiting the space of the text.

There are thus three different positions of meaning: 1) the *thematic* interpretation that the "I"-hero gives of his "madness"; 2) the *ironic* interpretation that the "I"-narrator proposes of the madness of the "I"-hero, rhetorically deconstructing his *thematic* reading; 3) the ironic interpretation of the narrator's irony, demonstrating how the irony of the text rhetorically deconstructs the irony *thematized* by the voice of the narrator.

While the voice of the narrator operated a reversal, a rhetorical-

---

[14] J. Lacan, *Ecrits: A Selection* (New York: Norton, 1977).

ironical chaismus of the *theme* of the hero's madness, the narrator in turn *thematized* this gesture of reversal, explicitly articulating it as the *theme* of the madness of doubt. As a result, although the "I"-narrator ironically, rhetorically demystifies the "I"-hero, the narrator's relation to himself is still mystified, remaining thoroughly thematic: it is a relation of consciousness and of self-presence—of *presence to self*—within the very "madness" of his doubting.

The thematic and the rhetorical positions of meaning thus confront and contest each other in two different ways, on two different levels of reading: first in the narrator's irony and then in the irony of the text. Let us summarize from this angle the strategic movement of our three readings: first, we read along with the hero from the *thematic* point of view; then came the demystifying perspective of the narrator, his *rhetorical* (ironic) re-inscription of the hero's thematic reading, as well as the *thematization* of this rhetorical re-inscription; and finally, the irony *thematized* was displaced, *rhetorically*, by the irony *textualized:* it was, thus, Flaubert's *writing* that effected the (ironic) *rhetoricization* of the *thematization* of the narrator's irony.

Rhetoric and thematics are thus engaged in a dynamic that is not symmetrical, or dialectical. The theme has no hold over the rhetoric; it can only misapprehend it, and hence cannot deconstruct it. On the other hand, even though the rhetoric often effects the deconstruction or the decentering of the theme, it is always stalked by its own thematization, which steals away and cancels out its ironic force. Only a theme can exist in the mode of presence and consciousness. Rhetoric cannot become conscious of itself; if it does, it vanishes, losing what is specifically rhetorical in its effect. Rhetoric cannot itself express its own essence. It cannot *know* what it knows; it cannot complete its own trajectory or attain the calm of a final truth. Any rhetorical movement that reaches consciousness, that makes its meaning explicit, that ends its motion in a finite thought, is transformed into a theme, which in turn will have to be demystified by another textual rhetoric, by another unthought, unthinkable rhetorical movement.[15]

---

[15]Of course, this does not exclude my own critical discourse, which can only *thematize* the irony of the text, and remains, therefore, to be deconstructed itself. It is in this respect that the third reading *resembles* the first two: it is why the third reading is in no way privileged or definitive. There is no final reading.

The narrator's mistake was precisely to believe he was situated on the *common* axis of the rhetoric and the thematics of his "madness." In fact, rhetoric and thematics do not operate on the same plane: because they are situated on two radically different levels, they *have no common axis*. The relation that simultaneously links and separates them is comparable to the relation Freud found to exist between the "dream-work" and the "waking thought": between the two, there is a "difference in nature," such that "they cannot be compared." The "dream-work" (like rhetoric) "does not think, calculate or judge in any way at all; *it restricts itself to giving things a new form.*"[16]

> The elements which stand out as the principal components of the manifest content of the dream are far from playing the same part in the dream thoughts. And, as a corollary, the converse of this assertion can be affirmed: what is clearly the essence of the dream-thoughts need not be represented in the dream at all. The dream is, as it were, *differently centered* from the dream-thoughts.[17]

In the same way, the elements that seem essential to the "content," to the thematics of a text, may be only secondary in the properly textual thought at work. What stands out as central in the content very often is not; the specifically textual work, the rhetoricity of the text, is *differently centered*. The "dream-content" and the "dream-thoughts" (a mode of thought specific to sleep), Freud goes on to write, "are presented to us like two versions of the same subject-matter in two *different languages*" (IV, 277). It could then be said that thematics and rhetoric are also two articulations of the same text in two different languages. In and of themselves, the two languages could never understand or come in contact with one another: only the outside intervention of an *interpreter* can translate one into the other.

The text-work is thus analogous to dream-work. But if the dream's major function is to be the "guardian of sleep,"[18] to satisfy the wish to sleep, the satisfaction of that wish is not always without obstacles. As Nietzsche affirms, "no small art is it to sleep: it

---

[16]Freud, *The Interpretation of Dreams*, in *Standard Edition* vols. IV and V (London: Hogarth Press, 1953), V, 507.

[17]*Ibid.*, IV, 305.

[18]*Ibid.*, V, 509–632.

is necessary for that purpose to *keep awake* all day."[19] Can it be said that the function of thematics is also to *keep awake* that *we may sleep,* to preserve the power of sleep that resides in language? For the theme blinds (us) by its very brightness; its task is to *obscure the rhetoricity* of the text, to make the rhetoric literally *unreadable.* Rhetoric, on the other hand, is whatever makes the theme malfunction, whatever makes the theme not work, *undo itself.*

That is why the task of reading is first of all, of course, to find the theme, but afterward to try to *lose* it. And losing the theme is sometimes more difficult than finding it.[20]

*   *   *

Losing the theme: isn't that precisely the movement outlined by Flaubert's work as a whole? Madness seems to invade the increasingly demented characters of Flaubert's later works: Bouvard and Pécuchet, Saint Julian the Hospitable, or Felicity, who in her delirium sees a parrot as the Holy Ghost. Delirium deepens, but statements about madness, the word "madness" itself, have disap-

---

[19]*Thus Spake Zarathustra* (New York: Random House), pt. I, p. 26.

[20]Cf. the beautiful passage in which Heidegger comments on both the madness and the thought of Nietzsche: "But to encounter Nietzsche's thinking at all, we must first find it. Only when we have succeeded in finding it may we try to lose again what that thinking has thought. And this, to lose, is harder than to find. . . . Nietzsche knew of these relations of discovery, finding, and losing. . . . What he still had to say in this respect is written on one of those scraps of paper which Nietzsche sent out to his friends about the time he collapsed in the street (January 4, 1889) and succumbed to madness. These scraps are sometimes called 'epistles of delusion.' Understood medically, scientifically, that classification is correct. For the purposes of thinking, it remains inadequate. One of these scraps is addressed to the Dane Georg Brandes, who had delivered the first public lectures on Nietzsche at Copenhagen, in 1888.

Postmark Torino, 4 Jan. 89

To my friend Georg!
After you had discovered me, it was no trick to find me: the difficulty now is to lose me . . .

The Crucified.

Did Nietzsche know that through him something was put into words that can never be lost again? Something that cannot be lost again to thinking, something to which thinking must forever come back again the more thoughtful it becomes?" (Heidegger, *What Is Called Thinking?* trans. F. D. Wieck and J. G. Gray [New York: Harper & Row, 1968], pp. 52–53.)

peared. As madness increases, the *theme* of madness recedes, and is lost.

But already in the *Memoirs of a Madman,* the rhetorical movement of madness acts to erase its meaning, to lose its title; "madness" loses its title to *authorize* meaning. The sign "madness" constantly negates itself, erases itself as a concept, as something identical to itself. It is as though the *Memoirs* actually intended to recount the failure of the *Memoirs of a Madman* to name the *true meaning* of madness. "It is a madman," we were told at the very beginning of the text, "who has written these pages": that was an illusion of autonomy on the part of the subject of madness, who, assured of his being ("it *is* a madman"), believed he in effect determined his own writing (*"who has written* these pages") as his *relative subordinate.* But in the action of the text, *the "writing" functions so as to subvert and lose the "being"*—the "being" of "madness" as a subject, theme or meaning—as a signified center of the text.

"Madness," in the end, concretizes—emblematically—the slippage of meaning, its way of fleeing us each time we think we have it. The lexeme "madness" thus polarizes the unresolvable tension between the will, the irreducible desire to name truthfully, and that which—as text, signifying play, rhetoric—irreducibly escapes that truth.

Madness is not the *origin* of (the) writing, the *cause* of meaning, but an *effect of discourse*—as is the subject himself. The question posed by the *Memoirs of a Madman* can, once again, be expressed in Lacanian terms:

> Is the place that I occupy as the subject of a signifier concentric or eccentric, in relation to the place I occupy as the subject of the signified?—That is the question. It is not a question of knowing whether I speak of myself in a way that conforms to what I am, but rather of knowing whether I am the same as that of which I speak.[21]

The madness of the *Memoirs of a Madman* is an *eccentricity of the subject in relation to the theme of which he speaks. The* sign "madness" is spoken only insofar as it *excludes* the subject: insofar as it *articulates* the subject *outside meaning.* The space of the *Memoirs of a Madman* is a space in which the "I"-signified is

[21]Lacan, *Ecrits: A Selection,* p. 165.

always disappearing; it is a space where the *writing* of "madness" is not preceded by its *being*.

It is doubtless for this reason that, in looking for the *beginning* of his being, for the *origin* of his madness, the narrator can only *re*-begin his story and his history, discover each time that the writing has *already begun:*

CHAPTER I
I am going to put down on paper . . . my ideas and my memories . . . (p. 230)
CHAPTER II
I am thus going to write the story of my life. (p. 230)
CHAPTER IX
Here is where the Memoirs truly begin . . . (p. 236)
CHAPTER XV
But I am going to go back further . . . the fragment that you are about to read was composed in part last December, before I had the idea of writing the *Memoirs of a Madman*. (p. 239)

At the presumed point of departure, of origination, of essence, what is found is already a figure of rebeginning—the rebeginning of a figure: a figure that is an illusion and a lie; a figure that does not circumscribe the identity of a past, nor the past of an identity, but rather the passage, the trace of a certain language. It is the figure of a past that never took place, a past that was never present:

What! Nothing of all that will return? . . . I recalled those long, hot summer afternoons when I talked to her without ever suspecting that I loved her. . . . Indeed, how could she have seen that I loved her, because *I didn't love her then, and in all that I have said to you, I lied;* it was now that I loved her, that I desired her. (XXI, p. 246)

Adieu! And yet, *how I would have loved you . . .* ! My soul melts with delight at every *madness* that my love invents. Adieu! (XXII, p. 247)

The *Memoirs* lead only to the "madness" of the past conditional: "how I would have loved you!" The past of the indicative, the past in the indicative, is a lie: "because I didn't love her then, and in all that I have said to you, I lied."

But what is the lie here, if not time itself: time insofar as it is the discord in language, the corrosion of presence and of the permanence of meaning?

O bells! You will ring thus also for my death, and a minute after for a baptism; you are, like the rest, a mockery and a *lie*. (XIII, p. 247)

If I told you that I had loved other women, *I would be lying*. I believed it though . . . (XC, p. 239)

"I would be lying"; "I lied to *you*." It goes without saying that the "lie" the "I" tells the "you" is not a simple lie; it is not *psychological*. "I lied" means "I believed." I believed in meaning and in language, as if time—death—did not pass through it, as if language were not fundamentally at odds with itself. The "lie," then, is the *non-integrity of the theme, which is precisely what constitutes rhetoric:* the non-coincidence of the theme with itself, of the word with itself; the arbitrary nature of the sign, the indefinite displacement of signifiers, and thus the *non-integrity of signifieds.*

Since the "lie" necessarily constitutes, liguistically (and not psychologically), the very basis of the author-reader relation, that relation is also rhetorical: a relation not of transparency (of the signifieds) and presence (of the statements), but of interpretation, displacement, and mutation. "I lied to you," for neither my thought nor my past knew itself; my memory lies to me as well, because it, too, functions *rhetorically* and not *thematically*.

"To lie" is thus to write the very text of the *Memoirs of a Madman:* to write a madness which has no memory; to discover, in plumbing the madness of the past, to what degree I have already forgotten myself; to rebegin then—and forever—the Memoirs of my own forgetting.

5

Honoré de Balzac: Madness, Ideology, and the Economy of Discourse

—Madness and the Novel
—"The Mystified Mystifier"
—The Rhetoric of the Text: Metaphor and Metonymy
—Madness and the Illusion of Realism
—Exchange and Reversibility: The Economy of the Text
—Madness and Irony: The Three Dimensions of the Textual Space

Madness and the Novel

Is there a relationship between madness and the novel? Out of context, this question might appear absurd. One has only to bring to mind, however, *Don Quixote* to realize that the novel as a genre is fundamentally involved in a relationship with madness, and that the implications of this relationship can be verified on a thematic as well as on a structural level.

Thematically, *Don Quixote* sets forth a triangular relationship which links madness on the one hand to desire and on the other hand to language; Don Quixote's delirium is, in effect, a mode of reference, a way of referring desire back to language. Every novel is a voyage within language. Every novel is an adventure of desire.

Don Quixote reveals a desire which is already, in and of itself, language, a text written by books. The challenge of that desire is to *live* the "novelesque" [*le romanesque*], to live *up to* the novel, to keep the promise made by books. For Don Quixote, reading novels is already a form of madness: a delirious rewriting of the World. Through Don Quixote's madness, the novel dramatizes its own reading which it decodes as a desire for itself: a desire for the "novelesque." The source of the novel is desire; the source of desire is the novel. What wonder, then, if the text-made man be doomed to be quixotic, to chase the vertiginous windmill of his own reading-writing? This textual delirium constitutes the very principle of the "novelesque." The novel as a genre is, above all, the enactment—and the irony—of its own madness.

Writers have always been well aware of this novelistic madness. "Here is another *novel-bred madness* which I have never been able to cure myself of," writes Jean-Jacques Rousseau.[1] Stendhal similarly evokes a childhood friend: "There was nothing *novelesque* about him. . . . The absence of that *madness* made him dull in my eyes."[2] Inversely and without metaphor, it is not to this madness of the novel but to the very novel of his madness that Gérard de Nerval refers when speaking of his illness: "Fortunately," he writes from the asylum, "the *illness* has receded almost entirely today; that is, the exaltation of a mind which is much too *novelesque* [*romanesque*], so it seems."[3]

As soon as the great novelists have understood that the very essence of the "novelesque" is this supreme risk, this seductiveness of madness, every true novel would seem to implicate a subtle therapeutic structure. Every novel contains simultaneously the temptation of madness and the negation of this temptation, in a reflexive narrative system, where the "novelesque" at once dis-

[1] *Confessions*. Cf., "My mother had left some novels. We began to read them (. . .). I had no idea of things, no idea that all feelings were already known to me; I had thought of nothing; I had felt everything. These vague emotions that I felt one by one did not damage the Reason that I was yet to acquire; but they did form a Reason of another stamp and gave me *bizarre and novelesque, fictional notions* about life which experience and reflection have never been able to cure." *Confessions* (Paris: Gallimard, Bibliothèque de la Pléiade), Book I, p. 8. My italics.

[2] *La Vie de Henri Brulard*, in *Oeuvres intimes* (Paris: Gallimard, Bibliothèque de la Pléiade), p. 392.

[3] Letter to Mme Emile de Girardin, April 27, 1841, in *Oeuvres*, I, 851. Nerval's italics.

closes and denounces its own madness. The novel thus involves a sort of schizophrenic structure, built up so as to entail its own destruction, and whose mode of functioning is its own negation.

This structural schizophrenia is quite easily discernible in the modern novel. Since it appears to me to be constitutive, however, of the very genre, I have chosen here to test it in a text reputed to be a classic. The present study will thus deal with a short novel by Balzac, whose preoccupation with the phenomenon of madness is indeed well known. But although many have already remarked on the psychological interest that madness held for Balzac, especially in its relationship to "passion," no one has yet taken into consideration the *functioning* of madness in Balzac's work: madness as an operational model that organizes the novel as a system whose very mode of functioning is to undo itself. It is this textual dynamic that I propose to analyze in an exemplary text whose astonishing richness has not yet received the critical attention it deserves: "The Illustrious Gaudissart."

"The Mystified Mystifier"

The story—to recall it briefly—is about an indefatigable traveling salesman called the Illustrious Gaudissart, who goes to Touraine on behalf of an insurance company and a group of newspapers: *The Children's Newspaper, The Movement,* and *The Globe.* To get rid of the traveling salesman, the inhabitants of the locality introduce Gaudissart to the village madman, Margaritis, telling him that the madman is a businessman, a famous banker. Now, one of the obsessions of this madman is his overwhelming desire to sell two barrels of wine which don't even exist. A long dialogue ensues between Gaudissart and the madman. To the great merriment of the populace, not only does the salesman not notice that his interlocutor is mad, but he is totally fooled by him and, becoming in his turn a buyer, signs an order confirming his purchase of the nonexistent barrels of wine.

In 1833, finding himself short several pages to make up a volume, Balzac wrote this tale in a single night. It was, no doubt, the rapidity of the text's composition that predisposed its readers not to take it altogether "seriously." It is no coincidence, however, that this tale has been systematically misread, since the text itself is full of snares. What is at stake in Balzac's irony is far more serious than the apparent farce the text appears to be. Nor does the story's thrust lie in the political and economic "portrait of manners" that the traditional readings of this text extol. Suzanne Bérard writes, for example:

> Even if we forget the interest provided by the political and economic study of a certain group of speculators after the July Revolution; even if we disdain those fine, brilliant pages on Parisian commerce and its extensions into the provinces, we still cannot rid ourselves of the character of Gaudissart himself.[4]

This appraisal is symptomatic. The critical consensus would attribute Balzac's achievement solely to the portrait of the salesman. But what about the no less important "portrait" of the madman? Haven't we gotten rid of him a little too quickly and too easily? "The intrusion of this madman in Gaudissart's adventure," writes Bernard Guyon, "may be explained in the following way: (. . .) Balzac (. . .) wanted to amuse us (. . .). He made a mistake. Let us pass quickly over this lapse of taste."[5] It is certainly not by chance that the exegetes of "The Illustrious Gaudissart" have systematically repressed the importance of the madman in this text, for there precisely lies the text's problematic aspect, its inherent difficulty: What is the meaning of the intrusion of pathology into the very discourse of the novel? What is at stake in literature is meaning; but a madman's speech is *a priori* meaningless; at any rate, it is unreadable, incomprehensible. Madness integrated into literature immediately raises the question of how the unreadable can as such be read: How and why does nonsense produce sense?

We cannot gauge the import of delirious language without reflecting simultaneously on the language we call "normal": the speeches of the madman take on significance and meaning only by their immediate reference to Gaudissart's discourse—to which, in fact, they constitute a reply.

Examined from this point of view, Balzac's text appears beyond all else to be a dramatized meditation on language: what takes

[4]S. Bérard, Preface to *L'Illustre Gaudissart* (Paris: Garnier-Flammarion, 1968), p. 34.

[5]B. Guyon, Introduction to *L'Illustre Gaudissart* (Paris: Garnier, 1970), p. xxvii.

place is nothing other than the exchange of speech. Not only is it by means of speech—the madman's—that Gaudissart is conquered, but it is also by means of speech—his own—that Gaudissart hoped to win. Like his victory, Gaudissart's defeat depends on language.

If Gaudissart represents—as the text tells us in a phrase that cannot be over-emphasized—*the genius of civilization*,[6] it is insofar as he is at once the master and the slave of the power of language:

> Nobody in France suspects the incredible power wielded by traveling salesmen (. . .). How can one forget these admirable maneuvers which mold the minds of the population by *dealing in words* with the most refractory masses (. . .)?
>
> Do you want to know *the power of language* and the great pressure that a sentence places on the most rebellious money? (. . .) *Listen to the discourse* of one of these high dignitaries of Parisian industry (. . .). Thus *eloquence*, labial flux, counts for nine-tenths of the ways and means of our exploitation. (p. 192)[7]

There is nothing surprising, then, in the fact that Gaudissart's face and physique are compared to "those classic figures adopted by the sculptors of every country for the *statues of Abundance, Law, Force, and Commerce*." An intention to dominate—one might almost say to seduce—animates the salesman's enterprise: for him, speech is a field of forces in which his will to power is affirmed; language is, above all, the place where the other can be captured. As Balzac puts it:

> Speaking, making oneself heard, isn't that *seducing?* A government with two chambers, a woman listening with both ears are both equally lost. (p. 193)

However, the salesman's plan depends on a mistaken premise: Gaudissart does not know to what extent he is himself determined by speech; he thinks he can dominate language just as language has enabled him to dominate others. What Balzac's text teaches us,

[6]Balzac, *L'Illustre Gaudissart*, in *La Comédie humaine* (Paris: Editions du Seuil, Collection "L'Intégrale," 1966), III, 192. All references will be to this edition.

[7]In the texts quoted, all italics are mine unless otherwise indicated.

however, is that language has no master: this demystification is the function of the madman's discourse.

On the very first page, Gaudissart's character is defined by three oxymorons: "This human pyrophorus is an *ignorant scholar,* a *mystified mystifier,* an *unbelieving priest* who talks all the more glibly about his dogma and mysteries" (p. 192). We could invert these oxymorons to define the madman: he is a credulous disbeliever, a knowledgeable ignoramus, and a mystifying—or demystifying—dupe. Again, it is not by chance that the narrator compares the madman's physiognomy to that of an "old professor of rhetoric" (p. 200): indeed, a whole *rhetoric* of madness can be found in this novel, a rhetoric that precisely counterbalances the rhetoric of "Law, Force, and Commerce" represented by the traveling salesman. Madness is there in order to demystify the formidable mystification of our civilization.

The Rhetoric of the Text: Metaphor and Metonymy

"Though this be madness, yet there is method in it." What is this method which presides over the discourse of meaninglessness? What linguistic techniques transform delirious logic into a coherent counter-rhetoric, into a rhetoric of demystification?

> "You were in business, sir . . ." began Gaudissart.
>
> "Public business," replied Margaritis interrupting him. (. . .)
>
> "Oh, indeed," answered Gaudissart, "then we will understand each other perfectly."
>
> "I am listening," answered Margaritis taking the pose of a man sitting for his portrait (. . .).
>
> "Sir," said Gaudissart, "sir, if you were not a man of superior qualities . . ." (here the madman bowed), "I would restrict myself to counting out the material gains of this transaction (. . .). Of all the forms of social wealth, isn't time the most precious? To save time is to save money, isn't it? Now (. . .) is there anything which consumes more time than the lack of a guarantee to give to those you ask for money when, momentarily impecunious, you are rich in hopes?"
>
> "Money, now we've got to the point," said Margaritis.

"Well, sir (. . .), I will make myself clear by material examples (. . .). Instead of being a landholder living off your income, you are a painter, a musician, an artist, a poet . . ."

"I'm a painter," the madman added by way of parenthesis.

"Well, so be it, since you take to my metaphor, you are a painter, you have a promising future, a rich future. But I'll go even further."

Upon hearing these words, the madman studied Gaudissart with an uneasy look to see if he intended to go away and was reassured only upon seeing him remain seated.

"You are as yet nothing at all," continued Gaudissart, "but you feel yourself . . ."

"I feel myself," said the madman. (p. 200)

As one reads this dialogue, one is tempted to compare it with André Breton's observations in the *Manifesto of Surrealism:*

The forms of Surrealist language adapt themselves best to the dialogue. Here, two thoughts confront each other (. . .). My attention, prey to an entreaty it cannot in all decency reject, treats this opposing thought as an enemy; in ordinary conversation, it *"takes up"* almost always on *the other's words* (. . .). It puts me in a position to turn it to my advantage by distorting them. This is true to such a degree that in certain *pathological states of mind* where sensorial disorders occupy the patient's complete attention, he will respond to questions by seizing the last word spoken in his presence or the last portion of a Surrealist sentence some trace of which he finds in his mind (. . .). There is no conversation in which some trace of this disorder does not occur.

Poetic Surrealism has focused its efforts up to this point on reestablishing dialogue in its absolute truth, by freeing both interlocutors from any obligations of politeness. Each of them simply pursues his soliloquy (. . .). Words are only so many springboards for the mind of the listener.[8]

Surrealist before its time, the dialogue between Gaudissart and the madman has less the effect of a *communication* of speech than of a *displacement* of discourse. This displacement is produced, first of all, by repetition: by repeating snatches of sentences, excerpts of Gaudissart's discourse, the madman confers a new emphasis, a different value on them; through this new interpretation,

[8]*Manifestoes of Surrealism*, trans. R. Seaver and H. R. Lane (Ann Arbor: University of Michigan Press, 1969), pp. 34–35.

the madman's echo puts the salesman's statements into question, shows them to be problematic: the mere act of repeating becomes a radical interrogation. The rhetoric of repetition is in fact a rhetoric of discontinuity.

Discontinuity between sign and signified: madness appears in discourse as a passion for the signifier, as a repetition of signs—without regard for what is signified.

As a result, it is not only the message which is short-circuited, but specifically, the way the message is articulated and represented. For in the phrases he repeats, Margaritis in effect suppresses the symbolic, analogical or metaphorical dimension of the salesman's language:

> "I'm a painter," the madman added by way of parenthesis.
> "Well, so be it, since you take to my metaphor, you are a painter, you have a promising future, a rich future. But I'll go even further."
> Upon hearing these words, the madman studied Gaudissart with an uneasy look to see if he intended to go away (. . .). (p. 200)
> "Have you measured the spread of the *Globe?*"
> "Twice . . . on foot." (p. 203)

By taking figurative statements literally, by constantly shifting the symbolic onto the real, the madman systematically demolishes the foundation of the salesman's mystifying discourse—its metaphorical fictitiousness. For metaphor, he substitutes metonymy. Whatever words happen to appear, he substitutes the metonymical relationships of contiguity for the metaphorical relationships of continuity which, in Gaudissart's discourse, postulate a possible coincidence of sign and signified, of fiction and reality: the madman's discourse, in this way, undoes itself in the pure difference of a linguistic sign which insofar as it refers, precisely, to another sign, alienates its meaning, and is dissolved by repetition.

But in the process of this self-subversion and linguistic auto-dissolution, the madman's discourse also unhinges and unmasks the salesman's language, not so much by demonstrating its *falseness*, but rather by reducing it simply to the linguistic *fiction* upon which it is founded and which it specifically attempts to conceal. As Nietzsche says, there is no contradiction between "true" and "false"; contradiction exists rather between "the abbreviations of signs and the signs themselves." Doesn't the madman have exactly the same relation to the salesman as the abbreviations of signs to the signs themselves? Gaudissart's discourse is thus dislocated by its own echo and is itself dissolved in the pure vacuity of language.

Madness and the Illusion of Realism

Might not this fundamental interaction of the characters' speech patterns constitute, on another level, the very action of the novel? The structure of interlocution, the circulation of messages between two actants—one the emitter, the other the recipient—would then suggest by homology the transmission of the story itself between the author and the reader: the novel would thus reflect its own reading-writing.

The fact that in this *mise en abyme* the role of the reader is played by a madman brings us back to the fundamental structure of the quixotic, to that madness which, at its limits, subtends any reading of a novel. If the reader is a madman, it is first of all because Margaritis, like Don Quoxote, takes himself for a character in a novel: face to face with Gaudissart, the madman in effect lives a fiction and arrogates to himself various imaginary titles; as he strives to achieve a desired image in the other's eyes, he assumes all the fanciful roles assigned to him by this false mirror.

"You were in business, sir . . ." began Gaudissart.

"Public business," replied Margaritis (. . .). "I pacified Calabria during the reign of King Murat."

"Goodness, he has been to Calabria now!" said Mr. Vernier in a whisper (. . .).

"I am listening," answered Margaritis taking the pose of a man sitting for his portrait.

"Sir," said Gaudissart turning his watch-key absent-mindedly around in a regular twirling motion which fascinated the madman and perhaps helped keep him quiet, "Sir, if you were not a man of superior qualities . . . (here the madman bowed) I would restrict myself to counting out the material gains of this transaction (. . .). Instead of being a landholder living off your income, you are a painter, a musician, an artist, a poet . . ."

"I'm a painter," the madman added by way of parenthesis (. . .).

"(. . .) I see that you have been in business."

"Yes," said the madman, "I was the founder of the Territorial Bank, Rue des Fossés-Montmartre in Paris in 1798." (pp. 200–201)

If it is specifically by virtue of being a madman and under the bond of delirium that a character in a novel makes himself into a character in a novel, doesn't that imply a questioning of the psychological realistic notion of the traditional "character in a novel"? Margaritis is no longer a character in the conventional sense of the term: he is a pure signifier, a sign that generates other signs. His delirious confabulation does not point to a referent of a psychological order, but rather to the dynamics of a language game. He is not defined by his motivation, but by his role in the narration and by his place in discourse. He is not even an entity, but rather the functional possibility of permutation of signifiers between speaker and addressee. Therefore, the madman is not, strictly speaking, a person: he is *no one,* a blank, an empty speech receptacle. And it is insofar as he is "no one," a nul set or an empty square, that he makes the system function.

If we pursue this radical suspicion madness harbors in this text, we come to understand that Balzac, whose function as the celebrated messenger of "Realism" is for some his main title to glory, was not himself the dupe of the realist pretension borne by his writing.

It is this realist pretension that is incarnated here in the discourse of the salesman: it consists in making others believe that language "expresses" something which is not itself a sign but a reality already there, pre-existing and outside of language, a reality the signifier would only mirror and "represent."

Doesn't Balzac, however, tell us that Gaudissart, that would-be "realist," is a "mystified mystifier"? And isn't the role of madness precisely to despoil that referential illusion, that novelistic mystification? While the realist pretension tries to occult, to hide the discursive origins of the narrative, madness is there to bring "the story" back to its sole origin in discourse.

What is at stake in the discursive match between Gaudissart and the madman is thus, in fact, the confrontation between two general tendencies of the novel: the tendency toward narrative, toward representation; and the tendency toward discourse, toward the exploration of the play of language in and for itself. In effecting the permutation of narrative into discourse, madness appears as an agent of transformation in the text: the novel gives up the temptation to reproduce a space exterior to it in order to become an experience that produces its own space.

Exchange and Reversibility:
The Economy of the Text

The *exchange* of discourse between Gaudissart and the madman is accompanied by a parallel *exchange* of merchandise: narrative and discourse are both founded on the same dynamic. A subtle structural correspondence is thus established between the level of narrative's utterance and the level of its statement. This correspondence is emphasized by the fact that the commercial exchange, like the discursive exchange, has no referent: since the two barrels of wine are only the dream of a madman, the business deal is a bargain of fools, and the exchange—on the level of narrative as well as on the level of discourse—consists of the transmission of an object that is not there.

The text is organized, nonetheless, according to an economy of exchange, that is, it neutralizes oppositions in favor of a system of correlations: since everything is exchanged, everything is interchangeable. The madman and the salesman are, by this very token, shown to be themselves equivalents over and above their contradictions. For if the madman's language is the reverse side of the salesman's, it is also at the same time, as we have already noted, its parodic repetition. Both discourses resemble each other in their basic intention to seduce, to fascinate, to dominate the other so as to sell him things that do not exist.

Where then can we draw the line between the demented and the "reasonable," the delirious and the sensible behavior? Where does reason end and madness begin? Which of the two is crazier, Gaudissart or Margaritis? Doesn't Gaudissart also incarnate a kind of madness, "the madness of our era" (p. 194)? And doesn't Margaritis—an assiduous reader of the newspaper who "for seven years never noticed that he was still reading the same issue" (p. 199)—represent, by contrast, a certain "good" sense, a reason-in-reverse, whose point it is precisely to reject the "madness of our era"?

In this way, the text teaches us that "sense" and "non-sense" might in their turn be interchangeable; that "reason" and "madness" are *reversible* dialectical terms.[9] As are, moreover, the oxy-

[9]Cf. the reversal of terms, p. 205: " 'What!' replied Vernier (. . .), 'Do you think we don't have the right to make fun of a gentleman who lands in Vouvray with an air

morons whose polar terms determine, in their narrative reversals, the dynamics of the novel: reverisble and interchangeable, caught by turns in the story's traps, are the disbelievers and the believers, the ignorant and the learned, the mystified and the mystifiers.

For if the madman is not seduced by the mystifying structures of the salesman's discourse, he can demystify that discourse only by mystifying, in his turn, both the salesman and himself. Demystification takes thereby the form of a supreme mystification. The process of disillusionment becomes itself already the construction of a new illusion. We can escape enchantment only by yielding, subtly and surreptitiously, to a different enchantment. We are caught in the spider web of language, and there is no exit, no definitive way out.

Madness and Irony: The Three Dimensions of the Textual Space

Madness in Balzac's text has thus a primarily *ironic* function: this surrealistic dialogue could be considered at the same time as a parody of Socratic dialogue, in which the madman plays the role of a clownish Socrates, an unwitting pedagogue who transmits an ironic teaching for which, of course, he is not responsible and of which he is not aware.

In point of fact, the "professor of rhetoric" is not the madman: it is Balzac; Balzac, that is, the structure of the text, the system of relationships between the different levels of discourse.

Contrary to what some critics have asserted, this novel is admirably well built. The extent to which the structure of the text approaches that of theater, for instance, is remarkable: not only is dialogue in general a specifically theatrical form, but in this tale, the dialogue itself is actually *staged* by the townsman Vernier, who turns the plot into a spectacle to be observed by a hidden

---

and a flourish to ask us for our money under the pretext that we are great men, painters, verse-mongers; (. . .) By my sacred word of honor, *old Margaritis talks more sense* (. . .).'

'Very well, sir, I admit you have been insulted, (. . .) and *I will not give you a reason for it, because there is not enough reason in all this affair* for me to give you any.' "

audience. By this means, the spectators are themselves incorporated into the text:

> To indicate the merriest, the most *eloquent*, the most sarcastic of all the *gossip-mongers* of the region was as much as to tell Mrs. Vernier to gather *witnesses* to observe the *scene* which would take place between the salesman and the madman, so that they could amuse the town with it for months to come. (p. 199)

The piquancy of the dialogue lies in the paradoxical fact that it is a *three-way* dialogue, which comprises three discursive centers: Gaudissart, Margaritis, and the audience among whom is "the most eloquent gossip-monger of the region." Whatever position we take in this text, we encounter eloquence, but a kind of eloquence that becomes each time more repetitious and more parodic: the gossip will *repeat* the remarks made by the madman who *repeats* the remarks made by the salesman. In addition to the three centers of discourse, there are three centers of audition: the two interlocutors are, of course, supposed to be listening to each other, but, in fact, they only *understand* each other to the extent that they *do not listen* to each other, that they listen only to themselves. The dialogue is thus as much an exchange in *deafness* as it is an exchange of speech. And it is, paradoxically enough, this mutual deafness to the Other that makes *communication* possible and brings about the apparent mutual understanding. This ironical relationship between hearing and mis-understanding, between understanding and mis-hearing is outlined by Balzac himself, through his play on the two senses of the word *entendre* (to "hear" and/or to "understand") and his frequent use of the related verb *écouter* (to "listen"):

> "Mr. Margaritis," said Mrs. Vernier, "(. . .) Here is a gentleman sent to you by my husband, and you should *listen* [*écouter*] to him carefully (. . .)."
> The three women went into Mrs. Margaritis' room so they could *hear everything* [*tout entendre*] (. . .).
> "Oh, indeed," answered Gaudissart, "then *we will understand each other* [*nous nous entendrons*] perfectly."
> "*I am listening* [*je vous écoute*]," answered Margaritis (. . .).
> "Sir," said Gaudissart (. . .), "*Listen!* [*Ecoutez*]."
> "*So you have reached an understanding*" [*Vous vous êtes donc*

113

entendus?], said the relentless Mitouflet with the utmost calm. "That is funny." (. . .)

"Sir," said the Prince of Salesmen (. . .), "you must give me a reason for the insult you have just done me by putting me in relation with a man you knew to be mad. *Do you hear me* [*m'entendez-vous*], Mr. Vernier?" (. . .)

"(. . .) What are you complaining about? *You understand each other perfectly* [*Vous vous êtes parfaitement entendus*]." (pp. 200, 204–205)

The successive transformation of the words *écouter* and *entendre* can stand as model for the predicament of all words exchanged in this text: the ironic tension generated by these words is a function of their repeated *transposition* from one speaker to another, from one context to another. But only those at the third listening post, the hidden audience, are capable of perceiving this transposition. Only this audience, like the author and the reader, possesses the ironic knowledge which, as always, evades the protagonists. Thus, dramatic irony is itself *dramatized* in this novel.

In this way, the text writes itself as, fundamentally, a reading. Through the process of its constant self-reflection, the novel is engaged in its own self-parody and self-relativization. By virtue of its discursive centers, the textual space is radically decentered, diffusing any discourse that is bi-dimensional. Both the "novel" of the madman and the "novel" of the salesman—both the fiction of realism and the fiction of imagination—are transgressed, surpassed, and fundamentally negated: the fictitiousness of Realism is as fake as the Imaginary is gratuitous. The novel, thus, is nothing other than the vertiginous play of mirrors through which it ceaselessly demystifies itself.

This dizzying mirror-game, this reflexive play, is not without its dangers, and the presence of madness in this text is no accident. Indeed, madness is an integral part of every ironic structure. If madness here appears to be an extreme irony, it is because the extreme of irony is, precisely, madness: the madman is not just the *instrument* of ironic knowledge, he incarnates as well the imminence of the *peril* that threatens reflexive consciousness, always endangered by its own internal split, by the very tension that grounds it in its own contradiction. Balzac is well aware of this, as his own words in the *Théorie de la démarche* suggest: "I put myself at the exact point where knowledge touches on madness, and I refuse to put up any safety rail [*garde-fous*]."[10]

And Louis Lambert, "that immense brain which cracked to pieces as if it were too vast an empire," succumbed, as we know, because he flew too high "across the spaces of thought."[11]

Thus for Balzac, ironic consciousness is in reality an anguished consciousness, and one that is lucid in its anguish. In Balzac's work, comedy and tragedy meet and merge in madness: Balzac's irony is the reverse side of his pathos.

Balzac's salvation lies in his own doubleness: at once a madman and a salesman, he too is a seducer, speechifier, master and slave of language; he too is at the same time "mystified" and "mystifier"; but he is a "mystified mystifier" who, unlike the others, knows it.

[10]*Traité de la vie élégante,* followed by *La Théorie de la démarche* (Paris: Bossard, 1922), p. 129.
[11]*Louis Lambert* (Livre de Poche), pp. 178, 165.

PART THREE

MADNESS AND

PSYCHOANALYSIS

I situate myself at the exact point where
knowledge touches upon madness, and I can
erect no safety rail.
                    Balzac, Théorie de la démarche

6

Jacques Lacan: Madness
and the Risks of Theory
(The Uses of Misprision)

—Meaning and Knowledge
—Grammar and Rhetoric
—A Shade of Enthusiasm
—The Status of Teaching: An Ethic of the Unconscious
—Knowledge Presumed to be a Subject: The Drop of Ink
—"Don't You See I'm Burning?" or Lacan and Philosophy

Meaning and Knowledge

"The truth pursued by science," writes Georges Bataille, "is true only on condition that it be devoid of meaning, and nothing can have meaning except insofar as it is fiction."[1] This proposition could define at once the doctrine and the difficulty of psychoanalysis, as a *practice*—and a *science*—of the *fiction* of the subject. "What is truth, if not a complaint?" says Lacan. Now, "it is not the *meaning* of the complaint that is important, but whatever might be found beyond that meaning, that might be definable as real." The "real," here, refers specifically to what is not dependent upon the idea the subject has of it: "that which is not affected by my thinking about it."[2] "There is no other truth," Lacan affirms,

[1] G. Bataille, "L'Apprenti Sorcier," *Oeuvres complètes* (Paris: Gallimard, 1973), I, 526.
[2] "Les Non-dupes errent" (seminar), April 23, 1974 (unpublished).

"than mathematicized truth, that is, *written* truth"; truth, in other words, "can hinge only on axioms: truth proceeds only from what has no meaning."[3] There is truth only where there is no meaning.

Does psychoanalysis, then, aspire to meaning—or to truth? What is the meaning *of* psychoanalysis? This question, whose urgency has become evident in the current field of theory (but we know—from psychoanalysis—that evidence is, precisely, that which is *least seen*), this now unavoidable question of *the meaning of psychoanalysis*, is in fact a contradiction in terms, since "meaning" is forever but a fiction and since it is psychoanalysis itself which has taught us that. But contradiction, as we know, is the mode of functioning par excellence of the unconscious, and consequently, also of the logic of psychoanalysis. To reckon with psychoanalysis is to reckon with contradiction, including its disequilibrium, without reducing it to the specular illusion of symmetry or of a dialectical synthesis. If, indeed, the specular illusion, the "Imaginary," to use the Lacanian term, is itself a constitutive principle of *meaning*, being precisely "that which *blocks* the decoding of the *Symbolic*," which in turn acts as a vehicle for the Real only by being "always encoded," then "the Imaginary is a dimension [*dit-mension*, a speech-dimension] as important as the others."[4] The Imaginary is an irreducible dimension because within language, the "sememe"—the semantic unit—is always occupied by the body: it makes up for the fact that there is nothing else to lead the body toward the Other. There is no *natural* relationship: the only relationship with the Other is by "the intermediary of what *makes sense* in language."[5] We must not, then, resolve the contradiction, but resolve to accept it: we must articulate the question of the *meaning* of psychoanalysis on the basis of its own contradiction: we must consider this contradiction not as a contingent fact, but as the condition that makes possible the very question of psychoanalysis: of psychoanalysis *as a question*. Psychoanalysis introduces into the field of theory nothing less than the necessity of a new kind of articulation of its own question: the subversive urgency of psychoanalysis, its momentousness for

[3]*Ibid.*, February 11, 1973.
[4]*Ibid.*, November 13, 1973.
[5]*Ibid.*, June 11, 1974.

culture, lies in the need it has brought out and in the henceforth irreversible search it has inaugurated for *a new status of discourse.*

If, by its most radical dimension, psychoanalysis subverts the very status of meaning, even while it is thereby constrained to call *itself* in question and to subvert *its own* meaning, it does so because, as Lacan says, "meaning *knows itself*": meaning is, above all else, that which is present to itself; it is therefore a form of knowledge—knowledge of self—of consciousness. Now, if Freud's discovery of the unconscious "makes sense" (we see here again the pervasive problem of meaning that language cannot eliminate, the problem of the apprehension by consciousness of the unconscious which escapes it), this "id" (this "it") which speaks yields a *language* which *knows,* but without any subject being able to assume such a knowledge or being able to know that he/she knows. Lacan makes it clear that we are in no way dealing with the myth of "non-knowledge" [*non-savoir*] that a superficial avant-garde used to its advantage: for not only is it not *sufficient* not to know; the very ability not to know is not granted to us,[6] and cannot thus be taken for granted. What we are dealing with is a knowledge that is, rather, indestructible; *a knowledge which does not allow for knowing that one knows;*[7] a knowledge, therefore, that is not supported by *meaning* which, by definition, *knows itself.* The subject can get a hold on this unconscious knowledge only by the intermediary of his *mistakes*—the effects of non-sense his speech registers: in dreams, slips of the tongue, or jokes.

"A question suddenly arises (. . .): in the case of the knowledge yielded solely by the subject's mistake, what kind of subject could ever be in a position to know it in advance?"[8] The "subject who is presumed to know," that basic myth of Western culture, of the University, and of philosophic discourse, can only be "God Himself": a reflection in which the "knowledge" of consciousness contemplates itself, a phantom of potency produced by the narcissistic, self-inflating spell of the mirror. "Here he is, the God of the philosophers, dislodged from his latency in every theory. *Theoria,* might that not be the place in the world for the theo-logy?"[9]

[6]*Ibid.,* April 23, 1974.
[7]*Ibid.,* February 2, 1974.
[8]"La Méprise du sujet supposé savoir," *Scilicet,* no. 1 (1968), 38.
[9]*Ibid.,* p. 39.

The "subject presumed to know" lives in delusions and fantasies. By subverting this subject, psychoanalysis has radicalized a theory of non-transparency, a theory of what Baudelaire calls "the universal misunderstanding," and Proust "that perpetual error that we call, precisely, life." But within this theory, the position of psychoanalysis is itself problematic since it arises from the contradiction which determines its own discourse, namely: How can one construct a *theory* of the mistake essential to the very subject of theory as such? And if error is universal, how is one to escape error oneself? To what sort of listening or understanding can one appeal in a theory of radical *mis-understanding?* Lacan is fully aware of the untenable position he has nevertheless taken and taken on with an unparalleled intensity of effort and desire: "Retain at least what this text, which I have tossed out in your direction, bears witness to: my enterprise does not go beyond the act in which it is caught, and therefore, its only chance lies in its error—in its misprision [*elle n'a de chance que de sa méprise*]."[10] To my mind, the staggering originality of Lacan's work and discourse resides precisely in this untenable theoretical position. I would like, then, to attempt here an (overtly) brief meditation on this *méprise*—this misprision[11]—and on the significance of Lacan's gesture of giving it its chance.

Grammar and Rhetoric

Misprision, for Lacan, is of course an outgrowth of "the trickiness of the unconscious," which in language "is revealed by the rhetorical overload Freud shows it utilizes to make its argument":[12] the symptom functions like a metaphor, desire like a metonymy; the narcissistic mechanisms of defense and resistance employ all kinds of "tropes" and "figures of speech"—periphrasis, ellipsis, denial, digression, irony, litotes, etc.[13] A theory of mispri-

---

[10]*Ibid.*, p. 41.

[11]"A misunderstanding, a mistake (arch.)" (*Oxford English Dictionary*). This is the closest, and the only perfectly accurate, English equivalent to Lacan's word, *méprise.*

[12]"La Méprise du sujet supposé savoir," p. 32.

[13]"The Agency of the Letter in the Unconscious," *Ecrits: A Selection*, trans. A. Sheridan (New York: Norton, 1977), p. 156.

sion will thus be a theory of the *rhetoric* of the unconscious: "On the basis of the manifestations of the unconscious with which I deal as an analyst, I came to develop a theory of the effects of the signifier through which I rejoin the preoccupations of rhetoric."[14] Alongside this inquiry into rhetoric, there is in Lacan's work a second project, focusing on *grammar*: "Such are the structural conditions which determine—as *grammar*—the system of encroachments constitutive of the signifier."[15] The accomplishment of this double project should thus establish a *grammar of rhetoric*.

The logical coherence of such a project may seem self-evident. However, for a logician like Charles Sanders Peirce, the logical affiliation between rhetoric and grammar cannot be taken for granted: in fact, Peirce makes a distinction between "pure rhetoric" and "pure grammar." What he calls "pure rhetoric" is the well-known process by which one sign engenders another: a system of reference from sign to sign in which meaning is but another sign, requiring for its establishment the intervention of a *third* element which Peirce calls the *interpretant*. "Pure grammar," on the other hand, postulates the possibility of a continuous, binary relationship between sign and meaning not requiring the intervention of a third element. In general, we think of grammar as a logical system *par excellence* and, as such, identical to itself, universal, and generative, that is, inscribing the possibility of infinite combinations and transformations stemming from a *single, unified model* without the intervention of another model that would interfere with or subvert the first.[16] By contrast, rhetoric can be perceived only through a *discontinuity* that subverts or, at the very least, contradicts the logical *continuity* of the grammatical model. Rhetoric, to borrow out of context a Lacanian expression, always has an *"incongruous dimension* which analysts have not yet entirely given up because of their justified feeling that their conformism is of value only on the basis of that dimension."[17]

But if the grammatical model of continuity and the rhetorical

[14]"La Métaphore du sujet," *Ecrits* (Paris: Seuil, 1966), p. 889.

[15]"The Agency of the Letter," p. 152. Translation modified; emphasis added.

[16]These comments, as well as the epistemological distinction between rhetoric and grammar, are based on the remarkable article by Paul de Man, "Semiology and Rhetoric," *Diacritics*, no. 3 (1973). Reprinted in *Allegories of Reading* (New Haven: Yale University Press, 1979).

[17]"The Agency of the Letter," p. 152.

model of discontinuity are not congruent, how are we to understand, as a whole, the Lacanian project of establishing a *grammar of rhetoric?* It would seem that Lacan's scientific project is to reduce the rhetorical mystifications of the unconscious to the rigor of a grammar. The unconscious as an operation and psychoanalysis as a science would, as a result, be modeled on two different epistemologies and would be distinguished from each other just as grammar is distinguished from rhetoric. "If the symptom is a metaphor, it is not a metaphor to say so," Lacan affirms.[18] To "grammaticalize" rhetoric would then be to formalize it, to abstract a concept from it, to state a theory of rhetoric in a language itself rid of rhetoric: it would be to make the uttering of a statement coincide perfectly with what is stated, concerning, but also contradicting, rhetoric itself which is precisely "the law by which the utterance of a statement can never be reduced to the statement itself of whatever discourse."[19] Man pursues his dream, Lacan says elsewhere, "and as he does, it sometimes happens that he wishes to stop dreaming."[20] By the same token, Lacan himself, at times, dreams of dreaming no more: "If all that is articulated in sleep only enters into analysis through its narration, doesn't this presuppose that the structure of narration does not succumb to sleep?"[21] The task Lacan assigns himself is to break away from sleep so as to talk about it, to break away from the very mechanisms of the unconscious in order to *say the unconscious itself.*

Is this project feasible? Lacan is the first to recognize and to affirm that one cannot *get out of* the unconscious; therefore, it is not possible to say the unconscious itself, it is not possible to free oneself from its fundamental function as deception in order to enunciate, without deceiving oneself, the absolute law of deception: "We don't even know if the unconscious has a being in itself, and (. . .) it is because one could not say *that's it* that it was named the 'it' [*id*]. In fact, one could only say of the unconscious, *that's not it*, or rather, *that's it*, but *not for real.*"[22] Lacan formulates the same logical principle when he states "that no metalanguage can be spoken, or, more aphoristically, that there is no Other of the

---

[18]*Ibid.*, p. 175.
[19]"La Métaphore du sujet," p. 889.
[20]"Les Non-dupes errent" (seminar), March 12, 1974.
[21]"De la psychanalyse dans ses rapports avec la réalité," *Scilicet*, no. 1, p. 35.
[22]"La Méprise du sujet supposé savoir," p. 35.

Other."[23] What, however, is a *grammar* (a formalized grammar) if not the epitome of metalanguage? Grammar is thus—and Lacan knows it—one more impossible desire: the desire to establish a norm, a rule of *correctness*, to avoid precisely the misprision inherent in the enterprise, to be for once a *non-dupe*. But who knows better than Lacan that "non-dupes err"?[24] Lacan's writing thus articulates the very torment which inhabits logic. And the chances taken by Lacan's text—what gives it a chance and what makes its chance ours—is the spark struck up in language by the inner tension of a discourse struggling with itself, struggling with its double, contradictory desire: the desire for grammar and its counterpart, the desire for rhetoric. It is precisely through this contradiction that Lacan's discourse rejoins the *Real:* "the real," says Lacan, "is the *impossible.*"

A Shade of Enthusiasm

Lacan's language registers this contradictory desire both as a complication and as a simplification: on the one hand, as the ironic and sophisticated complication of a theory of misprision which excepts—in all conscience—neither its author nor its recipients; and on the other hand, as the affective simplification of the pathos of failure which prevades that discourse,[25] a pathos countered by the intensity of Lacan's affirmations and by the urgency of his enthusiasm. "The originality we are allowed," says Lacan, "is limited to the scrap of enthusiasm we have brought (. . .) to what Freud was able to name."[26] The urgency of the enthusiasm in Lacan's text serves to wrest affirmation from uncertainty, from the doubt occasioned by its own contradictions and complications. It manifests, in the very midst of logic, the function of desire,[27] that

---

[23]"The Subversion of the Subject and the Dialectic of Desire in the Freudian Unconscious," *Ecrits: A Selection*, p. 311.

[24]The title (translated) of Lacan's seminar of 1973–1974.

[25]Cf. "La Psychanalyse: Raison d'un échec," *Scilicet*, no. 1, pp. 42–50.

[26]"Introduction to 'Scilicet,'" *Scilicet*, no. 1 (1968), 5–6.

[27]Cf. Lacan's insistence on "the desire of the analyst" in *The Four Fundamental Concepts of Psychoanalysis*, trans. A. Sheridan (New York: Norton, 1977), p. 158.

"function of haste"[28] necessary to produce an affirmation within a plural logic. Each time the urgency passes, the enthusiasm inevitably subsides again into a sense of failure, in recognition of its own inescapable naïveté, of the blindness of its own intoxication. Lacan takes stock—within his desire for *grammar*—of his own unconscious *rhetoric*. "A shade of enthusiasm is the surest trace to leave behind in a writing to make it dated—in the worst sense of the word." That is the way Lacan introduces nothing less than his famous Rome Report, "The Function and Field of Speech and Language in Psychoanalysis": "We wish to discuss," writes Lacan, "the subject put in question by this report, since putting the subject here in its place, at the place in which we ourselves have not failed to illustrate it, is but to do justice to the place where it lies in wait for us."[29] The movement of Lacan's text thus obeys the principle outlined by Bachelard: "Let us begin by admiring. Later, we shall see whether it will be necessary, through criticism or reduction, to organize our disappointment."[30]

"A shade of enthusiasm" is thus the surest trace to leave behind in a writing to make it dated. But what does "to make dated" mean here? When we are dealing with Lacan, it means, first of all, to mark a memorable date, to introduce a new articulation into cultural discourse, a "renewal of the alliance with Freud's discovery."[31] But since this innovation, this "renewal of the alliance" rallies specifically to an elusive structure, consisting in the linguistic articulation of the very mechanisms of repression through which truth escapes, modernity can be attained only within a radical dimension of loss. Modernity is precisely what gets lost: what gets lost in and through the very welling up of the enthusiasm of having discovered it. Enthusiasm thus becomes the hallmark of the "missed chance," that peculiar movement through which we move away from that toward which we want to go. "If it is true that psychoanalysis rests on a fundamental conflict, on an initial radical drama as far as everything that might be included under the heading psychical is concerned, the innovation to which I have referred (. . .) makes no claim to a position of exhaustiveness with

[28]Cf. "Le Temps logique et l'assertion de certitude anticipée," *Ecrits*, pp. 197–229.
[29]"Du sujet enfin en question," *Ecrits*, p. 229.
[30]Georges Bachelard, *La Poétique de l'espace* (Paris: P.U.F., 1958), pp. 197–198.
[31]*The Four Fundamental Concepts*, p. 128.

respect to the unconscious, since it is, itself, an intervention in the conflict (. . .). This indicates that the cause of the unconscious (. . .) must be conceived as, fundamentally, a lost cause. And it is the only chance one has of winning it."[32]

This radical dimension of loss is, therefore, nothing other than the loss of the security of a metalanguage, the loss of a "claim to a position of exhaustiveness" which would precisely be the claim of *grammar:* we are faced, once again, with the inescapable dimension of *rhetoric,* that "stumbling block" which forces discourse to discover that it can only define rhetoric rhetorically, by participating in it, i.e., by stumbling, by elaborating not a grammar of rhetoric but a *rhetoric of rhetoric:* "Stumbling, faltering, splitting. In a spoken or written sentence something slips (. . .). It's there that something else is asking to be realized—something which appears as intentional, of course, but partaking of *a strange temporality.*"[33] This "strange temporality" is the lack of a present, the non self-presence characteristic of the rhetorical mode. It is also in this sense that the rhetoric of desire and enthusiasm is bound to be *dated:* for this rhetoric is not contemporaneous with its own statement. "There is no present," writes Mallarmé, "no—a present does not exist. (. . .) Ill-informed is he who would proclaim himself his own contemporary."[34]

To say that enthusiasm makes a text "dated" is to say that the enthusiasm has had a future that has come to point to it as past; that, from its own enthusiasm, the text has gleaned both more and less than it had expected; that urgency—both emotional and logical—has inscribed in language a vanishing point where the writing becomes *self-transgressive.* It is to say that the text—as it must—has organized our disappointment, has disappointed its own enthusiasm, subverted its own fantasy, and recanted the authority of its own rhetoric.

Inescapably, enthusiasm is what passes; it is, therefore, *nothing:* nothing, in any case, other than what is doomed—like us—to pass. "It is here that is inscribed that final *Spaltung* by which the subject articulates himself in the Logos, and on which Freud was beginning to write, giving us, at the ultimate point of a work that has the

---

[32]*Ibid.,* pp. 127–128.
[33]*Ibid.,* p. 25.
[34]"L'Action restreinte," *Oeuvres complètes,* p. 372.

dimensions of being, the solution of the 'infinite' analysis, when his death applied to it the word Nothing."[35]

> Nothing, this foam, virgin verse
> Denoting only its cut.[36]

"A shade [*un rien*] of enthusiasm" has a good chance of amounting to the *nothingness* [*rien*] of enthusiasm. But isn't that the source, precisely, both of the misprision and of the chance inherent in psychoanalytic *transference*? "At that turning point where the subject experiences the collapse of the assurance provided him by that fantasy whereby each individual fashions his view of the Real, what becomes evident is that the hold of desire is *nothing* but the hold of an un-being."[37]

In the "transference of intensity"[38] constitutive of desire's repetitions and structuring not just psychoanalytic treatment but also "that perpetual error that we call, precisely, life," what seeks realization is a kind of metaphoric operation, a desire for analogy—for metaphor. But the result is, each time, the abortion of the specular analogy, the failure of the metaphor to attain and name its proper meaning. "If the psychoanalyst cannot respond to the demand, it is only because to respond to it would of necessity be to disappoint it, since what is demanded is, in any case, Something-Else; and *that is precisely what one must come to understand.*"[39] While the analyst, in the transferential operation, occupies the precise place of the "nothing" of enthusiasm, the place of the primordial partial

---

[35]Lacan, "The Direction of the Treatment and the Principles of Its Power," *Ecrits: A Selection*, p. 277.

[36]Mallarmé, "Salut," *Selected Poems*, trans. C. F. MacIntyre (Berkeley: University of California Press, 1957), p. 2.

[37]Lacan, "Le Psychanalyste de l'école," *Scilicet*, no. 1 (1968), 25. My italics.

[38]Cf. Freud, *The Interpretation of Dreams*, in the *Standard Edition* (London: Hogarth, 1956), V, 560, 562–563, 564: "I am now in a position to give a precise account of the part played in dreams by the unconscious wish . . . the psychology of the neuroses [shows us] that an unconscious idea as such is quite incapable of entering the preconscious and that it can only exercise any effect there by establishing a connection with an idea which already belongs to the preconscious, by *transferring its intensity* on to it and by getting itself 'covered' by it. Here we have the fact of 'transference' . . . It will be seen that the day's residues . . . not only borrow something from the unconscious . . . namely the instinctual force which is at the disposal of the repressed wish—but that they also offer the unconscious something indispensable—namely the necessary point of attachment for a transference."

[39]Lacan, "La Psychanalyse: Raison d'un échec," p. 44. My italics.

object—*l'objet petit a*—which materalizes the non-being of desire, the end point of analysis—the naming of the Nothing—teaches the subject that the blind metaphor of his destiny is deprived of any proper meaning since all it can name is a metonymy (*l'objet petit a*). That is to say that the psychoanalyst, in playing the role of the non-proper (*non-propre*) (which the analysand deceives himself into reading as a proper name [*nom propre*]), occupies the radically other position of the pre-eminently rhetorical; and that the therapeutic goal is then to deconstruct the grammatical illusion of identity—of the proper—in order to reconcile the subject to his own rhetoric.

The Status of Teaching: An Ethic of the Unconscious

If transference is "the enacting of the reality of the unconscious,"[40] then, clearly, its manifestations will go beyond the strictly professional limits of psychoanalysis and become evident wherever effects of language are produced through regular interlocution: particularly, in the classroom situation. As Lacan points out, the transferential structure of the teaching relation is evoked in exemplary fashion in Plato's *Symposium:* "Who has expressed better than Alcibiades that the snares of love in transference have only one purpose, and that is to secure that of which he takes Socrates to be the unprepossessing container? But who knows better than Socrates that he bears only the meaning he engenders by containing this very *nothing?*"[41] The "Master" teacher, the illusory "subject presumed to know," occupies in the Real, like the analyst, the radically other position of the *"nothing"* of enthusiasm. However, far from challenging this instance of transference, teaching ought, rather, to assume it: "My seminar has been criticized precisely for playing, in relation to my audience, a role considered . . . dangerous, that of intervening in the transference. Now, far from denying it, I would regard this intervention as radical, as constitutive of the renewal of the alliance

---

[40]Lacan, *The Four Fundamental Concepts*, p. 174.
[41]Lacan, "Le Psychanalyste de l'école," p. 22.

with Freud's discovery."[42] Lacan proposes here a praxis of teaching in which he puts himself against one of those three tasks declared by Freud to be impossible, since their effectiveness is based precisely on the mirage that governs their performance: psychoanalyzing, governing, educating. But here again, the impossible becomes for Lacan an imperative of the Real; and, in his view, the status of the unconscious is not ontological but *ethical:* "The status of the unconscious, which, as I have suggested, is so fragile on the ontic plane, is ethical. In his thirst for truth, Freud says, *Whatever may happen, it is imperative to go there.*"[43] Lacan's practice of teaching, whose intensity derives at once from the pathos of a "vocation" and from the keenness of an intellectual awareness, from the "cruelty" (as Artaud would say) of a lucidity and of a rigor always striving toward that "extreme point of existence, the wager"[44]—embodies Lacan's quest not only for a new status of discourse, but also for a radically new kind of teaching.

It seems to me that this wager, which implicates us all, is the measure of Lacan's unprecedented move to confront psychoanalysis with its own madness, to push it—with all the risks involved—to the limits of its logical consequences.

"How are we to teach what psychoanalysis teaches us?" asks Lacan in a question posed not to the technicians of psychoanalytic treatment, but to the "practitioners of widely diverse disciplines."[45] What kind of teaching would assume in full consciousness its transferential function, assume, in other words, misprision with all its uses and abuses, with all its risks and possibilities? It would be, first of all, a teaching that would break with the mirror game of "the subject presumed to know," as well as with that false, narcissistic understanding inherent in all dual relationships; it would be a teaching based on a "firmer otherness,"[46] in which the "Master" would assume and articulate the radical *non-mastery* implied by the unconscious, making explicit his "rank"[47] (his position or his status) as the "nothingness of enthu-

---

[42]*The Four Fundamental Concepts*, p. 128. Translation modified.
[43]*Ibid.*, p. 33. Translation modified.
[44]Lacan, "La Raison d'un échec," p. 48.
[45]Lacan, "La Psychanalyse et son enseignement," *Ecrits*, pp. 439, 440.
[46]*Ibid.*, p. 44.
[47]Cf. Lacan's comments regarding the analyst: "This place that belongs to nobody . . . —the place of a rank to occupy, in semblance: the role of the analyst." "Les Non-dupes errent" (seminar), April 9, 1974.

siasm," so as to subvert fantasy and to *"transform the trap into a question."*[48] It would be, consequently, an eminently ironic teaching, that is, once again, radically *rhetorical* (strategic): it would be, as Lacan puts it (speaking of Saussure, but his words apply to his own case as well), "a teaching worthy of the name, that one can come to terms with only in its own terms."[49] Such teaching would then mobilize the resources not so much of transparency as of obstacles: it would teach *about* and *through* misprision, about and through interpretive stumbling blocks and textual distortions: "Any return to Freud founding a teaching worthy of the name will occur only on that pathway where truth . . . becomes manifest in the revolutions of culture. That pathway is the only training we can claim to transmit to those who follow us. It is called—a style."[50]

But what is a style?

Knowledge Presumed to Be a Subject: The Drop of Ink

A "style," of course, is something that occurs in language; it is an event—or an advent—of textuality, that is, of writing. The writing of Lacan incorporates in turn the risk and the potential of misprision. It moves through the difficult and obstructed paths of desire. It writes, in Mallarmé's expression, "black on white," that is to say, darkening with the very inkwell of the unconscious, producing a *light* only by projecting *shadows* somewhere else.

> To write—
> The inkwell, crystal as a consciousness, with its drop,
> at the bottom, of shadows . . . casts the lamp aside.[51]

Lacan's writing, so like Mallarmé's, is not just well aware of its deliberate *literary* quality; it furthermore fully assumes its irreducible share of ambiguity, its irreducible involvement in that

[48]On "transference," cf. *Ecrits*, p. 452.
[49]*Ecrits: A Selection*, p. 149.
[50]Lacan, "La Psychanalyse et son enseignement," p. 458.
[51]Mallarmé, "L'Action restreinte," p. 370.

linguistic blindness which paradoxically *informs* flashes of clear-sightedness and insight. Misprision is, indeed, given its chance through the textual reverses suffered by the "subject presumed to know" [*le sujet supposé savoir*]: "I propose," Lacan says, "as a formula defining writing, the *knowledge presumed to be a subject* [*le savoir supposé sujet*]."[52] The fact that this aphoristic formula on writing's knowledge operates a playful chiasmus on Lacan's other well-known formula concerning knowledge; the fact that *le savoir supposé sujet* is a strict (syntactic and rhetorical) reversal of *le sujet supposé savoir,* is no gratuitous play on words: it suggests that what is at stake in writing is precisely a reversal, a subversion of subjective knowledge (of that knowledge which believes it knows itself), a subversion of the self and its self-knowledge. Writing's knowledge, then, although usually "presumed to be a subject"—believed to be an attribute of the (writing) subject—is nothing other in effect than the textual knowledge of what links the signifiers in the text (and not the signifieds) to one another: *knowledge that escapes* the subject but through which the subject is precisely constituted as the one who *knows how to escape*—by means of signifiers—his own self-presence: "The subject," says Lacan, "doesn't presume anything, he is presumed. Presumed, as we have taught, by the signifier which represents him to another signifier."[53]

If Lacan's writing lingers with so much emphasis and "insistence" on the opacity of the letter, on the *materiality* of the signifier in its puns and its anagrammatical surprises, it does so in order to try to "meet misprision in its own place,"[54] in that place of language where precisely writing is located: where we ourselves are being *played with*. This is the way Lacan's difficult writing—his "dis-spelling," as he puts it—should be understood: "The written as what means not-to-be-read" is "a demand for interpretation."[55] To interpret is to stumble on the *arbitrariness* of the sign so as to find out that chance, paradoxically, does not exist; to stumble on the arbitrariness of the sign so as to learn to interpret the *non-arbitrariness* of the connection between the signifiers.

[52]"Les Non-dupes errent" (seminar), April 9, 1974.

[53]Lacan, "Le Psychanalyste de l'école," p. 19.

[54]"De la psychanalyse dans ses rapparts avec la réalité," *Scilicet*, no. 1 (1968), 56.

[55]Lacan, "Postface," *Les Quatre concepts fondamentaux de la psychanalyse* (Paris: Seuil, 1973), p. 252. (This section does not appear in the English translation.)

This, precisely, is what poets have always known: the insight into the non-arbitrariness of the arbitrary is constitutive of poetic knowledge in general, and specifically the poetic dimension inherent in Lacan's style. "And as Plato pointed out long ago, it is not at all necessary," says Lacan, "that the poet know what he is doing, in fact, it is preferable that he not know. That is what gives a primordial value to what he does. We can only bow our heads before it. . . . Freud always repudiated . . . the interpretation of art; what is called 'psychoanalysis of art' is to be avoided even more than the famous 'psychology of art' which is itself an insane notion. From art we should take seeds—take seeds for something else."[56]

Lacan does not indeed "interpret" poetry; he "takes seeds from it," incorporates it, writes it—and cites it. One of the reasons his texts are so difficult to approach is that he is (as he himself says about Freud) "an encyclopedia of the arts and muses."[57] But it is necessary to come to terms with this difficult, all but incomprehensible status of quotation—"the written as what means not-to-be-read"—in Lacan's texts. Lacan may quote Heidegger, for instance, while nonetheless keeping his distance from Heidegger's philosophic doctrine: "When I speak of Heidegger, or rather when I translate him, I at least make the effort to leave the speech he proffers us its sovereign significance."[58] *Sovereign significance* means that in the body of the text the quotation remains a foreign body; that it functions not as *meaning* (which "knows itself") but as a *signifier* which is always displaced, always imported from another text, another scene. Like the signifier, the quotation is incorporated into the text only through the unarticulated gap of its own displacement. The connection between the signifiers, the *articulation* between the various references quoted is what, by definition, can never be *thematized*, never be self-present in the text.

It is precisely this original stylistic feature of Lacan's text that philosophic discourse has refused to understand or to accept. Indeed, the unprecedented status of his quotations has been considered, by some philosophers, to be a major flaw. The "sovereign significance" that Lacan would like to leave, for example, to

---

[56]"Les Non-dupes errent" (seminar), April 9, 1974.
[57]"The Agency of the Letter," pp. 169–170.
[58]*Ibid.*, p. 175.

Heidegger's word, appears to these philosophers as a lack of seriousness, a philosophic "flippancy":

> One could say that his is clearly a way of not *reading* Heidegger's discourse, of avoiding or of refusing to read it. . . . One could also say that there is a certain flippancy (or excess cleverness) involved in this moving so flashily from one level to another and in "miraculously" resolving all the problems involved in the text's signifying process through a mere gesture of evocation.[59]

Upon encountering a writing as theoretically surprising, indeed as "flashy" as Lacan's, philosophic discourse—in a way specific to its reasoning—cannot but *miss the encounter* (all encounters are of course, in one way or another, missed: the difference here again is one of "style"). This particular philosophic way of missing the encounter—of giving form to "misprision"—here produces in effect, in a philosophically remarkable analysis, the "sovereign significance" of what might be called the *rigorist misunderstanding:* a radical misapprehension of the status of quotation in Lacan's works and, as a consequence, the rejection of his ellipsis and his "inarticulation," the rejection of his discourse as fundamentally a discourse *of the text,* "written as what means not-to-be-read." Philosophic discourse thus rejects Lacan's text insofar as the meaning of the latter can be neither reflected nor exhausted in its own self-knowledge, insofar precisely as the stake of its particular mode of *articulation* is to convey, put into play, and say the *maximum possible inarticulation.*

"Don't You See I'm Burning?" or Lacan and Philosophy

It is thus that, in their critical reading of Lacan's essay, "The Agency of the Letter in the Unconscious" (in which Lacan "transfers" the Freudian discovery onto Saussure), the philosophers have formulated the following critique: "The issue here is to articulate psychoanalysis with linguistics. . . . Yet this is precisely what is

[59]J.-L. Nancy and P. Lacoue-Labarthe, *Le Titre de la lettre, Une lecture de Lacan* (Paris: Galilée, 1973), pp. 136–137.

lacking . . . the articulation is missing."[60] Curiously enough, in (the very) place of what is missing, the critics find in Lacan's text a singular metaphor. Lacan writes:

> But haven't we felt for some time now that, having followed the pathways of the letter in search of the Freudian truth, we are getting very warm indeed, that something's burning all about us?[61]

The philosophers make the following comment: "But what this fire burns and lays waste here is nothing other, finally, than the articulation itself. At the place where the systematic linking of Saussure and Freud should take place, it burns, with the result that in this constitution of the science of the letter, we are in danger of having nothing left to decipher but ashes."[62]

What philosophy thus cannot accept is a discourse that *burns its way along*, skipping, in the process, its own logical (methodological) steps [*un discours qui brûle les étapes*]. For its part, philosophic discourse is defined by a demand for exhaustiveness of articulation—for *articulated*, thematized articulation. Even when philosophic discourse follows—as it currently does—more and more tortuous paths which, exhausting all possible detours and turns, "lead nowhere," it is still, despite all its denials, based on a fundamental demand for a linear course, requiring its progress to be uninterrupted and its detours to be kept in check; it is still based on a constitutive belief in the continuity (and exhaustiveness) of the Path. The paradox and the contradiction of contemporary philosophy reside in the fact that it attempts to express, by means of paths that are *continuous*, the radical nature of *discontinuity*. Lacan's position seems diametrically opposed to this: while it can be said that Lacan wishes to articulate the *continuity* of a logic and a mathematics of the unconscious, it is clear that he goes about it along paths remarkable for their *discontinuity*. These two positions, symmetrically contradictory and contradictorily asymmetrical, are symptomatic both of the difficulty and of the ambiguity of what is at stake in modern culture, namely, the search for a new status of discourse.

If contemporary psychoanalysis and philosophy both find them-

---

[60]*Ibid.*, pp. 84–85.
[61]"The Agency of the Letter," quoted in *ibid.*, p. 83.
[62]*Ibid.*, p. 86.

selves wrestling with the dramatic necessity, the ineluctable urgency, of breaking away from "Meaning," of radically "getting out of" the epistemology of presence and of consciousness, they are wrestling as well with the difficulty (the impossibility?) of raising their own discourse to the level of their discoveries and projects, of measuring up to the immeasurable demands, the unprecedented radicality, of the Freudian revolution.

Rimbaud:

—The mind is in authority, it insists that I remain in the West. It will have to be silenced if I am to end as I intended.[63]

Both Lacanian and ("post-phenomenological") philosophic discourse have thus produced "horrible toilers,"[64] engaged in rejecting the claims of both the "concept" and the "knowledge" it entails. This rejection, however, is articulated in two different ways: poetically by Lacan, discursively by the philosophers. Now, between philosophers and poets, the latter, paradoxically, are perhaps the least naïve. For if today's philosophers think they know that they don't know, the poets, for their part, know that they do know, but don't know what.

Lacan counters the philosophic, discursive variety of deconstruction with his own textual, rhetorical, and anagrammatical deconstruction. But, as we have seen, Lacan's (impossible) desire is to establish—rhetorically—a *grammar* of *rhetoric*. Conversely, philosophic discourse could be defined as the desire to exhaust the resources of grammar, in order to elaborate—*grammatically*—a radical *rhetoricity:* a rhetoric of rhetoric.

Hence, on the one hand, philosophic discourse reproaches Lacan for that moment of "denial" of radical "rhetoricity,"[65] when he seems to wish to pin down—to "arrest" or "immobilize"—the movement of rhetoric and metaphor (especially in his emphasis on the verb *to be:* "If the symptom *is* a metaphor, it is not a metaphor to say so"). But on the other hand, this same philosophic reading of Lacan's text in turn focuses on metaphor (in this case, Lacan's metaphor of fire: this "fire" of the Freudian truth "that is burning

---

[63]Rimbaud, "The Impossible," *Complete Works*, trans. P. Schmidt (New York: Harper & Row, 1967), p. 210. Translation modified.

[64]Rimbaud, "Lettre dite du 'voyant,'" *Oeuvres* (Paris: Garnier, 1960), p. 346.

[65]Nancy and Lacoue-Labarthe, *Le Titre de la lettre*, p. 149.

all about us") merely to arrest and immobilize it: the philosophic reading, in other words, inquires not into the "rhetoricity" of the metaphor, into its textual, rhetorical *functioning* in Lacan's writing, but rather into its *meaning*, its *proper* meaning. The metaphor is thus quickly pinned down, and its "closure" effected. *"It is well known* that Revelation is inscribed in letters of fire. Or, at any rate, that what is revealed is fire."[66]

By their own admission, these authors can learn from the "fire" metaphor only what is already "well known." And if it is indeed well known today that "God is dead," it is no less well known that "post-Nietzschean" philosophic discourse, for all that, still hasn't finished *killing* him off, killing off his ghost. Thus, the philosophic reading of Lacan's text rushes to the fire—to put it out. With the risk of fire averted, the (henceforth) philosophic path will be followed diligently, in the safety of a "comfortable pace"[67] that no longer "burns its way along."

To resolve this enigma of fire, Freud, however, proceeds quite differently, specifically in his discussion of the remarkable dream of a fire burning a corpse.[68] "And now we come upon a dream," Freud tells us (though it could just as well be said in reply to any philosophic reading), "and now we come upon a dream which raises no problem of interpretation and the meaning of which is obvious, but which, as we see, nevertheless retains the essential characteristics that differentiate dreams so strikingly from waking life and consequently call for explanation. It is only after we have disposed of everything that has to do with the work of interpretation that we can begin to realize the incompleteness of our psychology of dreams . . . Hitherto, . . . all the paths along which we have traveled have led us toward the light—toward elucidation and fuller understanding. But as soon as we endeavor to penetrate more deeply into the mental process involved in dreaming, every path will end in darkness. There is no possibility of *explaining* dreams . . . since to *explain* a thing means to *trace it back to something already known.*"[69]

Let us recall briefly the content and the circumstances of the dream in question, because the fire burning there will allow us to

66*Ibid.*, p. 86. My italics.
67*Ibid.*, p. 96.
68*The Interpretation of Dreams*, V, 509–511.
69*Ibid.*, pp. 510–511. My italics.

examine more fully the impact of the metaphor of fire on Freud's discovery, as well as its specific *rhetoricity* in Lacan's text. An old man had been engaged to keep vigil over the body of a child who had just died after a long illness; the father, worn out with fatigue, dozed off in the next room, and dreamed "that *his child was standing beside his bed, caught him by the arm and whispered to him reproachfully: 'Father, don't you see I'm burning?'* He [the father] woke up, noticed a bright glare of light from the next room, hurried into it and found the old watchman had dropped off to sleep and that the wrappings and one of the arms of his beloved child's dead body had been burned by a lighted candle that had fallen on them."[70]

Freud uses this dream to analyze, precisely, the question of awakening, and the dynamic relations between sleep and waking life. From this striking example, he concludes that if the dream, stimulated by the sleeper's perception of light from the real fire, nevertheless prolongs sleep despite the urgent need to awaken, it is because the dream functions not only to fulfill the father's wish to prolong his child's life but also to satisfy a bodily need, to integrate reality into the dream in order to fulfill the *wish to sleep.* Incited by the enigma of this dream, Freud proceeded, in his usual brilliant way, to ask a radical, unprecedented question: *What causes us to wake up?* and, by the same token, *What prevents awakening?*

In his usual brilliant way Lacan, in turn, picks up on Freud's question but displaces it somewhat, radicalizes it in a new way, by asking: "Where is *the reality* in this accident?"[71] I will translate the question thus: Is the reality of the desire that governs us and writes us of the order of the "fire" of our sleep, or of the order of the fire to which we awaken? Where exactly *is* the fire in this dream adventure? Which is the *real fire:* the one burning the living person in the dream, or the one burning, by metonymic repetition, the corpse in the next room and thus continuing, fatally and fantasmatically, to consume the body of a dead love? The rhetoricity of the Lacanian "fire," but also the rhetorical "burning" involved in every text, occurs precisely at the level of just such a missed encounter, of an *unarticulated* but dynamically metonymic, en-

---

[70]*Ibid.*, p. 509. Freud's italics.
[71]*The Four Fundamental Concepts*, p. 58.

counter between sleep and waking. Here, we can do no better than to quote Lacan, leaving to his writing its "sovereign significance": "Where is the reality in this accident, if not that something even more fatal is being repeated *by means of* reality, a reality in which the person who was supposed to be watching over the body still remains asleep, even when the father reemerges after having woken up? Thus the encounter, forever missed, has occurred between dream and awakening, between the person who is still asleep and whose dream we will never know and the person who has dreamt merely in order not to wake up. . . . It is only in the dream that this truly unique encounter can occur . . . memorable encounter—for no one can say what the death of a child is, except the father *qua* father, that is to say, no conscious being. For the true formula of atheism is not *God is dead*—even by basing the origin of the function of the father upon his murder, Freud protects the father—the true formula of atheism is *God is unconscious.*"[72]

As we see here, the question Lacan asks is not the philosophic question, "What is the (im)*proper meaning* of the fire?" but rather a question I would call literary, the question par excellence of the textual, or of the rhetorical: *"Where is the fire that consumes, that burns us?"* But this question is precisely one of undecidability— the very question of the undecidable—since the fire is of course burning in *both* rooms, in sleep and in waking life alike. The fire shifts in a dynamically metonymic burning that "catches all around us" only because *we don't know where it is.* "In this entirely sleeping world, only the voice is heard, *Father, can't you see I'm burning!* This sentence is itself a firebrand—of itself it brings fire where it falls—and one cannot see what is burning, for the flames blind us to the fact that the fire bears on the *Unterlegt,* on the *Untertragen,* on the real."[73]

Lacan's writing disconcerts us precisely because it is consumed by a "fire" that can never be *located* by the discourse of Meaning. Reading Lacan is like going through a Nervometer [*Pèse-Nerfs*];[74] it is like surrendering ourselves to a blindness that *works us over* and *thinks us through* without our necessarily ever achieving an

[72]*Ibid.*, pp. 58–59. Translation modified.
[73]*Ibid.*, p. 59.
[74]The implicit reference here is to a collection of prose poems by Artaud, entitled *Le Pèse-Nerfs* ("The Nervo-Meter").

exhaustive understanding of it. Thus it is that Lacan's text, whose singular articulation conveys the greatest possible degree of inarticulation, thinks beyond its means, and thinks *us* beyond ours.

> To bear down, according to the page, on the white, which inaugurates it, its simplicity, in itself, forgetful even of the title which would speak too loudly; and when there is aligned in a break, the least, disseminated break, chance vanquished word by word, indefectibly the white returns, gratuitous before, certain now, to conclude that nothing is beyond, and to authenticate silence.[75]

Lacan has effected in the current theoretical field an extremely subtle and complex *transferential operation*—in all the senses the word "transference" might possibly entail. To see that is to see, no doubt, that he is nothing but "the *Shade*"—the "*Nothing*"—of our own "enthusiasm"; but also, that he holds, in our cultural history, the undeniable "privilege of the Other": that he has given, that is, to psychoanalysis and to the field of culture and of theory precisely *"the gift of what he does not have; namely, his love."*[76]

[75]Mallarmé, "Le Mystère dans les lettres," *Oeuvres*, p. 387.
[76]Lacan, "The Signification of the Phallus," *Ecrits: A Selection*, p. 286.

7

Henry James: Madness and the Risks of Practice (Turning the Screw of Interpretation)

What* does the act of turning a screw have to do with literature? What does the act of turning a screw have to do with psychoanalysis? Are these two questions related? If so, might their relationship help to define the status of literature? It is these rather odd questions that the present study intends to articulate, so as to give them a further turn, to investigate and interrogate them on the basis of Henry James's famous short novel, *The Turn of the Screw.*

*This chapter is not translated; it is the author's original English version.

I. An Uncanny Reading Effect

> I didn't describe to you the purpose of it (. . .) at all, I described to you (. . .) the *effect* of it—which is a very different thing.
> H. James, *The Sacred Fount*

> The mental features discoursed of as the analytical are, in themselves, but little susceptible of analysis: we appreciate them only in their effects.
> E. A. Poe, *The Murders in the Rue Morgue*

The plot of *The Turn of the Screw* is well known: a young woman answering a want ad in a newspaper goes to meet a "perfect gentleman," a "bachelor in the prime of life," who hires her to take charge of his niece Flora and his nephew Miles, two little orphans who live in a secluded country house belonging to him. The young woman is to become the children's governess, but under the strict condition set down by her employer—"the Master"—that she assume "supreme authority" for her two charges, that is, that she solve singlehandedly any problems concerning them, without at any time turning to him for help or even contacting him for any reason. This condition is no sooner accepted than it begins to weigh heavily upon the governess (who is also the narrator)—especially when a letter arrives informing her, without giving the reason, that little Miles has been expelled from school: this unexplained punishment makes the child's apparent innocence seem somehow mysterious, suspect, ambiguous. In addition, the governess discovers that the house is haunted: several times she finds herself confronted by strange apparitions, whom, with the help of information about the house's past history gleaned from the housekeeper, Mrs. Grose, she finally identifies as the ghosts of two servants, Peter Quint and Miss Jessel, now dead, but formerly employed by the Master in this very house, and whose shady intimacy had, it seems, "corrupted" the children. The governess becomes steadily more convinced that the ghosts have come back to pursue their nefarious intercourse with the children, to take possession of their souls and to corrupt them radically. Her task is thus to *save* the children from the ghosts, to engage in a ferocious moral struggle against "evil," a struggle whose strategy consists of an attempt to catch the children in the very act of communing with the spirits, and thereby to force them to admit that communion, to confess their knowledge of the ghosts and their infernal complicity with them. Total avowal, the governess believes, would exorcise the children. The results of this heroic metaphysical struggle are, however, ill-fated: Flora, the little girl, caught by the governess in presence of the phantom of Miss Jessel, denies seeing the vision and falls seriously ill following the vehement accusations directed at her by the governess, whom she thenceforth holds in abhorrence; Miles, the little boy, on the other hand, having seemingly "surrendered" by pronouncing—under the governess's pressure—the *name* of Peter Quint face to face with his ghost, at that very moment dies in the arms of the governess as she clasps him to her breast in moral triumph. It is with this pathetically ironical embrace of a corpse that the story ends.

If the strength of literature could be defined by the intensity of its impact on the reader, by the vital energy and power of its *effect*, *The Turn of the Screw* would doubtless qualify as one of the strongest—i.e., most *effective*—texts of all time, judging by the quantity and intensity of the echoes it has produced, of the critical literature to which it has given rise. Henry James was himself astounded by the extent of the effect produced on his readers by his text, the generative potency of which he could measure only *a posteriori*. Ten years after the first appearance of *The Turn of the Screw*, in his New York Preface (1908), he writes:

> Indeed if the artistic value of such an experiment be measured by the intellectual echoes it may again, long after, set in motion, the case would make in favour of this little firm fantasy—which I seem to see draw behind it today a train of associations. I ought doubtless to blush for thus confessing them so numerous that I can but pick among them for reference.[1]

Few literary texts indeed have provoked and "drawn behind them" so many "associations," so many interpretations, so many exegetic passions and energetic controversies. The violence to which

[1]Unless otherwise specified, all quotes from The New York Preface and from *The Turn of the Screw* are taken from the Norton Critical Edition of *The Turn of the Screw*, ed. Robert Kimbrough (New York: Norton, 1966); hereafter abbreviated "Norton." As a rule, all italics within the quoted texts throughout this paper are mine; original italics alone will be indicated.

the text has given rise can be measured, for example, by the vehement, aggressive tone of the first reactions to the novel, published in the journals of the period: "The story itself is distinctly repulsive," affirms *The Outlook* (LX, October 29, 1898, p. 537; *Norton*, p. 172). And *The Independent* goes still further:

> *The Turn of the Screw* is the most hopelessly evil story that we have ever read in any literature, ancient or modern. How Mr. James could, or how any man or woman could, choose to make such a study of infernal human debauchery, for it is nothing else, is unaccountable. . . . The study, while it exhibits Mr. James's genius in a powerful light, affects the reader with a disgust that is not to be expressed. The feeling after perusal of the horrible story is that one has been assisting in an outrage upon the holiest and sweetest fountain of human innocence, and helping to debauch—at least by helplessly standing by— the pure and trusting nature of children. Human imagination can go no further into infamy, literary art could not be used with more refined subtlety of spiritual defilement. (*The Independent*, LI, January 5, 1899, p. 73; *Norton*, p. 175)

The publication of *The Turn of the Screw* thus meets with a scandalized hue and cry from its first readers. But, interestingly enough, as the passage just quoted clearly indicates, what is perceived as the most scandalous thing about this scandalous story is that *we are forced to participate in the scandal*, that the reader's innocence cannot remain intact: there is no such thing as an innocent reader of this text. In other words, the scandal is not simply *in* the text, it resides in *our relation to the text*, in the text's *effect on us*, its readers: what is outrageous in the text is not simply that *of which* the text is speaking, but that which makes it speak *to us*.

The outraged agitation does not, however, end with the reactions of James's contemporaries. Thirty years later, another storm of protest very similar to the first will arise over a second scandal: the publication of a so-called "Freudian reading" of *The Turn of the Screw*. In 1934, Edmund Wilson for the first time suggests explicitly that *The Turn of the Screw* is not, in fact, a ghost story but a madness story, a study of a case of neurosis: the ghosts, accordingly, do not really exist; they are but figments of the governess's sick imagination, mere hallucinations and projections symptomatic of the frustration of her repressed sexual desires. This psychoanalytical interpretation will hit the critical scene like a bomb. Making its author into an overnight celebrity by arousing as much interest as James's text itself, Wilson's article will provoke a veritable barrage of indignant refutations, all closely argued and based on "irrefutable" textual evidence. It is this psychoanalytical reading and the polemical framework it has engendered that will henceforth focalize and concretely organize all subsequent critical discussion, all passions and all arguments related to *The Turn of the Screw*. For or against Wilson, affirming or denying the "objectivity" or the reality of the ghosts, the critical interpretations have fallen into two camps: the "psychoanalytical" camp, which sees the governess as a clinical neurotic deceived by her own fantasies and destructive of her charges; and the "metaphysical," religious, or moral camp, which sees the governess as a sane, noble savior engaged in a heroic moral struggle for the salvation of a world threatened by supernatural Evil. Thus, as John Silver astutely puts it, "If the ghosts of 'The Turn of the Screw' are not real, certainly the controversy over them is."[2]

Would it be possible to say, indeed, that the *reality of the debate* is in fact more significant for the impact of the text than the reality of the ghosts? Could the critical debate itself be considered a *ghost effect?* Even more than the debate's content, it is its *style* which seems to me instructive: when the pronouncements of the various sides of the controversy are examined closely, they are found to repeat unwittingly—with a spectacular regularity—all the main lexical motifs of the text. Witness the following random examples, taken from a series of polemical essays:

—The motif of a danger which must be averted:

> The *danger* in the psychoanalytic method of criticism lies in its apparent plausibility.
>
> (Nathan Bryllion Fagin)[3]

—The motif of a violent aggression inflicted upon an object by an injurious, alien force:

---

[2]"A Note on the Freudian Reading of *The Turn of the Screw*," in: *A Casebook on Henry James's "The Turn of the Screw*," ed. Gerald Willen, 2d ed. (New York: Thomas Y. Crowell, 1969), p. 239. This collection of critical essays will hereafter be abbreviated *Casebook*.

[3]"Another Reading of *The Turn of the Screw*," in *Casebook*, p. 154.

> The Freudian reading of Henry James' 'The Turn of the Screw'
> [. . .] *does violence* not only to the story but also to the Preface.
>
> (Robert Heilman)[4]

—The motif of attack and defense, of confrontation and struggle: in a rebuttal to the Freudian reading, Oliver Evans proposes that Wilson's theory be

> *attacked* point by point.
>
> (Oliver Evans)[5]

—The motif of final victory, of the enemy's defeat:

> Here is one place where I find Freud completely *defeated.*
>
> (Katherine Anne Porter)[6]

It could perhaps be objected that a vocabulary of aggression, conflict, and maybe even danger is natural in a conflictive critical debate, and that it is just a coincidence that this vocabulary seems to echo and repeat the combative spirit that animates the text. Such an objection could not, however, account for some other, more specific, more peculiar stylistic echoes of the text which reemerge in the very language of the critics, in the very style of the polemic: the motif, for instance, of neurosis and of madness, of hysterical delusion. Robert Heilman thus accuses Wilson of alleged "hysterical blindness" (FR, *MLN,* p. 434), which alone would be able to account for the latter's errors in interpretation. Wilson, argues Heilman, is misreading James's use, in his New York Preface, of the word "authority." In Heilman's view, James's statement that he has given the governess "authority" is referring but to her *narrative* authority, to the *formal* fact that the story is being told *from her point of view*, and not, as Wilson would have it, to "the relentless English 'authority' which enables her to put over on inferiors even purposes which are totally deluded." How is this misreading possible? "Once again," explains Heilman, "the word *authority* has brought about, in an unwary liberal, an emotional

---

[4]"The Freudian Reading of *The Turn of the Screw,*" in *Modern Language Notes,* LXII, 7, Nov. 1947, p. 433. This essay will hereafter be referred to as: FR, *MLN.*
[5]"James's Air of Evil: *The Turn of the Screw,*" in *Casebook,* p. 202.
[6]"James: *The Turn of the Screw.* A Radio Symposium," in *Casebook,* p. 167.

spasm which has resulted in a kind of hysterical blindness" (FR, *MLN*, p. 434). Wilson's reading is thus polemicized into a *hysterical* reading, itself viewed as a neurotic symptom. What is interesting—and seems to me instructive—about this is that it is the very critic who *excludes* the hypothesis of neurosis from the *story* who is rediscovering neurosis in Wilson's critical *interpretation* of the story, an interpretation which he rejects precisely on the grounds that *pathology as such cannot explain the text:*

> It is probably safe to say that the Freudian interpretation of the story, of which the best known exponent is Edmund Wilson, no longer enjoys wide critical acceptance. (. . .) We cannot account for the evil by treating the governess as pathological. . .[7]

But the hypothesis of madness, or "pathology," which is indeed brought up by the governess herself, is not nearly so easy to eliminate as one might think, since, expelled from the text, it seems to fall back on the text's interpreter, and thus ironically becomes, through the very critical attempt at its elimination, ineradicable from the critical vocabulary, be it that of the "Freudians" or that of the "metaphysicians."

Another textual motif which crops up unexpectedly in the very language of the critical controversy is that of *salvation*. While insisting on the fact that *The Turn of the Screw* is in truth a drama of salvation, that is, a rescue operation to save the children from the evil ghosts, Robert Heilman writes:

> *The Turn of the Screw* may seem a somewhat slight work to call forth all the debate. But there is something to be said for the debate. For one thing, it may point out the danger of a facile, doctrinaire application of formulae where they have no business and hence compel either an ignoring of, or a gross distortion of, the materials. But more immediately: *The Turn of the Screw* is *worth saving.* (FR, *MLN*, p. 443)

The rescue operation, the drama of salvation described by the text thus *repeats itself* in the critical arena. But *from what* must the text be saved? From being reduced, explains Heilman, to "a commonplace clinical record." But again, let us notice the terms of the

[7]Robert Heilman, "*The Turn of the Screw* as Poem," in *Casebook*, p. 175.

objection, which associates the psychoanalytical reading's abuses with the more general abuses of science as such:

> We run again into the familiar clash between scientific and imaginative truth. This is not to say that scientific truth may not collaborate with, subserve, and even throw light upon imaginative truth; but it is to say that the scientific prepossession may seriously impede the imaginative insight. (FR, *MLN*, p. 444)

Another critic, repeating and emphasizing the term "preposession," agrees: "We must agree, I think, that Freudian critics of the tale are *strongly prepossessed*."[8] But what precisely is a "prepossessed" critic if not one whose mind is in advance in the *possession* of some demon, one who, like James's children, is himself *possessed?* Possessed—should we say—by the ghost of Freud? It is clear, in any case, that the urgency of rescuing, of *saving the text*, in a critical account like Heilman's, strongly resembles the exorcistic operations of the governess *vis-à-vis* her "possessed" charges, and that the critical confrontation appears itself as a kind of struggle against some ghost-effect that has somehow been awakened by psychoanalysis. The scene of the critical debate is thus a *repetition* of the scene dramatized in the text. The critical interpretation, in other words, not only elucidates the text but also reproduces it dramatically, unwittingly *participates in it*. Through its very reading, the text, so to speak, acts itself out. As a reading effect, this inadvertent "acting out" is indeed uncanny: whichever way readers turn, they can but be turned by the text, they can but *perform* it by *repeating* it. Perhaps this is the famous trap James speaks of in his New York Preface:

> It is an excursion into chaos while remaining, like Blue-Beard and Cinderella, but an anecdote—though an anecdote amplified and highly emphasized and returning upon itself; as, for that matter, Cinderella and Blue-Beard return. I need scarcely add after this that it is a piece of ingenuity pure and simple, of cold artistic calculation, an *amusette* to catch those not easily caught (the "fun" of the capture of the merely witless being ever but small), the jaded, the disillusioned, the fastidious. (*Norton*, p. 120)

[8]Mark Spilka, "Turning the Freudian Screw: How Not to Do It," in *Norton*, pp. 249–250.

We will return later on to this ingenious prefatory note so as to try to understand the distinction James is making between naïve and sophisticated readers, and to analyze the way in which the text's return upon itself is capable of trapping *both*. Up to this point, my intention has been merely to suggest—to make explicit—this uncanny trapping power of Henry James's text as an inescapable *reading-effect*.

Taking such reading-effects into consideration, we shall here undertake a reading of the text which will at the same time be articulated with a reading of its readings. This two-level reading—which also must return upon itself—will be concerned with the following questions: What is the nature of a reading-effect as such? and by extension: what is a reading? What does the text have to say about its own reading? What is a "Freudian reading" (and what is it *not*)? What in a text *invites*—and what in a text *resists*—a psychoanalytical interpretation? In what way does literature *authorize* psychoanalysis to elaborate a discourse about literature, and in what way, having granted its authorization, does literature *disqualify* that discourse? A combined reading of *The Turn of the Screw* and of its psychoanalytical interpretation will here concentrate, in other words, not only on what psychoanalytical theory has to say about the literary text, but also on what literature has to say about psychoanlaysis. In the course of this double reading, we will see how both the possibilities and the limits of an encounter between literature and psychoanalytical discourse might begin to be articulated, how the conditions of their meeting, and the modalities of their not meeting, might begin to be thought out.

II. What Is a Freudian Reading?

> The Freudians err in the right direction.
>
> Mark Spilka

I would like, as a starting point, to begin by subscribing to the following remarks by Mark Spilka:

> My concern (. . .) is with the imaginative poverty of much Freudian criticism, its crudeness and rigidity in applying valid psychological

insights, its narrow conception of its own best possibilities (. . .) Over the past four decades Freudian critics have made James's tale a *cause célèbre*. The tale sustains the *"cause"* through erotic ambiguities. Since it also arouses childhood terrors, and perhaps arises from them, we may say that the Freudian approach works here or nowhere. Yet opponents charge that Freudian critics have reduced the tale to a "commonplace clinical record." Though they are perfectly correct, my own charge seems more pertinent: these Freudian critics have not been sufficiently Freudian. (*Norton*, p. 245)

These subtle, challenging remarks err only in the sense that they consider as resolved, non-problematic, the very questions that they open up: how Freudian is a Freudian reading? Up to what point can one be Freudian? At what point does a reading start to be "Freudian enough"? *What* is Freudian in a Freudian reading, and in what way can it be defined and measured?

The one characteristic by which a "Freudian reading" is generally recognized is its insistence on the crucial place and role of sexuality in the text. The focal theoretical problem raised by a psychoanalytical reading would thus appear to be the definition of the very status of sexuality as such *in a text*. Wilson's reading of *The Turn of the Screw* indeed follows the interpretative pattern of accounting for the whole story in terms of the governess's sexual frustration: she is in love—says Wilson—with the Master, but is unable to admit it to herself, and thus obsessively, hysterically projects her own desires upon the outside world, perceives them as exterior to herself in the hallucinated form of fantasmatic ghosts.

> The theory is, then, that the governess who is made to tell the story is a neurotic case of sex repression, and that the ghosts are not real ghosts but hallucinations of the governess.[9]

In order to reinforce this theory, Wilson underlines the implicitly erotic nature of the metaphors and points out the numerous phallic symbols:

> Observe, also, from the Freudian point of view, the significance of the governess's interest in the little girl's pieces of wood and of the fact

[9]Edmund Wilson, "The Ambiguity of Henry James," in *The Triple Thinkers* (Penguin, 1962), p. 102. This essay will hereafter be referred to as *Wilson*.

that the male apparition first takes shape on a tower and the female apparition on a lake. (*Wilson*, p. 104)

What, however, was it in James's text that originally called out for a "Freudian" reading? It was, as the very title of Wilson's article suggests, not so much the sexuality as "the *ambiguity* of Henry James." The text, says Wilson, is ambiguous. It is ambiguous, that it, its meaning, far from being clear, is itself a *question*. It is this question which, in Wilson's view, calls forth an analytical response. The text is perceived as questioning in three different ways:

1) *Through its rhetoric:* through the proliferation of erotic metaphors and symbols *without* the direct, "proper" naming of their sexual nature.[10]

2) *Through its thematic content*—its *abnormal* happenings and its fantastic, strange manifestations.[11]

3) *Through its narrative structure* which resembles that of an enigma in remaining, by definition, elliptically incomplete.[12]

Solicited by these three modes of textual questioning—narrative, thematic, and rhetorical—the "Freudian" critic, in Wilson's view, is called upon to *answer*. In the case of the narrative question of the elliptical, incomplete structure of the enigma, he answers with the riddle's missing word, with the mystery's solution: the governess's sexual desire for the Master. In the case of the thematic question of uncanny strangeness, of fantastic happenings, he answers with a *diagnosis:* the ghosts are merely the symptoms of pathological, abnormal sexual frustration and repression. In the case of the rhetorical question of symbolic ambiguity, he answers with the "proper name," with the *literal* meaning of the phallic metaphors.

[10]Cf., for example, *Wilson*, p. 126: "Sex *does* appear in his work—even becoming a kind of obsession," but we are always separated from it by "thick screens."

[11]Cf. *ibid.,* "The people who surround this observer tend to take on the diabolic values of *The Turn of the Screw,* and these diabolic values are almost invariably connected with sexual relations that are always concealed and at which we are compelled to guess."

[12]Cf. *ibid.,* p. 108: "When one has once got hold of the clue to this meaning of *The Turn of the Screw,* one wonders how one could ever have missed it. There is a very good reason, however, in the fact that nowhere does James unequivocally give the thing away: almost everything from beginning to end can be read equally in either of two senses."

Considered from the "Freudian point of view," sexuality, valorized as both the foundation and the guidepost of the critical interpretation, thus takes on the status of an *answer* to the *question* of the text. Logically and ontologically, the answer (of sexuality) in fact pre-exists the question (of textuality). The question comes to be articulated (rhetorically, thematically, and narratively) only by virtue of the fact that the answer is as such *concealed*. Indeed the question is itself but an answer in disguise: the question is the answer's hiding place. The Freudian critic's job, in this perspective, is but to pull the answer out of its hiding place—not so much to give an answer *to* the text as to answer *for* the text: to be *answerable for* it, to answer *in its place*, to replace the question with an answer. It would not be inaccurate, indeed, to say that the traditional analytical response to literature is to provide the literary question with something like a reliably professional "answering service."

Such an operation, however, invites two fundamental questions: Does "James" (or James's text) authorize this way of answering *for* him? Does "Freud" (or Freud's text) authorize this way of answering *through* him?

The question of the possibility of answering for the text, as well as that of the status of such an answer, is in fact raised by James's text itself in its very opening, when Douglas, having promised to tell his dreadful story, intimates that it is a *love story*, which was confided to him by the heroine (the governess):

> Mrs. Griffin, however, expressed the need for a little more light. "Who was it she was in love with?"
>
> "The story will tell," I took upon myself to reply. (. . .).
>
> "The story *won't* tell," said Douglas; "not in any literal, vulgar way." (Prologue, *Norton*, p. 3; James's italics)

In taking upon himself "to reply," to make *explicit* who it was the governess was in love with, in locating the riddle's answer in the governess's repressed desire for the Master, what then is Edmund Wilson doing? What is the "Freudian" reading doing here if not what the text itself, at its very outset, is precisely indicating as that which it *won't* do: "The story *won't* tell; not in any literal, vulgar way." These textual lines could be read as an ironic note through which James's text seems itself to be commenting upon Wilson's reading. And this Jamesian commentary seems to be suggesting that such a reading might indeed be inaccurate not so much because it is incorrect or false, but because it is, in James's terms, *vulgar.*

If so, what would that "vulgarity" consist of? And how should we go about defining not only an interpretation's accuracy, but what can be called its *tact?* Is a "Freudian reading"—by definition—tainted with vulgarity? *Can* a Freudian reading, as such, avoid that taint? What, exactly, makes for the "vulgarity" in Wilson's reading? Toward whom, or toward what, could it be said that this analysis lacks tact?

"The difficulty itself is the refuge from the vulgarity," writes James to H. G. Wells (*Norton,* p. 111). And in the New York Preface to *The Turn of the Screw,* he elaborates further the nature of that difficulty, of that tension which underlies his writing as a question:

> Portentous evil—how was I to *save that,* as an intention on the part of my demon spirits, from the drop, the *comparative vulgarity,* inevitably attending, throughout the whole range of possible brief illustration, the offered example, the imputed vice, the cited act, the limited deplorable presentable instance? (*Norton,* p. 122)

What is vulgar, then, is the "*imputed* vice," the "offered example," that is, the explicit, the specific, the unequivocal and immediately referential "illustration." *The vulgar is the literal,* insofar as it is unambiguous: "the story won't tell; not in any *literal, vulgar* way." The literal is "vulgar" because it *stops the movement* constitutive of meaning, because it blocks and interrupts the endless process of metaphorical substitution. The vulgar, therefore, is anything that misses, or falls short of, the dimension of the symbolic, anything that rules out, or excludes, meaning as a loss and as a flight—anything that strives, in other words, to eliminate from language its inherent silence, anything that misses the specific way in which a text *actively* "won't tell." The vulgarity that James then seeks above all to avoid is that of a language whose discourse is outspoken and forthright and whose reserves of silence have been cut, that of a text inherently *incapable* of silence, inherently unable to hold its tongue.

If vulgarity thereby consists of the *reduction of rhetoric* as such, of the elimination of the indecision which inhabits meaning and of the *ambiguity* of the text, isn't that precisely Wilson's goal? Isn't Wilson's critical and analytical procedure that, precisely, of a *literalization* (i.e., in James's terms, of a "vulgarization") of sexuality in the text? Wilson, in fact, is quite aware of the text's rhetorical, undecidable question:

> The fundamental question presents itself and never seems to get properly answered: What is the reader to think of the protagonist? (*Wilson*, p. 112)

But he only points out that question in order to *reduce* it, *overcome* the difficulty of the ambiguity, *eliminate* the text's rhetorical indecision by supplying a prompt *answer* whose categorical *literality* cannot avoid seeming rudimentary, reductive, "vulgar." What are we to think of the protagonist?

> We find that it is a variation on one of his [James's] familiar themes: the thwarted Anglo-Saxon spinster; and we remember unmistakable cases of women in James's fiction who deceive themselves and others about the origins of their aims and their emotions. (. . .)
> James's world is full of these women. They are not always emotionally perverted. Sometimes they are apathetic. (. . .)
> Or they are longing, these women, for affection but too inhibited or passive to obtain it for themselves. (*Wilson*, pp. 110–111)

Is this type of literalization of textual sexuality what a "Freudian point of view" is really all about? Invalidated and disqualified by James, would this "vulgarizing" literalization in truth be validated, authorized, by Freud? If for James the *literal* is *vulgar*, can it be said that from a Freudian point of view the *sexual* as such is *literal*? In order to investigate this question, I would like to quote, at some length, Freud himself, in a little-known text which appeared in 1910 under the title " 'Wild' Psychoanalysis":

> A few days ago a middle-aged lady (. . .) called upon me for a consultation, complaining of anxiety-states. (. . .) The precipitating cause of the outbreak of her anxiety-states had been a divorce from her last husband; but the anxiety had become considerably intensified, according to her account, since she had consulted a young physician in the suburb she lived in, for he had informed her that the *cause* of her

anxiety was her *lack of sexual satisfaction*. He said that she could not tolerate the loss of intercourse with her husband, and so there were only three ways by which she could recover her health—she must either return to her husband, or take a lover, or obtain satisfaction from herself. Since then she had been convinced that she was incurable (. . .)

She had come to me, however, because the doctor had said that *this was a new discovery for which I was responsible,* and that she had only to come and ask me to confirm what he said, and *I should tell her that this and nothing else was the truth* (. . .). I will not dwell on the *awkward predicament* in which I was placed by this visit, but instead will consider the conduct of the practitioner who sent the lady to me (. . .) connecting my remarks about "wild" psycho-analysis with this incident.[13]

It is tempting to point out the analogy between the rather comical situation Freud describes and the so-called "Freudian" treatment of the governess by Wilson. In both cases, the reference to Freud's theory is brutally and crudely literal, reducing the psychoanalytical explanation to the simple "lack of sexual satisfaction." Here therefore is Freud's own commentary on such procedures. Curiously enough, Freud, like James, begins with a reminder that the validity of an interpretation is a function not only of its truth, but also of its *tact:*

> Everyone will at once bring up the criticism that if a physician thinks it necessary to discuss the question of sexuality (. . .) he must do so with tact. (*Standard*, p. 222)

But tact is not just a practical, pragmatic question of "couchside manner"; it also has a theoretical importance: the reserve within the interpretative discourse has to allow for and to indicate a possibility of error, a position of uncertainty with respect to truth.

> Besides all this, one may sometimes make a wrong surmise, and *one is never in a position to discover the whole truth.* Psycho-analysis provides these definite technical rules to replace the indefinable

---

[13] "'Wild' Psycho-Analysis," in *The Standard Edition of the Complete Psychological Works of Sigmund Freud*, Vol. XI (1910), pp. 221–222. This edition will hereafter be abbreviated *Standard*.

"medical tact" which is looked upon as a special gift. (*Standard*, p. 226)

The analysis of the "wild psychoanalyst" thus lacks the necessary tact, but that is not all.

> Moreover, the physician in question was ignorant of a number of *scientific theories* [Freud's italics] of psycho-analysis or had misapprehended them, and thus showed how little he had penetrated into an understanding of its nature and purposes.
> (. . .) The doctor's advice to the lady shows clearly in what sense he understands *the expression "sexual life"—in the popular sense,* namely, in which by sexual needs nothing is meant but the need for coitus (. . .) *In psychoanalysis the concept of what is sexual comprises far more; it goes lower and also higher than its popular sense.*
> (. . .) Mental absence of satisfaction with all its consequences can exist where there is no lack of normal sexual intercourse (. . .)
> (. . .) By emphasizing exclusively the somatic factor in sensuality he undoubtedly simplifies the problem greatly. (*Standard*, pp. 222–223)

Sexuality, says Freud, is not to be taken in its literal, popular sense: in its analytical *extension,* it goes "lower and also higher" than its literal meaning, it extends both beyond and below. The relation between the analytical notion of sexuality and the sexual act is thus not a relation of simple, literal adequation, but rather a relation, so to speak, of *inadequation:* the psychoanalytical notion of sexuality, says Freud, comprises both *more* and *less* than the literal sexual act. But how are we to understand an *extension* of meaning which includes not only *more,* but also *less* than the literal meaning? This apparent paradox, indeed, points to the specific complication which, in Freud's view, is inherent in human sexuality as such. The question here is less that of the meaning *of* sexuality than that of a complex *relationship between sexuality and meaning;* a relationship which is not a simple *deviation* from literal meaning, but rather a *problematization of literality as such.*

The oversimplifying literalization professed by the "wild psychoanalyst" thus essentially misconstrues and misses the complexity of the relationship between sex and sense. It entails, however, another fundamental error, which Freud goes on to criticize:

A second and equally *gross misunderstanding* is discernible behind the physician's advice.

It is true that psycho-analysis puts forward *absence of sexual satisfaction* as the cause of nervous disorders. *But does it not say more than this?* Is its teaching to be ignored as too complicated when it declares that *nervous symptoms arise from a conflict between two forces*—on the one hand, the libido (which has as a rule become excessive), and on the other, a rejection of sexuality, or a repression (which is over-severe)? No one who remembers this *second* factor, which is *by no means secondary in importance*, can ever believe that sexual satisfaction in itself constitutes a remedy of general reliability for the sufferings of neurotics. *A good number of these people are, indeed, (. . .) in general incapable of satisfaction.* (*Standard*, p. 223)

Nervous symptoms, Freud insists, spring not simply from a "lack of sexual satisfaction" but from a *conflict between two forces*. Repression is constitutive of sexuality: the *second* factor is by no means *secondary* in importance. But the second factor as such is precisely the *contradiction* of the first. Which means not only that the literal meaning—the first factor—is not simply first and foremost, but also, that its *priority*, the very *primacy* in which its literality is founded, its very *essence of literality*, is itself *subverted* and *negated* by the second, but not secondary, meaning. Indeed, sexuality being constituted by these *two* factors, *its meaning is its own contradiction:* the *meaning* of the sexual as such is *its own obstruction*, its own deletion.

The "lack of satisfaction," in other words, is not simply an *accident* in sexual life, it is essentially inherent in it: "All human structures," says Lacan, after Freud, "have as their essence, not as an accident, the restraint of pleasure—of fulfillment."[14]

Here, then, is another crucial point which Wilson misses, *opposing* as he does sexuality to the "lack of satisfaction," considering the frustration of the governess (defined as the "thwarted Anglo-Saxon spinster") as an abnormal *accident* to be treated as pathogenic. What would "the abnormal" be, however, in Wilson's view, if not precisely that which is *not literal*, that which *deviates* from

---

[14]Jacques Lacan, "Discours de clôture des journées sur les psychoses chez l'enfant," in *Recherches*, special issue on "Enfance aliénée," 11 décembre 1968, pp. 145–146; translation mine. Unless otherwise indicated, all quotations from Lacan's work in this paper are in my translation.

the *literal?* Literal (normal) sex being viewed as a simple, positive *act* or *fact*, it is simply inconceivable that it would constitutively miss its own aims, include its own negation as its own inherent property. For Wilson, sex is "simple," i.e., adequate to itself.[15] Wilson can thus write of *The Sacred Fount*, another enigmatic Jamesian story—"What if the hidden theme of *The Sacred Fount* is *simply sex* again?" (*Wilson*, p. 115). But for Freud, as we have seen, not only is the status of sexuality not *simple:* composed as it is by two dynamically contradictory factors, sexuality is precisely *what rules out simplicity as such.*

It is indeed because sexuality is essentially the violence of its own non-simplicity, of its own inherent "conflict between two forces," the violence of its own division and self-contradiction, that it is experienced as anxiety and lived as terror. The terrifying aspect of *The Turn of the Screw* is in fact linked by the text itself, subtly but suggestively, precisely to its *non-simplicity.* After promising to tell his story, Douglas adds:

> "It's quite too horrible." (. . .) "It's beyond everything. Nothing at all that I know touches it."
> "For sheer terror?" I remember asking. He seemed to say *it was not so simple as that;* to be really at a loss how to qualify it. (Prologue, p. 1)

If, far from implying the simplicity of a self-present literal meaning, sexuality points rather to a multiplicity of conflicting forces, to the complexity of its own divisiveness and contradiction, its meaning can by no means be univocal or unified, but must necessarily be *ambiguous.* It is thus not rhetoric which disguises and hides sex; sexuality *is* rhetoric, since it essentially consists of ambiguity: it is the coexistence of dynamically antagonistic meanings. Sexuality is the *division and divisiveness of meaning;* it is meaning *as* division, meaning *as* conflict.

---

[15]And if that adequation does not appear in James's work, it is, in Wilson's view, because James, too, like the governess, missed out on the simplicity of the normal status of normal sex and knew only the lack of satisfaction involved in its pathological manifestations: cf. *Wilson*, p. 125: "*Problems of sexual passion* (. . .) *were* beginning to be subjects of burning interest. But it is probable that James had by this time (. . .) come to recognize *his unfittedness for dealing with them* and was far too honest to fake."

And, indeed, what is the *subject* of *The Turn of the Screw* if not this very conflict which inhabits meaning, the inherent conflict which structures the relationship between *sex* and *sense?* "The governess," John Lydenberg pertinently writes, "may indistinctly consider the ghosts as the essence of evil, and, as Heilman points out, she certainly chooses words which identify them with Satan and herself with the Saviour. But our vantage point is different from the governess's: we see her as one of the combatants, and as the story progresses we become even more uncertain who is fighting whom."[16]

In thus dramatizing, through a clash of meanings, the very functioning of meaning as division and as conflict, sexuality is not, however, the "text's meaning": it is rather that through which meaning in the text *does not come off,* that which in the text, and through which the text, *fails to mean,* that which can engender but a *conflict of interpretations,* a critical debate and discord precisely like the polemic that surrounds *The Turn of the Screw* and with which we are concerned here. "If analytical discourse," writes Lacan, "indicates that meaning is as such sexual, this can only be a manner of accounting for its *limits.* Nowhere is there a last word. (. . .) Meaning indicates only the direction, points only at the sense toward which it fails."[17]

III. The Conflict of Interpretations: The Turns of the Debate

> Et ma tête surgie
> Solitaire vigie
> Dans les vols triomphaux
>   De cette faux
>
> Comme rupture franche
> Plutôt refoule ou tranche
> Les anciens désaccords
> Avec le corps
>
>   Mallarmé, *Cantique de St-Jean*

[16]J. Lydenberg, "The Governess Turns the Screws," in *Casebook*, p. 289.
[17]J. Lacan, *Le Séminaire—Livre XX: Encore* (1972–73) (Paris: Seuil, 1975), p. 66. This work will henceforth be referred to as *Encore*.

In repeating as they do the primal scene of the text's meaning as division, the critics can by no means master or exhaust the very meaning of that division, but only act the division out, perform it, be part of it.

To participate in a division is, however, at the same time, to fight *against* division: it is indeed to commit oneself to the elimination of the opponent, hence to the elimination of the heterogeneity of meaning, the very scandal of contradiction and ambiguity. One after another, the critics thus *contest* Wilson's reading by negating or denying his assumption that the very *meaning* of *The Turn of the Screw* can at all be *divided* or equivocal:

> "Almost everything from beginning to end," [Wilson] declares, "can be read equally in either of two senses." "Almost everything": *But what if there is one thing, one little thing, that cannot be read in either of two senses, that can be read only in one sense?* What then? How strange that Mr. Wilson does not see that any such fact (. . .) could be the sharp little rock on which *his theory must split.* (A. J. A. Waldock)[18]
>
> The Freudians misread the internal evidence almost as valiantly as they do the external. In the story, of course, there are passages that it is possible to read ambivalently; but *the determining unambiguous passages* from which the critic might work are so plentiful that *it seems hardly good critical strategy to use the ambiguous ones as points of departure.* (Robert Heilman, FR, *MLN*, p. 436)
>
> Granted that the text has various levels of meaning, it would appear on the whole unwise to have them mutually contradictory. (Alexander Jones)[19]

The attempt, however, to eliminate contradiction itself partakes of the contradiction: the affirmation of meaning as *undivided* is simultaneously one that *excludes* the position of the opponent; the homogeneity of meaning can be asserted but through the expulsion of its heterogeneity. In precisely trying to *unify* the meaning of the text and to proclaim it as unambiguous, the critics only mark more forcefully its constitutive *division* and duplicity. Contradiction reappears with ironical tenacity in the very words used to banish it:

[18]"Mr. Edmund Wilson and *The Turn of the Screw*," in *Casebook*, p. 172.
[19]"Point of View in *The Turn of the Screw*," in *Casebook*, p. 301.

[My] interpretation (. . .) has the virtue of *extreme inclusiveness,* though I fear *there is no room in it* for (. . .) Mr. Wilson. (Oliver Evans, *Casebook,* p. 211)

But here again, to affirm contradiction in the very act of denying it, as does the *critics' story,* their story of the "true" interpretation of the story, is precisely to bear witness to the *double bind* which is constitutive of the very framework of the *governess's narrative,* to be caught in the dynamically conflictive impasse which confronts the governess herself *as narrator.* To affirm contradiction in the very act of denying its existence in the text is therefore to repeat, oneself, the *textual act,* to perform the very act of textuality triggered by the ambiguity of sexuality. It becomes thus clear that the critical debate, in its intentions and contentions, itself partakes of the textual *action.* "The Turn of the Screw," writes James, "was an action, desperately, or it was nothing" (New York Preface, *Norton,* p. 121). The *actors,* or the agents of this textual action, are indeed the readers and the critics no less than the characters. Criticism, to use Austin's terminology, here consists not of a statement, but of a performance of the story of the text; its function is not *constative,* but *performative.* Reading here becomes not the cognitive observation of the text's pluralistic meaning, but its "acting out." Indeed it is not so much the critic who comprehends the text, as the text that comprehends the critic. Comprehending its own criticism, the text, through its reading, orchestrates the critical disagreement as the performance and the "speech *act*" of its own disharmony. "Irony," as Roland Barthes, in a different context, puts it, "irony is what is immediately given to the critic: not to see the truth, but, in Kafka's terms, to be it."[20]

In thus dramatizing, through their contradictory versions of the text's truth, the truth of the text as its own contradiction, James's critics, curiously enough, all hold *Freud* responsible for their disagreement: "Freud" is indeed believed to be the cause and is referred to as the demarcation line of their polemical divergence. The studies of *The Turn of the Screw,* according to their own self-presentation, divide themselves into so-called "Freudian" and so-called "anti-Freudian" readings. Thus it is that while Ezra Pound

[20]*Critique et vérité* (Paris: Seuil, 1966), p. 75.

calls James's story "a Freudian affair,"[21] while Wilson—as we have seen—invites us to "observe the Freudian point of view," and while Oscar Cargill celebrates "Henry James as a Freudian Pioneer" in the very title of the first version of his study of *The Turn of the Screw*, Katherine Anne Porter, on the other hand, singles out *The Turn of the Screw* as an illustration of Freud's "defeat": "Here is one place," she argues, "where I find Freud completely defeated" (*Casebook*, p. 167). So does Robert Heilman strike at Freud himself through Wilson, in entitling his polemical essay against the latter, "The Freudian Reading of *The Turn of the Screw*." The opening lines of the essay mark well the generalization of the methodological reproach at stake: "The Freudian reading of Henry James's *The Turn of the Screw* (. . .) does violence not only to the story but also to the Preface" (FR, *MLN*, p. 433). In a counter-attack on Heilman and other "anti-Freudian essays" listed in a footnote under this terminological heading, John Silver proposes "to lend support to Mr. Wilson's interpretation" in an essay which he entitles: "A Note on the Freudian Reading of *The Turn of the Screw*" (*Casebook*, p. 239). Between "Freudians" and "anti-Freudians," in the critical debate around *The Turn of the Screw*, Freud's ghost significantly and ironically thus seems to have become the very mark and sign of divisiveness and of division. It is as though "Freud" himself, in this strange polemic, had become the very *name* of the critical disagreement, the uncanny *proper name of discord*.

This symmetrical polar opposition between "Freudians" and "anti-Freudians" itself rests, however, on an implied presupposition, which is, in truth, as problematic, and as paradoxical, as the debate itself. The paradox can be summed up as follows: Whereas the two opposing critical sides believe themselves to be in spectacular *disagreement* over *James's* "true meaning," they demonstrate in fact a spectacular *agreement* over *Freud's* "true meaning," which, unlike that of James, is considered by both sides to be transparent, unequivocal, incontrovertible. But in reality the "true Freud" is no more immediately accessible to us than the "true James." For "Freud" is equally a text, known only through the difficulties and uncertainties of the act of reading and of interpreta-

---

[21]Quoted by Harold C. Goddard in "A Pre-Freudian Reading of *The Turn of the Screw*," in *Norton*, p. 182.

tion. What, indeed, if it were not enough to call oneself a "Freudian" in order to *be* one? And what if it were not enough to call oneself an "anti-Freudian," either, in order to, in truth, become one? In this sense, Freud's name can hardly be considered a *proper name*, but becomes in effect nothing other than a *ghost*, as ambiguous as James's ghosts, to the extent that it conveys not an established truth or a referential *knowledge*, but an *invitation to interpretation*. A "Freudian reading" is thus not a reading guaranteed by, grounded in, Freud's knowledge, but first and foremost a *reading of Freud's "knowledge*," which as such can never *a priori* be assured of knowing anything, but must take its chances *as* a reading, necessarily and constitutively threatened by error.

In thus examining the paradigm of the so-called "Freudian reading of *The Turn of the Screw*" and its distortion of Freud's theory as we could here but begin to *read* it in Freud's *text*, our intention has been to displace and dislocate the much-repeated, central question of the polemic: "is the Freudian reading true or false?" by suggesting that *we do not yet know what a Freudian reading really is*.

The question, therefore, can no longer be simply to decide whether in effect the "Freudian" reading is true or false, correct or incorrect. It can be both at the same time. It is no doubt correct, but it misses nonetheless the most important thing: it is blind to the very textuality of the text. The question of a reading's "truth" must be at least complicated and re-thought through another question, which Freud, indeed, has raised, and taught us to articulate: what does such "truth" (or any "truth") leave out? What is it *made to miss?* What does it have as its function to overlook? What, precisely, is its residue, the *remainder* it does not account for? Since, as we have seen, the critical scene of the polemic is both repetitive and performative of the textual scene, it can in fact be said that it is the very "falseness" of the readings that constitutes their "truth." The Freudian reading is no doubt "true," but no truer than the opposed positions that contradict it. And it is "false," indeed, to the extent that it *excludes* them. These opposed positions, which assert the text's contradiction in the very act of denying it, are thus "true" to the extent that they are "false." And a new, far more troubling question can no longer be avoided, with respect to James as well as with respect to Freud, and indeed *because of* both: is a reading of *ambiguity* as such really *possible?* Is

it at all possible to read and to interpret ambiguity *without reduc-*
ing it in the very process of interpretation? Are reading and ambiguity in any way *compatible?*

It should be noted that the expression "Freudian reading" is
itself an ambiguous expression that can refer either to Freudian
statements or to Freudian *utterance:* a reading can be called
"Freudian" with respect to *what it reads* (the *meaning* or thematic
content it derives from a text) or with respect to *how it reads* (its
interpretative *procedures,* the techniques or *methods* of analysis it
uses). While it is almost exclusively in the first of these two senses
that the concept "Freudian reading" is understood and used in the
American cultural context, in France, it is on the contrary rather in
the second sense that a new reading of Freud has been elaborated
by Jacques Lacan. For Lacan, indeed, the unconscious is not only
that which must be read, but also, and primarily, *that which*
reads. Freud's discovery of the unconscious is the outcome of his
reading of the hysterical discourse of his patients, i.e., of his being
capable of reading in this hysterical discourse *his own uncon-*
scious. The discovery of the unconscious is therefore Freud's discovery, within the discourse of the other, of what was actively
reading within himself: his discovery, in other words, or his reading, of what was reading—in what was being read. The gist of
Freud's discovery, for Lacan, thus consists not simply of the revelation of a new *meaning*—the unconscious—but of the *discovery of*
a new way of reading:

> [Freud's] first interest was in hysteria. (. . .) He spent a lot of time
> listening, and, while he was listening, there resulted something para-
> doxical, (. . .), that is, a *reading.* It was while listening to hysterics
> that he *read* that there was an unconscious. That is, something he
> could only construct, and in which he himself was implicated; he was
> implicated in it in the sense that, to his great astonishment, he
> noticed that he could not avoid participating in what the hysteric was
> telling him, and that he felt affected by it. Naturally, everything in
> the resulting rules through which he established the practice of psy-
> choanalysis is designed to counteract this consequence, to conduct
> things in such a way as to avoid being affected.[22]

[22]Transcribed from a recording of J. Lacan's talk at the "Kanzer Seminar" (Yale
University, November 24, 1975), which has been translated into English by Barbara
Johnson.

In the light of this Lacanian insight, I would like to propose a rereading of *The Turn of the Screw* which would try to replace the conventional idea of a "Freudian reading" with a different type of reading, one whose necessity and possibilities have been precisely opened up by Lacan's re-reading of Freud's discovery of reading. Throughout this paper, Lacan's work will be periodically referred to, not so much as an authoritative body of theoretical knowledge, but as a remarkably rich and complex analytical *text*, whose value lies for us less in any reified form of its pronouncements than in the suggestiveness of its rhetoric, less in what it states than in what it *understates*, leaves *open*—in its linguistic silences and their possible interaction with James's text.

Our reading of *The Turn of the Screw* would thus attempt not so much to *capture* the mystery's solution, but to follow, rather, the significant path of its flight; not so much to solve or *answer* the enigmatic question of the text, but to investigate its structure; not so much to name and make *explicit* the ambiguity of the text, but to understand the necessity and the rhetorical functioning of the textual ambiguity. The question underlying such a reading is thus not "*What* does the story mean?" but rather "*How* does the story mean?" How does the meaning of the story, whatever it may be, rhetorically take place through permanent displacement, textually take shape and take effect: *take flight.*

IV. The Turns of the Story's Frame: A Theory of Narrative

> It appeared that the narrative he had promised to read us really required for a proper intelligence a few words of prologue.
>
> *The Turn of the Screw*

> Literature is language (. . .); but it is language around which we have drawn a frame, a frame that indicates a decision to regard with a particular self-consciousness the resources language had always possessed.
>
> Stanley E. Fish

The actual story of *The Turn of the Screw* (that of the governess and the ghosts) is preceded by a prologue which is both posterior and exterior to it, and which places it *as* a story, as a speech event, in the context of the "reality" in which the story comes to be told. With respect to the story's *content*, then, the prologue constitutes a sort of *frame*, whose function is to situate the *story's origin*.

The narrated story is thus presented as the *center* of the *frame*—the focal point of a narrative space which designates and circumscribes it from the outside as *its inside*. Placed *around* the story which becomes its center, the narrative frame, however, frames *another* center within its *literal* space:

> The story had held us, *round the fire*, sufficiently breathless (. . .) He began to read to our hushed *little circle*, (. . .) kept it, *round the hearth*, subject to a common thrill. (pp. 1 and 4)

Since the narrative space of the prologue organizes both a *frame around the story* and a *circle around the fire*, since the fire and the story are both placed at the very *center* of the *narration*, the question could arise as to whether they could be, in any way, considered *metaphors of each other* in the rhetorical constellation of the text. This hypothesis in turn opens up another question: if the content of the story and the fire in the hearth *are* metaphors of each other, how does this metaphorical relation affect the centrality of the two terms?

Before pursuing these questions further, let us take another look at the prologue's status as the story's "frame." The prologue, in fact, frames the story not only spatially but also temporally: while it takes place long *after* the governess's story, it also tells of events that had occurred *before* it: the meeting between the governess and the Master which sets up the determining conditions of the subsequent events. The frame picks up the story, then, both *after its end* and *before its opening*. If the function of the frame is to determine the story's *origin*, then that origin must somehow be both anterior and posterior to the story.

Anterior to the story but recounted and accounted for *a posteriori*, the story's origin seems to depend on the authority of the storyteller, i.e., of the narrator, who is usually supposed to be both the story's literal source and the depository of the knowledge out of which the story springs and which the telling must reveal. But while the prologue's function would thus seem to be to *relate* the story to its narrator, the prologue of *The Turn of the Screw* rather *disconnects* the story from the narrator since it introduces not *one* narrator, but *three:* 1) the person who says "I," the first-person "general narrator" who transmits to *us* the story with which he himself had no direct connection, and which he heard from Douglas; 2) Douglas, who reads the story to the circle around the fire, but who did not participate in it himself. Douglas had known the governess, the story's heroine, as his sister's governess long after the story had taken place, and had been secretly in love with her although she was ten years his senior. It was, however, only later, on her deathbed, that the governess confided to him a written account of her story. 3) The third teller of the story is thus the governess herself, who is the first-person narrator of her own written narrative.

Having received and read the manuscript, Douglas had in turn kept the governess's story secret for forty years, until that night around the fire when at last, to his privileged circle of friends and most especially to the general narrator, he decided to reveal it. And finally, long after his own telling of the story around the fire, Douglas, on his own deathbed, confided the treasured manuscript to his friend the narrator, who tells us in the prologue that the story he is transmitting to us is his own transcription, made still later, of that manuscript, which he had heard Douglas read before the fire.

The existence of the story is thus assured only through the constitution of a *narrative chain*, in which the narrators relay the story from one to the other. The story's origin is therefore not assigned to any one voice which would assume responsibility for the tale, but to the deferred action of a sort of *echoing effect*, produced—"after the fact"—by voices which themselves re-produce previous voices. It is as though the frame itself could only multiply *itself*, repeat itself: as though, in its infinite reproduction of the very act of narration, the frame could only be its own self-repetition, its own self-framing. If the tale is thus introduced through its own reproduction, if the story is preceded and anticipated by a repetition of the story, then the frame, far from situating, as it first appeared, the story's *origin*, actually situates its *loss*, constitutes its infinite deferral. The story's origin is therefore situated, it would seem, in a *forgetting* of its origin: to tell the story's origin is to tell the story of that origin's obliteration. But isn't this forgetting of the story's origin and beginning, and the very story of this forgetting, constitutive, precisely, of the very story of psychoanalysis and of *analysis as a story?* *The Turn of the Screw* would seem to be very like a psychoanalytical tale. Through the spiral threads of its prologue, the story indeed originates in a frame through which it frames itself into losing its own origin: as is the case with the psychoanalytical story of the unconscious, it is here the very loss of the story's origin which *constitutes* the origin of the story. The New York Preface, in its turn, both underlines and illustrates this point: added *a posteriori* as a second preface to the beginning of the story, it is like a prologue to the prologue, an introduction to the introduction, as if to make up for the missing origin or beginning, but succeeding only in repeating it, in beginning once again the tale of the constitutive loss of the tale's beginning.

> The starting point itself—the sense (. . .) of the circle, one winter afternoon, round the hall-fire of a grave cold country house where (. . .) the talk turned, *on I forget what homely pretext,* to apparitions and night-fears, to the marked and sad drop in the general supply (. . .). The good (. . .) ghost stories appeared to have been told (. . .) Thus it was, I remember, that amid our lament for a beautiful *lost form,* our distinguished host expressed the wish *that he might but have recovered for us* one of the scantiest of *fragments* of this form at its best. He had never forgotten the impression made on him as a young man by the withheld glimpse, at it were, of a dreadful matter that had been reported years before, and with as few particulars, to a lady with whom he had youthfully talked. The story would have been thrilling *could she but find herself in better possession of it,* dealing as it did with a couple of small children in an out-of-the-way place, to whom the spirits of certain "bad" servants, dead in the employ of the house, were believed to have appeared with the design of "getting hold" of them. This was all, but *there had been more,* which my friend's old converser *had lost the thread of* (. . .). He himself could give us but *this shadow of a shadow*—my own appreciation of which, I need scarcely say, was exactly *wrapped up in that thinness.* (Norton, pp. 117–118)

A narrative frame that thus incarnates the very principle of repetition of the story it contains, and, through that repetition, situates both the loss of the story's origin and the story's origin *as* its own loss, is clearly not a simple backdrop, staging, from the circumstantial *outside,* the *inside* of the story's content, but constitutes rather a complication, a problematization of the relationship itself between the inside and the outside of the textual space. On the one hand, as Alexander Jones points out, the "outside" frame expands the "inside" of the story, bringing into it both the storyteller and the reader:

> By placing himself within the confines of the story as "I," the narrator, James makes himself one of the characters rather than an omniscient author. *No one is left on the "outside" of the story,* and *the reader is made to feel that he and James are members of the circle around the fire.* (*Casebook*, p. 299)

In including not only the content of the story but also the figure of the reader within the fireside circle, the frame indeed leaves no one *out:* it pulls the outside of the story into its inside by enclosing in it what is usually outside it: its own readers. But the frame at the same time does the very opposite, pulling the inside outside: for in passing through the echoing chain of the multiple, repetitive narrative voices, it is the very *content,* the *interior* of the story that becomes somehow *exterior to itself,* reported as it is by a voice inherently alien to it and that can render of it but "the shadow of a shadow," a voice whose intrusion compromises the tale's secret intimacy and whose otherness violates the story's presence to itself. The frame is therefore not an outside contour whose role is to display an inside content: it is a kind of exteriority which permeates the very heart of the story's interiority, an internal cleft separating the story's content from itself, distancing it from its own referential certainty. With respect to the story's content, the frame thus acts both as an inclusion of the exterior and as an exclusion of the interior: it is a perturbation of the outside at the very core of the story's inside, and as such, it is a blurring of the very difference between inside and outside.

No one, then, is left on the "outside" of the story, except the story's inside. Like the circle round the fire, the story's frame thus encloses not only the story's content, but, equally, its readers and its reading. But what if the story's content *were* precisely *its own reading?* What if the *reading* (outside the text) were none other than the story's *content* (inside the text), being also, at the same time, that which compromises that content's inside, preventing it from coinciding with itself, making it ex-centric, exterior to itself? If we stop to consider that this non-presence of the story to itself, this self-exteriority, this ex-centricity and foreignness of the content to itself, can define, as such, precisely, the *unconscious,* we can see that reading, here, might be just the key to an understanding of the essential link between the story and the unconscious. "That is what analytical discourse is all about: reading," says Lacan (*Encore,* p. 29). For has it not become obvious that the chain of narrative voices which transmits *The Turn of the Screw* is also, at the same time, a chain of *readings?* Readings that re-read, and re-write, other readings? In the chain transmission of the story, each narrator, to relay the story, must first be a *receiver* of the story, a *reader* who at once records it and *interprets* it, simultaneously trying to make sense of it and *undergoing* it, as a lived experience, an "impression," a *reading-effect.*

> I asked him if the experience in question had been his own. To this his answer was prompt. "Oh, thank God, no!"
> "And is the record yours? You took the thing down?"
> "Nothing but the impression. I took it here—" he tapped his heart. "I've never lost it." (Prologue, p. 2)

"The safest arena," writes James elsewhere, "for the play of moving accidents and of mighty mutations and of strange encounters, or whatever odd matters, is the field, as I may call it, rather of their second than of their first exhibition":

> By which, to avoid obscurity, I mean nothing more cryptic than I feel myself show them best by showing almost exclusively the way they are felt, by recognising as their *main interest* some *impression strongly made by them* and intensely received. We but too probably break down (. . .) when we attempt the prodigy (. . .) in itself; with its "objective" side too emphasized the report (. . .) will practically run thin. We want it clear, goodness knows, but we also want it thick, and *we get the thickness in the human consciousness that entertains and records, that amplifies and interprets it.* That indeed, when the question is (. . .) of the "supernatural", constitutes the only thickness we do get; here *prodigies,* when they come straight, come with an effect imperilled; *they keep all their character,* on the other hand, *by looming through some other history*—the indispensable history of somebody's *normal* relation to something.[23]

---

[23]Preface to "The Altar of the Dead," in Henry James, *The Art of the Novel, Critical Prefaces,* ed. R. P. Blackmur (New York: Charles Scribner's Sons, 1962), p. 256. Unless otherwise indicated, quotations from James's Prefaces will refer to this collection, hereafter abbreviated *AN.*

The "main interest" of the story is thus the "thickness" it acquires through its own *reading*—through "the human consciousness that entertains and records, that amplifies and interprets it." The very subject-matter of the story of the "supernatural," its narrative condition, is, says James, its way of *"looming through some other history,"* its narration *in the other,* and *out of* the other. And that "other" here is the reader. The reader—i.e., also each one of the narrators: Douglas with respect to the governess's manuscript; "I" with respect to Douglas's account of it. The reader-narrator is here that "other," his personal story is the "other history," and his reading (i.e., his narrative, his telling) is significant to the extent that it *interferes* with the tale it tells. Each one of these superimposed stories, each act of narration and each narrative, is here a *reading of the other;* each reading is a *story in the other,* a story whose signification is interfered with but whose interference is significant, a story whose very meaning *interferes* but whose interference *means.* And this, of course, brings us back to the very question of the unconscious, for what, indeed, is the unconscious if not—in every sense of the word—a *reader?* "In analytical discourse," writes Lacan, "the unconscious subject is presumed to be able to read. And that's what the whole affair of the unconscious amounts to" (*Encore,* p. 38). The story of the unconscious thus resembles James's tale, insofar as they both come to us, constitutively, *through the reader.*

Thus it is that the narrator presents us with his own transcription of the manuscript which Douglas, "with *immense effect,* (. . .) began to *read* to our hushed little circle" (p. 4). Douglas's performance as storyteller, as author-narrator, consists, thereby, of a literal act of *reading.* And if the first-person narrator retransmits the story, communicates to us a reproduction and a reading of that reading, it is doubtless the result of the "immense effect" Douglas's reading produced on him, and which he hopes in turn to produce on us. The very act of telling, of narration, proceeds then from the potentially infinite repercussion of an *effect of reading;* an effect that, once produced, seeks to reproduce itself as an effect yet to be produced—an effect whose *effect* is an effect to produce. Narrative as such turns out to be the trace of the *action* of a reading; it is, in fact, *reading as action.* In Douglas's very first remarks, on the opening page of the prologue, the very *title* of the story is uttered as the mark, or the description, of its own *reading-effect:*

"I quite agree—in regard to Griffin's ghost, or whatever it was—
that its appearing first to the little boy, at so tender an age, adds a
particular touch. (. . .) If the child gives the *effect* another *turn of the
screw*, what do you say of two children?"

"We say, of course," somebody exclaimed, "that they give two
turns! Also that we want to hear about them." (Prologue, p. 1)

It is by virtue of the reading-effect it produces that the text
receives its very name, its title. But that title, as a title, is not given
to it by the original author of the manuscript: it is added to it "after
the fact"—as the alien seal of the reader—by the third narrator, the
last reader-receiver in the narrative chain of readings:

The next night, by the corner of the hearth (. . .) [Douglas] opened the
faded red cover of a thin old-fashioned gilt-edged album (. . .). On the
first occasion the same lady put another question. *"What is your
title?"*

"I haven't one."

"Oh, *I** have"! *I said*. But Douglas, without heeding me, had begun
to *read* with a fine clearness that was like a rendering to the ear of the
beauty of his author's hand. (Prologue, p. 14; *James's italics; remaining italics mine)

Not only does the title precisely name "the turn of the screw" of
its own *effect:* the title is itself the *product* of such an effect, it is
itself the *outcome* of a *reading* of the story (and is itself thereby a
reading of the story), since the narrative is given its name and title
by the reader and not by the author. In this manner the prologue,
just as it displaced and dislocated the relationship between the
inside and the outside, deconstructs as well the distinction and the
opposition between reader and writer. The reader here becomes the
author, and the author is in turn a reader. What the narrator perceives in Douglas's reading as "a rendering to the ear of the beauty
of his author's hand" is nothing but Douglas's *performance* as a
reader, which becomes a metaphor of the original author's writing
through the very act of reading which that writing has inspired and
produced as one of its effects. In essence, then, when Douglas
answers the question "What is your title?" with "I haven't one,"
that answer can be understood in two different manners: he has no
name for his own narrative; or else, he has no *title to* that narrative
which is really not his own, he is not *entitled*, therefore, to give it a

title, he has no right or authority over it, since he is not its author, since he can only "render the beauty of his author's hand," "represent" the story's author, to the extent that he is the story's reader.

The story, therefore, seems to frame itself into losing not only its origin but also its very title: having lost both its name and the authority of its author, the narrative emerges, out of the turns of its frame, not only authorless and nameless, but also unentitled to its own authority over itself, having no capacity to denominate, no right to *name itself*. Just as the frame's content, the governess's narrative, tells of the *loss of the proprietor* of the *house*, of the "Master" (by virtue of which loss the house becomes precisely *haunted*, haunted by the usurping ghosts of its *subordinates*), so does the framing prologue convey, through the reader's (vocal) rendering of an authorship to which he has no title, the *loss of the proprietor of the narrative*. And this strange condition of the narrative, this strange double insistence, in the frame as in the story, on the absence of the story's master, of the owner of the property, cannot but evoke, once more, the constitutive condition of the unconscious, itself a sort of obscure knowledge that is, precisely, authorless and ownerless, to the extent that it is a knowledge no consciousness can *master* or *be in possession of*, a knowledge no conscious subject can attribute to himself, assume as *his own* knowledge. "Any statement of authority," writes Lacan with respect to the discourse of the unconscious, but in terms that can equally describe the very narrative conditions of *The Turn of the Screw*—"Any statement of authority [in this discursive space] has no other guarantee than that of its own utterance."[24]

If the story has thus managed to lose at once its author, its authority, its title, and its origin, *without losing itself*—without being itself suppressed, obliterated or forgotten—it is because its written record has been repeatedly and carefully *transferred* from hand to hand: bequeathed first by the dying governess to Douglas, and then by the dying Douglas to the narrator. It is thus *death* itself which moves the narrative chain forward, which *inaugurates* the manuscript's *displacements* and the process of the *substitution* of the narrators. By so doing, death paradoxically appears not as an end but rather as a starting point: the starting point of the *transferral* of the story, that is, of its *survival*, of its capacity to go

[24]*Ecrits* (Paris: Seuil, 1966), p. 813. Hereafter referred to as *Ecrits*.

on, to subsist, by means of the repeated *passages* it effects *from death to life,* and which effect the narrative.

For each of the people who receive and keep the manuscript of the story, that manuscript constitutes, well beyond the death of the addressor—the person who bequeathed it to them—, the survival of the giver's language and the giver's own survival *in* his language: a *return* of the dead *within the text.* And we hardly need recall that it is precisely the return of the dead which provides the central moving force of the narrative being thus transferred: the story of the governess's struggles with the servants' ghosts. While the prologue contains nothing supernatural in itself, it curiously foreshadows the question of the return of the dead by making the manuscript itself into a ghost, speaking from beyond several graves.

What, however, is the motivation for the narrative's transmission? For what reason is the manuscript at all transferred? Douglas, quite discreetly, alludes to the reason.

> "Then your manuscript—?"
> "(. . .) A woman's. She has been dead these twenty years. She sent me the pages in question before she died." They were all listening now, and of course there was somebody to be arch, or at any rate to draw the inference. But if he put the inference by without a smile it was also without irritation. "She was a most charming person, but she was ten years older than I. She was my sister's governess," he quietly said. "She was the most agreeable woman I've ever known in her position; she would have been worthy of any whatever. It was long ago, and this episode was long before. (. . .) We had, in her off-hours, some strolls and talks in the garden—talks in which she struck me as awfully clever and nice. Oh yes; don't grin: *I liked her extremely and am glad to this day to think she liked me too. If she hadn't she wouldn't have told me.* She had never told anyone. (Prologue, p. 2)

In an understatement, Douglas lets it be understood that if the manuscript has survived "these twenty years" beyond the death of its author, it is because of the love which had once drawn him to her and which had prompted her in turn to confide to him her ultimate deathbed secret. The cause for the transferral of the manuscript is, therefore, not just death, but love. For Douglas, the manuscript commemorates his encounter with a woman, and with her writing: the story is as such the outcome, the result of love, of death, of writing, of transferring.

If the story's origin is lost, then it is not just because, by virtue of the author's death, it is buried in an unrecoverable, distant past: it is also because that origin cannot be situated as a *fixed point*, but only as a movement, a dynamic: the story's origin is *in transference*. The beginning of the tale, in other words, is not ascribable to any of the narrators, but to the relationship between the narrators. The story's origin is not a *referent*, but the very *act of reference:* the very act—through love and death—of *referring* to *the Other;* the gesture of the transference of a story.

The narrators, in fact, constitute not only a self-relaying *chain* of narrative transmissions, but also a series of pairs or *couples:* the governess and Douglas; Douglas and the first-person narrator. Before the triangular narrative chain comes into being—by means of the repeated and successive transfers of the manuscript due precisely to the disruption of the couples, to the death, each time, of one of the two partners—the couples, during their lifetime, carry on a relationship that, in both cases, has a discreet erotic connotation but is primarily discursive and linguistic. Such is the relationship between the governess and Douglas:

> [and] we had, in her off-hours, some strolls and talks in the garden— talks in which she struck me as awfully clever and nice. Oh yes; don't grin: I liked her extremely and am glad to this day to think she liked me too. (Prologue, p. 2)

Later on, it is the same sort of relationship that structures the rapport between Douglas narrating and the first-person narrator listening:

> It was *to me in particular* that he appeared to propound this—appeared almost to appeal for aid not to hesitate (. . .). The others resented postponement, but it was just his scruples that *charmed me.* (Prologue, p. 2)

In both cases, the couples therefore become couples by virtue of a constitutive situation of dialogue and of *interlocution*, whose discursiveness subtly develops into a discreet game of *seduction*. Indeed, this structuring situation of the couples strikingly calls to mind the psychoanalytical situation *par excellence,* governed as it is by *transference,* in its most strictly analytical sense: it is quite clear that the narrator's fascination with Douglas, as well as Douglas's fascination with the governess, are both transferential fascinations—and so is the governess's fascination with the Master. The tale of transference thus turns out to be the tale of the transference of a tale. This transferential structure will, however, not only motivate, but also modify the narrative, becoming at once its *motive* and its *mask:* putting the narrative in motion as its dynamic, moving force, it will also hide, distort it through the specular mirages of its numerous mirrors of seduction.

The play of seduction is productive of mirages insofar as, inscribed within the very process of narration, it becomes a play of *belief*—belief in the narrator and therefore in the accuracy of his narrative. It is because Douglas is so charmed by the governess, on whom the discursive situation makes him transfer, with whom he becomes narcissistically infatuated, that he *adds faith* to the literality of her narrative and to the authority of her own idealized mirror-image of herself. Vouching for the governess, he grants her story the illusory authority of a delusive *credibility.* Douglas, in other words, endows the governess with a *narrative authority.* Authority as such, so crucial to *The Turn of the Screw,* nonetheless turns out to be itself a fiction, an error in perspective, created by and established through the illusions and delusions of the transferential structure.[25] In the same way, Douglas's account of the governess's story is in turn given authority and credibility by the play of mutual admiration and intuitive understanding between him and his charmed, privileged listener, who will himself become a narrator.

[25]Cf. James's own comments on the "authority" of the governess in the New York Preface: "I recall (. . .) a reproach made me by a reader capable evidently, for the time, of some attention, but not quite capable of enough, who complained that I hadn't sufficiently 'characterized' my young woman engaged in her labyrinth (. . .), hadn't in a word invited her to deal with her own mystery as well as with that of Peter Quint (. . .) I remember well (. . .) my reply to that criticism. "(. . .) We have surely as much of her own nature as we can swallow in watching it reflect her anxieties and inductions. It constitutes no little of a character indeed, in such conditions, (. . .) that she is able to make her particular *credible* statement of such strange matters. She has 'authority,' which is a good deal to have given her, and I couldn't have arrived at so much had I clumsily tried for more" (*Norton,* pp. 120–121).

The transferential narrative chain thus consists not only of the echoing effects of voices reproducing other voices, but also of the specular effect of the seductive *play of glances,* of the visual exchange of specular reflections, of the mirror-repetition of symmetrically—and therefore infinitely—self-reproducing, self-reflecting self-reflections. *The Turn of the Screw,* indeed, in every sense of the word, is a *reflection* of, and on, the act of *seeing.* The story's frame is nothing other than a *frame of mirrors,* in which the narrative is both reflected and deflected through a series of symmetrical, mutual glances of couples looking at themselves looking at themselves.

> ". . . she liked me too. If she hadn't she wouldn't have told me. She had never told anyone. It wasn't simply that she said so, but that I knew she hadn't. I was sure; *I could see.* You'll easily judge why when you hear."
>
> "Because the thing had been such a scare?"
>
> *He continued to fix me.* "You'll easily judge," he repeated; *"you* will."
>
> *I fixed him too. "I see.* She was in love."
>
> He laughed for the first time. "You *are** acute. Yes, she was in love. That is she *had** been. That came out—she couldn't tell her story without its coming out. *I saw it,* and *she saw I saw it;* but neither of us spoke of it (. . .)" (Prologue, pp. 2–3; *James's italics; remaining italics mine)

What, however, is the nature of the act of "seeing"? This is the crucial question raised by the appearance of the ghosts, not simply because the ghosts only appear when the governess sees them, but also because each of their appearances enacts the same specular confrontation as that between the other couples: the same exchange of symmetrical, dual glances occurs between the governess and the supernatural intruder. In this play of "seeing oneself seen by the other" and of "seeing the other see," through which the prologue, once again, foreshadows the main story, what, then, does "seeing" mean? "I saw it, and she saw I saw it"; "I was sure; I could see"; "He continued to fix me (. . .) I fixed him too. 'I see. She was in love.' " Clearly, in the play of these Jamesian sentences, "seeing" is *interpreting;* it is *interpreting love;* and it is also interpreting *by means of love.* Thus, in several ways and on several levels, love has here become, in both senses of the word, the *sub-*

ject of interpretation. In this double transferential structure, in this double love-relation, between the narrator and Douglas, and between Douglas and the governess, love has become both what is *seen* and what *"can see"*; both what is *read* and what *is reading*; both what is *to be interpreted* in this intense exchange of glances, and what is actively, through that exchange, *doing the interpreting*. Love interprets. And inversely, the interpreter as such, whether or not he knows it, wants it, or intends it, is caught up in a love-relation, in a relationship constitutively transferential.

Transference, says Lacan, is "the acting-out of the reality of the unconscious."[26] On the basis of the literary evidence we are analyzing, and within the framework of a theory of narrative, we are here prompted to raise the question whether the acting-out of the unconscious is always in effect the acting-out of a *story*, of a narrative; and whether, on the other hand, *all* stories and all narratives imply a transferential structure, that is, a love-relation that both organizes and disguises, deciphers and enciphers them, turning them into their own substitute and their own repetition. *The Turn of the Screw* at any rate would seem to confirm such a hypothesis.

It is therefore no coincidence that the *transferral* of the manuscript should be presided over by a pair of would-be *lovers*, nor that the story should be twice retold (and acted out) for love, precisely, of its previous narrator or teller. Nor is it a coincidence that the transferential couple is here identified with the couple *author-reader*. The love-relation, i.e., the acting out of the unconscious through a relation of performative interpretation, seems to inhere in, and to govern, the relationship between the addressor of the narrative ("author" or narrator) and its addressee (listener-receiver or reader-interpreter).

> I can see Douglas there before the fire (. . .) looking down at his converser with his hands in his pockets. "Nobody but me, till now, has ever heard. It's quite too horrible." (. . .) "It's beyond everything. Nothing at all that I know touches it."
> "For sheer terror?" I remember asking.
> He seemed to say that it wasn't so simple as that; to be really at a

[26] J. Lacan, *Le Séminaire—Livre XI: Les Quatre concepts fondamentaux de la psychanalyse* (Paris: Seuil, 1973), p. 158. This work will henceforth be referred to as *Quatre Concepts*.

loss how to qualify it. *He passed his hand over his eyes,* made a little wincing grimace. "For dreadful—dreadfulness!"

"Oh, how delicious!" cried one of the women.

He took no notice of her; *he looked at me, but as if, instead of me, he saw what he spoke of.* "For general uncanny ugliness and horror and pain." (Prologue, pp. 1–2)

The play of passionate glances becomes even more complex when the act of looking is revealed to be not so much a passive observation as an active operation of *substitution.* Paradoxically, the intensity of that emotive look directs both the seduction and the story, both the narrative and the emotion toward a rhetorical *place* rather than an individual object: "he looked at me, but *as if, instead of me,* he saw *what he spoke of.*" That sentence has two different implications: 1) "what the narrator *speaks of*" is equivalent to the *place* of the person he addresses, or *speaks to:* if the reader also finds himself in that place (spoken to), then the reader is indeed the *subject* of the story; 2) what Douglas actually "speaks of" is the "general uncanny ugliness and horror and pain" that has to do with *ghosts.* In becoming, by virtue of his *place* ("spoken *to*") the *subject* of the story ("spoken *of*"), the *reader* (as well as the first-person narrator) himself becomes a ghost, occupying the rhetorical *ghostly place,* bound up in the "uncanniness" of the odd relationship between love, death, and substitution.

If, by virtue of the storyteller's transference on the reader, the reader thus becomes the storyteller's *ghost* (the addressee of his unconscious), the reader, in his turn, transfers on the storyteller or the "author," to the extent that he invests the latter with the authority and prestige of the *"subject presumed to know."* "Transference," says Lacan, "is only understandable insofar as its starting point is seen in the subject presumed to know; he is presumed to know what no one can escape: meaning as such." It is, as we have seen, the first-person narrator who, in his role as fascinated reader and admiring interpreter, confers upon Douglas his prestige, upon the narrative its title, and upon the story the authority of the ultimate *knowledge* it is *presumed* to have of its own meaning: " 'The story will tell,' I took upon myself to reply" (p. 10). The "I" of the first-person narrator in his role of reader thus constitutes as the text's *knowledge* what his own reading does *not* know in precisely the same way as a psychoanalytical patient's transferential fantasy attributes to his analyst a knowledge which is really his own story as *unknown*.

In telling at once of transference and through transference, the story acts as a repetitive border-crossing, as a constant shuttle between opposed domains: speech and silence, life and death, inside and outside, consciousness and the unconscious, sleep and wakefulness:

> The case, I may mention, was that of an apparition in just such an old house as had gathered us for the occasion—an appearance, of a dreadful kind, to a little boy *sleeping* in the room with his mother and *waking her up* in the terror of it; *waking her not to dissipate his dread* and soothe him to sleep again, *but to encounter also, herself,* (. . .) *the same sight* that had shaken him. It was this observation that drew from Douglas—not immediately, but later in the evening—a reply that had the interesting consequence to which I call attention. (Prologue, p. 1)

It is noteworthy that, in these opening lines of the prologue, it is a child who is at the origin both of the dream and of the dreamlike tale that follows. But if the child, indeed, *awakens* here his mother, it is only so as to *include her in his dream*, to wake her *into his own sleep*. In straddling, in this manner, the line between waking and sleeping, the child's story thus subverts or at least distorts the possibility of telling the two apart. Like the child, the narrator, through the dreamlike narrative he puts in motion out of his own transferential illusions, can only *wake us* into *his own sleep*: into the transferential dream that becomes our own. What the tale awakens in us is finally nothing other than, precisely, *our own sleep*.

At this juncture, it could be illuminating to recall that the psychoanalytical notion of transference is for the first time brought up by Freud in *The Interpretation of Dreams*, precisely with respect to the question of the *relation between sleeping and waking:* in attempting to explain the interactions and exchanges that occur between sleep and wakefulness, Freud analyzes the role of the "day's residues" and their relation to the "dream wish":

> On this view dream might be described as *a substitute for an infantile scene modified by being TRANSFERRED on to a recent experi-*

ence. The infantile scene is unable to bring about its own revival and has to be content with returning as a dream.[27]

My supposition is that a conscious wish can only become a dream-instigator if it succeeds in AWAKENING an unconscious wish with the same tenor and in obtaining reinforcement from it. (Ibid., p. 591)

It is only possible to do so [to explain the part played by the day's residues] if we bear firmly in mind the part played by the unconscious wish and then seek for information from the psychology of the neuroses. We learn from the latter that an unconscious idea is as such quite incapable of entering the preconscious and that it can only exercise any effect there by establishing a connection with an idea which already belongs to the preconscious, by TRANSFERRING ITS INTENSITY on to it and by getting itself "covered" by it. Here we have the fact of "TRANSFERENCE," which provides an explanation of so many striking phenomena in the mental life of neurotics. (*Ibid.*, p. 601)

It will be seen, then, that the DAY'S RESIDUES (. . .) not only *borrow* something from the unconscious when they succeed in taking a share in the formation of a dream—namely the instinctual force which is at the disposal of the repressed wish—but that they also *OFFER* THE UNCONSCIOUS something indispensable—namely THE NECESSARY POINT OF ATTACHMENT FOR A TRANSFERENCE. (*Ibid.*, p. 603)

Let us summarize what we have learnt so far. (. . .) The unconscious wish links itself up with the day's residues and effects a transference on to them; this may happen either in the course of the day or not until a state of sleep has been established. A wish now arises which has been transferred on to the recent material; or a recent wish, having been suppressed, gains fresh life by being reinforced from the unconscious. This wish seeks to force its way along the normal path taken by thought-processes, through the preconscious (. . .) to consciousness. But it comes up against the censorship. (. . .) At this point it takes on the distortion for which the way has already been paved by the transference of the wish on to the recent material. So far it is on the way to becoming an obsessive idea or a delusion or something of

[27]S. Freud, *The Interpretation of Dreams*, trans. James Strachey (New York: Discus/Avon, 1967), p. 585. In this quotation and those that follow from *The Interpretation of Dreams*, the italics are Freud's; the capitalization is mine.

the kind—that is, *a thought* which has been intensified by transference and distorted in its expression by censorship. Its further advance is halted, however, by the sleeping state of the preconscious. (. . .) The dream-process consequently enters on a regressive path, which lies open to it precisely owing to the peculiar nature of the state of sleep, and it is led along that path by the attraction exercised on it by groups of memories; some of these memories themselves exist only in the form of visual cathexes and not as translations into the terminology of the later systems (. . . .) In the course of its regressive path the dream-process acquires the attribute of representability. (. . .) It has now completed the second portion of its zigzag journey. (*Ibid.*, pp. 612–613)

Freud's analysis of the movement of psychic energies back and forth between sleep and wakefulness *via* transference seems perfectly tailored to fit precisely the visual dream-like figures of the *ghosts. Seeing* is thus above all *transferring.* And if, as we have "seen" ourselves from the prologue, seeing is always reading, deciphering, *interpreting,* it is because reading is also transferring: just as a dream is a transference of energy between the "day's residue" and the unconscious wish, so does the act of reading invest the conscious, daylight signifiers with an unconscious energy, transfer on recent materials the intensity of an archaic sleep. Seeing, thus, is always in some manner sleeping, that is, looking with the very eyes of the unconscious—through the fabric of a dream, reading not literally but rhetorically.

Both senses of the term "transference" in Freud's text—transference as the mainspring of psychoanalysis, as the repetitive structural principle of the relation between patient and analyst, and transference as the rhetorical function of any signifying material in psychic life, as the movement and the energy of displacement through a chain of signifiers—thus come together in the prologue of *The Turn of the Screw:* it is their very interaction that gives rise to the story and carries out the narrative both as a *couple-relation* and as the displacement—the transferral—of a manuscript. The whole story is thus played out in the differential space between the transference of the narrators and the transference of the narrative, between an enterprise of seduction and of narcissistic capture and the displacement of a signifier, the transferral of a text, the work of an effect of writing:

"Well then," I said, "just sit right down and begin."

He turned round to the fire, gave a kick to a log, watched it an instant. Then as he faced us again: "I can't begin. I shall have to send to town. (. . .) *The story's written.* It's in a locked drawer—it has not been out for years." (Prologue, p. 2)

V. The Scene of Writing: Purloined Letters

Sans ce qui fait que le dire, ça vient à s'écrire, il n'y a pas moyen de faire sentir la dimension du savoir inconscient.

J. Lacan, 1974 Seminar

. . . l'histoire nous laisse ignorer à peu près tout de l'expéditeur, non moins que du contenu de la lettre (. . .) nous n'en pouvons retenir qu'une chose, c'est que la Reine ne saurait la porter à la connaissance de son seigneur et maître.

J. Lacan, *Séminaire sur la lettre volée*

The fact that "the story's written," underlined by the narrative suspense that that fact creates, has two important implications:

1) The story is a *text* and not just a series of events: it has its own *materiality* and its own *place;* it exists as a material object;

2) As a material object, the manuscript is independent of the narrator, who is, rather, himself dependent on *it:* the narrator is dependent on the place and materiality of the written word.

This double implication will in turn have three immediate consequences:

1) It is *impossible* for the narrator to *begin;* there seems to be a problem inherent in the beginning as such, since it is first *postponed,* and then *replaced* by a "prologue": "I can't begin. I shall have to send to town. (. . .) The story's written," says Douglas. However, when the manuscript has arrived, Douglas explains the need for "a few words of prologue" (p. 4) which will substitute for the beginning, since "the written statement took up the tale at a point after it had, in a manner, begun" (p. 4).

2) The manuscript's place is a "locked drawer"—a closed, secret place: for the story to be told, the lock has to be forced, the hideout

opened up: a seal of silence must be broken, and the story's "opening" is thus literally and figuratively an *outbreak:*

> "The story (. . .) has not been told for years. I could write to my man and enclose the key; he could send down the packet as he finds it." (. . .) he had *broken* a thickness of ice, the formation of many a winter; had had his reasons for a long silence. (Prologue, p. 2)

> Mrs. Griffin spoke. (. . .)
> ". . . It's rather nice, his long reticence."
> "Forty years!" Griffin put in.
> "With this *outbreak* at last."
> "The *outbreak*," I returned, "will make a tremendous occasion of Thursday night." (Prologue, p. 3)

3) In order for there to be a narrative at all, Douglas must have the manuscript *sent* to him through the mail. There is thus an *address* on the text: *the story is a letter.* Indeed, it is triply so: sent first by the governess to Douglas, then by Douglas to himself, then by Douglas to the narrator. As a letter, the narrative entails both a *change of location* and a *change of address.*

In fact, the manuscript-letter is itself a story about letters: the first narrative event of the governess's story is the cryptic letter announcing Miles's dismissal from school; then the governess mentions that she intercepts the children's letters to the Master; then there is the troubling question for the governess of the letter Mrs. Grose wants sent to the Master about the goings-on at Bly, which the governess promises to write herself; and finally, the governess's letter to the Master is intercepted and destroyed by Miles.

What is striking about these letters is that they all bear a curious resemblance to the letter of the manuscript itself. They are addressed and sealed: ". . . my letter, *sealed and directed*, was still in my pocket" (chap. 18, p. 65). To open them requires that a seal be broken, that violence be done; the letters' opening instigates a sort of crisis:

> The postbag, that evening (. . .) contained a letter for me, which, however, in the hand of my employer, I found to be composed but of a few words enclosing another, addressed to himself, with a *seal still unbroken.* "This, I recognize, is from the head-master, and the head-

master's an awful bore. Read him, please; deal with him; but mind you don't report (. . .)" *I broke the seal with a great effort*—so great a one that I was a long time coming to it; took the unopened missive at last up to my room and only *attacked it* just before going to bed. I had better have let it wait till morning, for it gave me a second sleepless night. (chap. 2, p. 10)

In the story as in the prologue, the materiality of writing, as the materiality of the manuscript, seems to create a problem of beginnings. Like Douglas, the governess finds it difficult to begin:

I went so far, in the evening, as to *make a beginning*. (. . .) I sat for a long time before a *blank sheet of paper* (. . .). Finally I went out. (chap. 17, p. 62)

We will later learn that this letter from the governess to the Master will never be, in fact, more than just an envelope containing that same blank sheet of paper: the beginning as such is only written as *unwritten*, destined to remain anterior and exterior to what can be learned from a letter:

"I've just begun a letter to your uncle," I said.
"Well then, finish it!"
I waited a minute. "What happened *before?*"
He gazed up at me again. *"Before* what?"
"Before you came back. And *before* you went away." . . . he was silent. (chap. 17, pp. 64–65)

Insofar as the narrative itself is an effect of writing and as such is dependent on the letter of its text, its very *telling* involves the non-possession of its beginning. If the story is a letter and if a letter is the materialization of the absence of the beginning of a story, then the very act of telling, of narrating, must begin as the transgressive breaking of a seal—the seal of the silence from which the story springs. The story then is nothing but the circulation of a violated letter which materially travels from place to place through the successive changes of its addressees, and through a series of "address-corrections." While the letter is never really begun, it is nonetheless ceaselessly *forwarded*.

The letters *in* the story, then, strikingly resemble the letter of the manuscript of the story. And although these letters either remain unwritten or are intercepted and destroyed, although their content is either missing or undecipherable, their *function* none-, theless, like that precisely of the manuscript-letter which contains them, is to *constitute a narrative*, to *tell the story* of the goings-on they partake of, the story that has necessitated their being written.

> "Do you mean you'll write?" Remembering she couldn't, I caught myself up. "How do you communicate?
> "I tell the bailiff. *He* writes."
> "And should you like him to *write our story?*"
> My question had a sarcastic force that I had not fully intended, and it made her (. . .) inconsequently break down (. . .).
> "Ah, Miss, *you write!*" (chap. 16, pp. 61–62)

Clearly, what the letter is about is nothing other than the very story that contains it. What the letters are to tell is the telling of the story: how the narrative, precisely, tells itself *as an effect of writing*. The letters in the story are thus not simply *metonymical* to the manuscript that contains them; they are also *metaphorical* to it: they are the reflection *en abyme* of the narrative itself. To read the story is thus to undertake *a reading of the letters*, to follow the circuitous path of their changes of address.

The first thing such a "letter-reading" must encounter is the fact that, paradoxically enough, it is not what the letters *say* that gets the story started, but what they *don't say*: the letters are as such *unreadable*, illegible as much for the reader as for the characters in the story, who are *all the more* affected by them for not being able to decipher them. The letters are thus unreadable in precisely the same way the unconscious is unreadable: like the letters, the unconscious also governs an entire (hi)story, determines the course of a whole life and destiny, without ever letting itself be penetrated or understood.

If the letters' very resistance to daylight, to transparency and to meaning, is indicative of their participation in an unconscious economy; if, as signifiers *par excellence* of that unconscious economy, they can only be meaningful *through their own censorship*, signify through their own *blacking-out*; if the very story of the unconscious is a story of the circulation of undecipherable letters—then the crucial theoretical question for both literature and psychoanalysis, for the reader of textual letters as well as for the interpreter of the text of the unconscious, would be the following one: how can *unreadable* letters be *read*, even as they demand to be *read as unreadable?* This question, which is indeed raised by *The Turn of the Screw* on all levels, is crucial as much for the reader as for the characters of the story, whose fortunes are wholly determined by the mystery that the letters at once point to and withhold.

How can we read the unreadable? This question, however, is far from simple: grounded in contradiction, it in fact subverts its own terms: to actually *read* the unreadable, to impose a *meaning* on it, is precisely *not* to read the unreadable *as unreadable,* but to *reduce* it to the readable, to interpret it as if it were of the same order as the readable. But perhaps the unreadable and the readable *cannot* be located on the same level, perhaps they are *not* of the same order: if they could indeed correspond to the unconscious and to the conscious levels, then their functionings would be radically different, and their modes of being utterly heterogeneous to each other. It is entirely possible that the unreadable as such could by no means, in no way, be made *equivalent* to the readable, through a simple effort at better reading, through a simple *conscious* endeavor. The readable and the unreadable are by no means simply *comparable,* but neither are they simply *opposed,* since above all they are not *symmetrical,* they are *not* mirror-images of each other. Our task would perhaps then become not so much to read the unreadable *as a variant of the readable,* but, to the very contrary, to *rethink the readable itself,* and hence, to attempt to read it *as a variant of the unreadable.* The paradoxical necessity of "reading the unreadable" could thus be accomplished only through a radical modification of the meaning of "reading" itself. To read on the basis of the unreadable would be, here again, to ask not *what* does the unreadable mean, but *how* does the unreadable mean? Not what is the meaning of the letters, but in what way do the letters *escape* meaning? In what way do the letters *signify via,* precisely, their own *in-*significance?

We have seen how the letters become a crucial dramatic element in the narrative plot precisely because of their unreadability: their function of "giving the alarm" (chap. 21, p. 78), of setting the story in motion and keeping it in suspense through the creation of a situation of tension and of contradiction in which ambiguity reigns, is correlative to the persistent opacity of their informative function and to the repeated failure of their attempts at narration, of their endeavor to tell the story of a beginning, to "write a story" that would itself know its own origin and its own cause. But it is precisely *because* the letters *fail* to narrate, to construct a coherent, transparent story, that there is a story at all: there is a story *because* there is an unreadable, an unconscious. Narrative, paradoxically, becomes possible to the precise extent that a story becomes *impossible*—that a story, precisely, *"won't tell."* Narrative is thus engendered by the displacement of a "won't tell" which, being transmitted through letters, forwards itself as a *writing-effect*.

It is indeed the unreadable which determines, in James's text, the narrative structure of the story. The narrative events themselves arise out of the "alarm" the letters invariably produce. And each of the letters will end up, indeed, giving rise to another letter. There is therefore a *chain* of letters, in much the same way as there is a *chain* of narrative voices, of narrators. The letters, however, relay each other or give rise to each other by means of the very *silences*, of the very *ellipses*, that constitute them: the letters are linked to each other only through the very "holes" in their contents. From the enigmatic letter of the Director of Miles's school, to the unfinished letter of the governess to the Master, which Miles intercepts and destroys, the story of *The Turn of the Screw* is structured around a sort of necessity short-circuited by an impossibility, or an impossibility contradicted by a necessity, of *recounting an ellipsis*, of writing, to the Master, a letter about the headmaster's letter, and about what was missing, precisely, in the headmaster's letter: the reasons for Miles's dismissal from school. The whole story springs from the impossibility, as well as from the necessity, of writing *a letter about what was missing in the initial, original letter*.

Thus it is that the whole course of the story is governed by the hole in a letter. The signifying *chain* of letters, constituted less by what the letters *have* in common than by what they *lack* in common, is thus characterized by three negative features that can be seen as its common attributes: 1) the message or content of the letters is elided or suppressed; 2) in place of the missing message, what is recounted is the story of the material movement and fate of the letters themselves: the letters' circuit, however, becomes, paradoxically enough, a short-circuit of the direct contact between receiver and sender; 3) the addressee, who determines the letters' displacements and circuit, becomes the privileged element in each one of the letters: the *address* is the only thing that is readable, sometimes the only thing even *written*. And, curiously enough, *all* the letters in *The Turn of the Screw*—including the one from the school director, forwarded to the governess—are originally addressed to one and the same person: the Master. What is the structural significance of this convergence of the unreadable upon one crucial address?

The need to write to the Master to inform him of the uncanny happenings for which Bly has become the arena stems from the fact that the Master is the *lawful proprietor* of Bly: for the governess and for the children as well, the Master embodies at once the supreme instance of Law as such and the supreme figure of Power. But the Master, before the story's beginning, in its unwritten part for which the prologue accounts, had precisely exerted his power and dictated his law to the governess through the express *prohibition* that any letters be addressed to him.

> "He told her frankly all his difficulty—that for several applicants the *conditions* had been *prohibitive*. (. . .) It sounded strange, and all the more so because of his main condition."
> "Which was—?"
> "That she should never trouble him—but never, never; neither appeal nor complain nor write about anything; only meet all questions herself; receive all moneys from his solicitor, take the whole thing over and let him alone. She promised to do this, and she mentioned to me that when, for a moment, disburdened, delighted, he held her hand, thanking her for the sacrifice, she already felt rewarded."
> "But was that all her reward?" one of the ladies asked.
> "She never saw him again." (Prologue, p. 6)

The paradoxical contract between the governess and the Master is thus from the outset a contract of *disconnection*, of *non-correspondence*. Constitutive of an aporia, of a relation of non-relation, the Master's discourse is very like the condition of the unconscious as such: Law itself is but a form of Censorship. But it is precisely this censoring law and this prohibitive contract that constitute, paradoxically, the story's condition of possibility: the condition of possibility of the story of the impossibility of writing the Master a letter about what was initially missing, *not said,* in yet another letter (equally addressed to, but refused by, the Master). Through the Master's inaugural act of forwarding *unopened* to the governess a letter addressed to him from the Director of Miles's school, mastery determines itself as at once a *refusal of information* and a *desire for ignorance.* Through its repressive function of blocking out, of suppressing, the instance of Law is established as the *bar* which will radically separate signifier from signified $(^S/_S)$,[28] placing the letters, by the same token, under the odd imperative of the *non-knowledge* of their own content, since, written *for* the Master, the letters are, from the outset, *written for their own Censor.* The situation, however, is even more complex than this, since the governess also, quite clearly, falls in love—right away—with the Master. The Master therefore becomes, at the same time, not only an authority figure as well as an instance of prohibition, but also an object of love, a natural focus of transference. Written not only *for* the very personified image of power, but also *for* their own censorship and their own prohibition, the letters addressed to the Master are in fact, at the same time, *requests for love* and demands for attention. What, then, is the nature of a demand addressed both to the instance of power and to the instance of active non-knowledge? What is the status of *love for the Censor*—of *love for what censures love?* And how can one write *to the Censor?* How can one write *for* the very figure who signifies the suppression of what one has to say to him? These are the crucial questions underlying the text of *The Turn of the Screw.* It is out of this double bind that the story is both recounted and written.

The letters to the Master can convey, indeed, nothing but silence. Their message is not only erased; it consists of its own erasure. This is precisely what Miles discovers when he steals the letter the governess has intended to send to the Master:

> "Tell me (. . .) if, yesterday afternoon, from the table in the hall, you took, you know, my letter."
> (. . .)
> "Yes—I took it."
> (. . .)
> "What did you take it for?"

[28]Cf. J. Lacan, "L'Instance de la lettre dans l'inconscient" (*Ecrits*), esp. pp. 497–498, 502.

"To see what you said about me."

"You opened the letter?"

"I opened it."

(. . .)

"And you found *nothing!*"—I let my elation out.

He gave me the most mournful, thoughtful little headshake. "*Nothing.*"

"*Nothing, nothing!*" I almost shouted in my joy.

"*Nothing, nothing,*" he sadly repeated.

I kissed his forehead; it was drenched. "So what have you done with it?"

"I've burnt it." (chaps. 23–24, pp. 84–86)[29]

It is no coincidence, doubtless, that the letters to the Censor end up being intercepted and materially destroyed. Just as the governess intercepts the children's letters to the Master, Miles intercepts the governess's letter to the Master and ends up throwing it into the *fire.* The reader may recall, however, that the fire, as of the very opening line of the prologue, appeared as the center of the narrative space of desire out of which the story springs: "The story had held us, *round the fire,* sufficiently breathless. . ." Symbolically narrative frame: in the center of the circle, in the center of the prologue, the same central place, with respect to the circle of readers-listeners, as that of the story's content with respect to the narrative frame: in the center of the circle, in the center of the frame, fire and story's content seemed indeed to act as foci—as *foyers*—upon which the space both of narration and of reading seemed to converge. But through Miles's gesture of throwing the governess's let-

---

[29]The fact that the letter of *Nothing* can in fact signify a *love letter* is reminiscent of Cordelia's uncanny reply to King Lear: by virtue of his imposing paternal and royal authority, King Lear, although soliciting his daughter's expression of love, can symbolically be seen as its censor. In saying precisely "nothing," Cordelia addresses her father with the only "authentic" love letter:

Lear:	. . . Now, our joy,
	Although the last, not least, to whose young love
	The vines of France and milk of Burgundy
	Strive to be interested, what can you say to draw
	A third more opulent than your sisters? Speak.
Cordelia:	Nothing, my lord.
Lear:	Nothing!
Cordelia:	Nothing.
Lear:	Nothing will come of nothing. Speak again. (*King Lear*, I, i)

ter into the fire, the *fire inside the story* turns out to be, precisely, *what annihilates the inside of the letter;* what materially destroys the very "nothing" that constitutes its *content.* And since the letters in the story are metaphorical to the manuscript of the story as a whole, i.e., to the narrative itself as an effect of writing, we can see that what the fire indeed consumes, in burning up the content of the letter, is nothing other than the very *content* of the story. If the story here is one of letters, it is because, in every sense of the expression, *letters burn.* As that which burns the letter and which burns up the letter, the fire is the story's center only insofar as it *eliminates the center:* it is analogous to the story's *content* only insofar as it consumes, incinerates at once the content of the story and the inside of the letter, making both indeed impossible to read, *unreadable,* but unreadable in such a way as to hold all the more "breathless" the readers' circle round it. "We do not see what is burning," says Lacan in another context, referring to another fire which, however, is not without resemblance in its fantastic funereal presence to the one that, here, is burning up the letter—"we do not see what is burning, for the flame blinds us to the fact that the fire catches (. . .) on the real."[30]

> Tout l'âme résumée
> Quand lente nous l'expirons
> Dans plusieurs ronds de fumée
> Abolis en autres ronds
>
> Atteste quelque cigare
> Brûlant savamment pour peu
> Que la cendre se sépare
> De son clair baiser de feu
>
> Ainsi le chœur des romances
> A la lèvre vole-t-il
> Exclus-en si tu commences
> Le réel parce que vil

[30]*Quatre Concepts,* p. 58. It is perhaps not indispensable, but neither would it be here out of place to recall the crucial importance of fire in Henry James's life, and its recurrent role, both real and symbolic, as a *castrating agent:* just as James's father lost a leg in attempting to put a fire out, James himself believed he had injured his back in the course of a fire, as a result of which he was afflicted for the rest of his life with a mysterious, perhaps psychosomatic back ailment. Cf. Dr. Saul Rosenzweig, "The Ghost of Henry James: A Study in Thematic Apperception," in *Character and Personality,* December 1943.

Le sens trop précis rature
Ta vague littérature
(Mallarmé)[31]

VI. The Scene of Reading: The Surrender of the Name

> It was a sense instinctive and unreasoned, but I felt from the first that if I was on the scent of something ultimate I had better waste neither my wonder nor my wisdom. I *was* on the scent—that I was sure of; and yet even after I was sure I should still have been at a loss to put my enigma itself into words. I was just conscious, vaguely, of being on the track of a law, a law that would fit, that would strike me as governing the delicate phenomena (. . .). The obsession pays, if one will; but to pay it has to borrow.
>
> H. James, *The Sacred Fount*

The Turn of the Screw is thus organized around a double mystery: the mystery of the letters' content and the mystery of the ghosts. Like the letters, the ghosts, too, are essentially figures of *silence:*

> It was the *dead silence* of our long gaze at such close quarters that gave the whole *horror,* huge as it was, its only note of the unnatural. (chap. 9, p. 41)

On the one hand, then, the ghosts—which are, by definition, "horrors" ("What *is* he? He's a horror" [chap. 5, p. 22]; "For the woman's a horror of horrors" [chap. 7, p. 32])—are as *mute,* that is, as *silent* as the letters. And on the other hand, the letters themselves, through their very silence, point to "horrors":

> My fear was of having to deal with the intolerable question of the *grounds of his dismissal from school,* for that was really but the question of the *horrors* gathered behind. (chap. 15, p. 57)

[31]"The whole soul when slow we breathe it out summed up in several rings of smoke abolished into others, attests to some cigar burning cannily as long as the ash falls away from its clear kiss of fire; just so, the chorus of old romances steals to the lip. Exclude them if you begin the real, because vile. A too precise meaning crosses out your vague literature." (My literal translation.)

In the governess's eyes, the word "horror" thus defines both what the ghosts *are* and what the letters *suppress*, leave out. Could it not be said, then, that the ghosts, whatever their horror may consist of, act as a kind of pendant to the missing *content* of the letters? Like that content, the ghosts are themselves erased significations, barred signifieds: just as the letter opened by Miles turned out to contain "nothing," the ghost seen by the governess is like "no-body."

> "What is he like?"
> "I've been dying to tell you, but he's like nobody." (chap. 5, p. 23)

Nothing, nobody; no-thing, no-body: marked by the very sign of negation and denial, prefixed by a "no" which bars them in the very act of calling them up, the ghosts—like the letters—manifest themselves only to negate themselves, but through this self-negation, carry out their own self-affirmation; their mode of being and of self-manifestation is that of their own contradiction. The double scandal implicated by the double reference to the "horrors," qualifying both what the ghosts reveal and what the letters conceal, could thus spring not from any essential *evil* inherent as such in the letters and the ghosts, but precisely from their structural self-contradictory way of functioning. In the ghosts as well as in the letters, it could be nothing other than this *economy* of contradiction that takes on the power to "horrify,"to scandalize and to appall.

If the ghosts, themselves marked with the sign of negation, come to fill in—so to speak—the letters' gaps, or at least to occupy a place homologous to the vacant interior of the letters, could it not be said that the ghosts are in reality nothing other than the letters' *content*,[32] and that the letters' content could thus itself be nothing other than a *ghost-effect?*[33]

---

[32]The signifying chain of letters would then by the same token be a chain of ghosts: the return of the erased letter would have something to do with the return of the dead; writing, in its blots, its omissions, and its changes of address, would reveal the insistence and mark the return of that which was considered dead and buried, but which has nonetheless come back; the story of the unconscious would be that of the return of the repressed through the insistence of the signifier. Cf. *The Turn of the Screw*, chap. 13, pp. 50–51: "The element of the unnamed and untouched became, between us, greater than any other, and (. . .) so much avoidance couldn't have been made successful without a great deal of tacit arrangement. It was as if, at

The suggestion that the ghosts are in fact contained in the letters, that their manifestations have to do with *writing*, is outlined by a remark of the governess herself, concerning Peter Quint: "So I saw him as I see the letters I form on this page" (chap. 3, p. 17). This remark, which creates a relation between the letters and the ghosts through the intermediary verb "to see," seems to posit an equivalence between two activities, both of which present themselves as a mode of seeing:

$$
\begin{array}{ccc}
& \text{as} & \\
\text{so I saw him} & = & \text{I see the letters} \\
\textit{to see ghosts} & = & \textit{to see letters}
\end{array}
$$

But what is "seeing letters," if not, precisely, *reading?*[34] In observing and in "seeing," as she says, the very letters that she forms "on this page" of the manuscript of her narrative, the governess is indeed *reading* her own story, which she is also writing in the form of a *letter* to be sent to Douglas. Contained within the letter, the ghosts are thus determined as both a *writing-* and a *reading-effect.*

The governess is in fact revealed to be an avid reader not only of her own story but also of the novels that fill the library at Bly. Is it not significant, indeed, that the ghosts are consistently associated in the governess's mind with the novels she has read? Quint's first appearance immediately calls up the memory of two such nov-

---

moments, we were perpetually coming into sight of subjects before which we must stop short, turning suddenly out of alleys that we perceived to be blind, closing with a little bang that made us look at each other—for, like all bangs, it was something louder than we had intended—the doors we had indiscreetly opened. All roads lead to Rome, and there were times when it might have struck us that almost every branch of study or subject of conversation skirted forbidden ground. Forbidden ground was the question of the return of the dead in general and of whatever, in especial, might survive, in memory, of the friends little children had lost."

[33]Since the letters, as we saw earlier, are metaphorical to the manuscript as a whole, and since the letters' content thus represents the content of the story, the inside of the "frame" outlined by the prologue, it is not surprising that the ghost first appears to the governess as precisely that which fills in a frame: "The man who looked at me over the battlements was as definite as *a picture in a frame*" (chap. 3, p. 16).

[34]The obverse of this equation, which indeed confirms its validity, is illustrated by Mrs. Grose: on the one hand, she never sees any ghosts, and on the other, she "cannot read," she is illiterate:

not to read letters = not to see ghosts

els:[35] the novels constitute *interpretations* of the ghost. The governess's third encounter with the apparition, on the other hand, occurs just after she has sleepily put aside the book she has been reading: through this metonymical, contiguous connection, the ghost, almost directly, seems to spring out of the pages of the book. It is here no longer fiction that interprets ghostly apparitions, but rather the ghost itself that constitutes a possible interpretation of the novel just read.

> *I sat reading* by a couple of candles (. . .) I remember that the book I had in my hand was Fielding's *Amelia;* also that I was *wholly awake.* I recall further both a general conviction that it was horribly late and a particular objection to looking at my watch. (. . .) I recollect (. . .) that, though I was deeply interested in the author, I found myself, *at the turn of a page* and with his spell all scattered, looking straight up from him and hard at the door of my room. (. . .)
> . . . I went straight along the lobby (. . .) till I came within sight of the tall window that presided over the great *turn of the staircase* (. . .). *My candle* (. . .) *went out* (. . .). Without it, the next instant, I knew that *there was a figure on the stair.* I speak of sequences, but I require no lapse of seconds to stiffen myself for a third encounter with Quint. (chap. 9, pp. 40–41)

To see ghosts, then, is to read letters, and to read letters is to stay up late at night: reading has to do with night as such, just as ghosts have to do with darkness. To read (to see letters, to see ghosts) is thus to *look into the dark,* to see in darkness ("My candle [. . .] went out [. . .]. Without it, the next instant, I knew there was a figure on the stair"). In order to look into the dark, to see in darkness (in order to read), should the eyes be opened or should they, on the contrary, be closed? The governess tells us that her eyes were open, that she was "wholly awake." If, however, a suspicion could arise that this was somehow not quite the case, the ghost itself

[35] "Was there a 'secret' at Bly—a mystery of Udolpho or an insane, an unmentionable relative kept in unsuspected confinement?" (chap. 4, p. 17). The allusions here are to Ann Radcliffe's *Mystery of Udolpho*, which depicts the presence of a ghost in an uncanny, supernatural environment, and to Charlotte Brontë's *Jane Eyre*, which tells of a romance precisely between a governess and her Master, untimely cut off by the revelation of the Master's former marriage to a woman, now mad, who is being sequestered in his house.

would turn out to be nothing but a *dream induced by letters;*
reading itself could then be suspected of being prey to sleep-appari-
tions, apparitions that would inextricably attend and suffuse the
written word as such.[36]

The governess is thus a *reader,* undergoing the effects of letters;
of letters that come through the mail or are written to be mailed, as
well as those that can be read on the printed pages of a book. The
governess's very first question, upon receipt of the letter from the
head-master of Miles's school, is indeed the question *par excellence* of the interpreter: *"What does it mean!* The child's dis-
missed his school" (chap. 2, p. 10). In her pursuit of *meaning*—the
meaning of the ghosts as well as that of the letters—in her constant efforts at *deciphering* the goings-on at Bly, the governess's
whole adventure turns out to be, essentially a *reading-adventure,* a
quest for the definitive, literal or proper meaning of words and of
events.

I had restlessly *read into* the facts before us almost all the *meaning*
they were to receive from subsequent and more cruel occurrences.
(chap. 6, pp. 27–28)

I (. . .) *read into* what our young friend had said to me the *fullness of
its meaning.* (chap. 15, p. 57)

I *extracted a meaning* from the boy's embarrassed back. (chap. 23, p.
82)

I suppose I now *read into* our situation a clearness it couldn't have
had at the time. (chap. 23, p. 84)

The search for meaning is prompted by a perception of *ambiguities:*—Ambiguities in the letters:

Deep obscurity continued to cover the region of the boy's conduct at
school. (chap. 4, p. 19)

[36]Cf. indeed the description of the Master: "a figure as had never risen, save in a
dream or an old *novel"* (Prologue, p. 4), and that of the house at Bly: "I had a view of
a castle of romance inhabited by a rosy sprite, such a place as would somehow (. . .)
take all colours out of storybooks and fairy-tales. *Wasn't it just a storybook over
which I had fallen a-doze and a-dream!* No . . ." (chap. 1, p. 10)

—Ambiguities in the ghosts:

> . . . I caught at a dozen possibilities (. . .) that I could see, in there having been in the house (. . .) a person of whom I was in ignorance. (. . .) My office seemed to require that there should be no such ignorance and no such person. (. . .) This visitant (. . .) seemed to fix me (. . .) with just the question, just the scrutiny (. . .) that his own presence provoked. (chap. 3, p. 17)

—Ambiguities in the spoken word:

> . . . my impression of her having accidentally said more than she meant (. . .)
> I don't know what there was in this brevity of Mrs. Grose's that struck me as ambiguous. (. . .) I felt that (. . .) I had a right to know. (chap. 2, pp. 12–13)

Thus, "seeing ghosts" and "seeing letters" both involve the perception of ambiguous and contradictory signifiers, the perception of *double* meanings. The act of reading and interpreting those ambiguities, however, reveals itself paradoxically to be an act of *reducing* and *eliminating* them:

> I (. . .) opened my letter again to repeat to her. (. . .) "Is he really bad?"
> The tears were still in her eyes. "Do the gentlemen say so?" "They go into no particulars. They simply express their regret that it should be impossible to keep him. *That can have but one meaning* (. . .): that he's an injury to the others." (chap. 2, p. 11)

> There was *but one* sane inference: (. . .) we had been, collectively, subject to an intrusion. (chap. 4, p. 18)

> I had an *absolute certainty* that I should see again what I had already seen. (chap. 6, p. 26)

> I began to take in with *certitude* and yet without direct vision, the presence, a good way off, of a third person. (. . .) There was *no ambiguity* in anything. (chap. 6, p. 29)

> *"If I had ever doubted, all my doubt would at present have gone.* I've been living with the miserable *truth*, and now it has only too much *closed round me* . . ." (chap. 20, p. 73)

In her endeavor to reduce the contradictory and the ambiguous to "but one meaning," the governess's method of reading her own adventure is thus not substantially different from that of James's readers, the critics of the text:

> But what if there is one thing (. . .) that cannot be read in either of two senses, that can be read *only in one sense?* (A. J. A. Waldock, *Casebook*, p. 172)

> The *determining unambiguous passages* from which the critics might work are so plentiful that it seems hardly good critical strategy to use the ambiguous ones as points of departure. (Robert Heilman, FR, *MLN*, p. 436)

In anticipating once again the strategies of its own reading, the text becomes a challenge to the reader, an invitation to a second-degree reading, which would attempt to read the text's own critical reading of its reading: the way in which the text *puts in perspective,* and reflects upon, its own dramatization of the quest for proper meaning, of the determining transition from a perception of the equivocal to the establishment of meaning as univocal, of the very process of truth's closing around the reader:

> "If I had ever doubted, all my doubt would at present have gone. (. . .) Truth (. . .) has only too much closed round me." (chap. 20, p. 73)

The elimination of uncertainty and doubt, the acquisition of *certainty* and *clearness* about the meaning of what had nonetheless appeared at first to be ambiguous and obscure—the successful culmination, in other words, of the reading process—is time and again formulated in the text as an epistemological assertion, as a cognitive achievement, as a claim to *knowledge:*

> "He was looking for little Miles." A portentous clearness now possessed me. *"That's* whom he was looking for."
> "But how do you know?"
> "I know, I know, I know!" My exaltation grew. "And *you* know, my dear!" (chap. 6, pp. 25–26; James's italics)

The reader's *certainty* is thus correlative to his claim to *know:* knowing, indeed, is first and foremost knowing *meaning.* "I don't *know* what you *mean,"* protests Flora (chap. 20, p. 73). "Knowing," however, is acquired by means of "seeing":

> Mrs. Grose, of course, could only gape the wider. "Then *how do you know?"*
> "I was there—*I saw with my eyes."* (chap. 7, pp. 30–31)

> "For the woman's a horror of horrors."
> "Tell me *how you know,"* my friend simply repeated.
> *"Know?* By *seeing* her! By the way she looked." (chap. 7, p. 32)

If "to know" is to know *meaning,* "to see" is, on the other hand, to perceive a figure *as a sign:*

> There was a figure in the ground, a figure *prowling for a sight.* (chap. 10, p. 44)

Seeing, in other words, is of the order of the *signifier* (that which is perceived as a *conveyer* of signification, in the very *process* of signifying), while *knowing,* on the other hand, is of the order of the *signified* (that which *has been meant;* the accomplished meaning that, as such, is mastered, known, possessed). "Knowing," therefore, is to "seeing" as the signified is to the signifier: the signifier is the *seen,* whereas the signified is the *known.* The signifier, by its very nature, is ambiguous and obscure, while the signified is certain, clear, and unequivocal. Ambiguity is thus inherent in the very essence of the act of seeing:

> . . . there are depths, depths! The more I go over it, the more I see in it, and the more I see in it, the more I fear. I don't know what I *don't* see—what I *don't* fear! (chap. 7, p. 31; James's italics)

By the same token, ambiguity is fundamentally excluded from the act and the domain of "knowing":

> The way this *knowledge* gathered in me was the strangest thing in the world (. . .). I began to take in with *certitude* (. . .) the presence (. . .) of a third person. (chap. 6, p. 29)

The reading strategy employed by the governess entails, thereby, a dynamical relation between *seeing* and *knowing,* a conversion of the act of seeing into the fact of knowing. We will now attempt to analyze more closely, within the very lexical tracks outlined by the vocabulary of the text, the functioning of this conversion and of this strategy, in order to explore the ways in which it governs the narrative diachrony, shaping it indeed into the story of the progress of a reading-process toward its ineluctable end.

Reading, then begins with an awareness, with a perception of ambiguous signifiers: an enigmatic letter, an unfamiliar and uncanny ghost. The *meaning* they imply is a *knowledge* from which the governess is barred ("He's—God help me if I *know what* he is!"; chap. 5, p. 22). If it is precisely out of *lack of knowledge* that the reading-process springs, the very act of reading implies at the same time the assumption that knowledge *is*, exists but is *located in the Other:* in order for reading to be possible, there has to be knowledge in the Other (in the text, for instance), and it is that knowledge in the Other, of the Other, that must be *read*, that has to be appropriated, taken from the Other. The governess naturally thus postulates that the signified she is barred from, the sense of what she does not know, exists and is in fact possessed by—or possessing—someone else. Knowledge haunts. The question of meaning as such, which seems indeed to haunt the pages of *The Turn of the Screw*, can thus be formulated as the question: "*What is it that knows?*" "If the unconscious has taught us anything," writes Lacan, "it is first of all this: that somewhere, in the Other, 'it' knows. 'It' knows because 'it' is supposed by those signifiers the subject is constituted by (. . .). The very status of knowledge implies that some sort of knowledge already exists, in the Other, waiting to be taken, seized." (*Encore*, pp. 81, 89)

Through reading, the governess tries indeed to seize the Other's knowledge, to read in the Other the signified she seeks. First she aims at seizing Mrs. Grose's knowledge:

Then *seeing* in her face that she already, in this (. . .) found a touch of picture, I quickly added stroke to stroke (. . .).
"You *know* him then?"
(. . .)
"You *do know* him?"
She faltered but a second. "*Quint! she cried.*" (chap. 5, pp. 23–24)

But it is most especially the knowledge of the children that the governess seeks to read:

"They *know;* it's too monstrous: they know, they know!" (chap. 7, p. 45; James's italics)

I was ready to *know* the very worst that was to be *known.* What I had then had an ugly *glimpse* of was that my eyes might be sealed just while theirs were most opened. (. . .)

What it was most impossible to get rid of was the cruel idea that whatever I had seen, Miles and Flora saw *more** —things terrible and unguessable and that sprang from dreadful passages of intercourse in the past. (chap. 13, pp. 52–53; *James's italics)

Having been the witness or the accomplices of the presumed liaison between the two dead servants, the children, in the governess's eyes, are in possession of a knowledge that is at once *knowledge of meaning* and *knowledge of sex:* "They know—it's too monstrous: they know, they know!" The very predicate of knowledge, while still maintaining here its cognitive sense or value, equally rejoins its Biblical, archaic, sense: "to know," indeed, is both "to possess valuable information" and "to have sexual intercourse with." The presumed knowledge of the Other, which the governess attempts to *read,* has to do, in some odd way, both with cognition and with pleasure, both with sense and with the senses: that which must be read is, uncannily, both an epistemological and a carnal knowledge.

The children become, then, in the governess's eyes, endowed with the prestige of the "subjects presumed to know." The reader will recall, however, that "the subject presumed to know" is what sustains, according to Lacan, precisely the relationship of *transference* in psychoanalytical experience: "I deemed it necessary, says Lacan, "to support the idea of transference, as indistinguishable from love, with the formula of the subject presumed to know (. . .). The person in whom I presume knowledge to exist, thereby acquires my love" (*Encore,* p. 64). "Transference *is* love (. . .) I insist: it is love directed toward, addressed to, knowledge."[37] Presuming the child to know, the governess does indeed—unwittingly—fall in love with him, and her love, her fascination, is directed toward his knowledge:

[37]J. Lacan, "Introduction à l'édition allemande des *Ecrits,*" *Scilicet,* no. 5 (Paris: Seuil, 1975), p. 16.

It was extraordinary how my absolute conviction of his secret pre-
cocity (. . .) made him (. . .) appear as accessible as an older person—
forced me to treat him as an intelligent equal. (chap. 17, p. 63)
. . . Miles stood again with his hands in his little pockets (. . .) We
continued silent while the maid was with us—as silent, it whim-
sically occurred to me, as some young couple who, on their wedding
journey, at the inn, feel shy in the presence of the waiter. (chap. 22, p.
81)

As was the case in the prologue, we find ourselves again dealing
with a relationship of *reading* which as such entails a relationship
of *transference:* reading is again revealed to be the repetition of a
love story, the story of a love addressed to and directed toward the
knowledge of the Other. The governess's reading, her search for a
signified located in the knowledge of the Other, thus paradoxically
places her in the role not of analyst but of analysand, of *patient*
with respect to the children presumed to know, who hence themselves occupy unwittingly the very place, the very structural position, of the *analyst.*

But of course this is not the way the governess herself sees
things. In her view, it is the children who are the "patients,"
whereas she herself is, to the contrary, the therapist:

His clear, listening face, framed in its smooth whiteness, made him
for the minute as appealing as some wistful *patient in a children's
hospital;* and I would have given, as the resemblance came to me, all I
possessed on earth really to be the nurse or the sister of charity who
might have helped to *cure* him. (chap. 17, p. 63)

Toward the end of the novel, the governess does indeed come up
with what she calls a "remedy" (chap. 21, p. 76) to cure Miles. The
remedy she has in mind is a *confession:*

"I'll get it out of him. He'll meet me—he'll confess. If he confesses,
he's saved." (chap. 21, pp. 78–79)

It is thus in her capacity as a therapist, as a soul-doctor, that the
governess brings about the story's denouement in the form of a
confession intended as a cure. The importance she thereby attributes to the therapeutic value of language and of *speech* as such,

to the exorcistic power of Miles's mere *naming* of the evil which possesses him, could be suggestive of a remote resemblance with the therapeutic project of the psychoanalytical "talking cure."

It is, however, not only as a would-be "therapist," but also as a *reader* that the governess desires to bring about Miles's confession: in demanding from the child the *whole truth* about *what he knows*, she seeks, precisely, to appropriate the knowledge that the Other is presumed to have: to force that knowledge to *reveal itself*, to reveal itself, indeed, both as cognition and as pleasure. Miles's expected double confession, the revelation of his misdeeds at school and the avowal of his complicity with the ghosts, would enable the governess to decipher, i.e., to *read*, both the *meaning* of the ghosts and the *content* of the letters. The child's confession would thus constitute the crowning achievement of the governess's enterprise of reading: the definitive *denomination*—by means of language—of both *truth* and *meaning*.

> They are in my ears still, his *supreme surrender of the name* and his tribute to my devotion. (chap. 24, p. 88)

This victory, this ultimate triumph of reading through the "supreme surrender of the name," remains, however, highly ambiguous and doubly problematic in the text. On the one hand, the very act of naming, which the governess takes to be the decisive *answer* to her questions, is in the child's mouth, in reality, itself a question:

> "It's *there*—the coward horror, there for the last time!"
> At this (. . .) he was at me in a white rage, bewildered, glaring vainly over the place and missing wholly, though it now, to my sense, filled the room (. . .). "It's *he?*"
> I was so determined to have all my proof that I flashed into ice to challenge him. "Whom do you mean by 'he'?"—"Peter Quint—you devil!" His face gave again, round the room, its convulsed supplication. "*Where?*" (chap. 23, p. 88; James's italics)

If the act of naming does indeed name the final truth, that truth is given not as an answer to the question about meaning, but as itself a *question* about its *location*. "Where?" asks Miles—and this interrogation is to be his last word, the last word, indeed, of his "confession." The final meaning, therefore, is not an answer, but is itself a question, which also questions its own pursuit. In considering that question as an answer, the governess in effect stifles its nonetheless ongoing questioning power.

On the other hand, the governess's triumph both as a reader and as a therapist, both as an interpreter and as an exorcist, is rendered highly suspicious by the death of what she had set out at once to *understand* and to *cure*. It therefore behooves the reader of *The Turn of the Screw* to discover the meaning of this murderous effect of meaning; to understand how a child can be killed by the very act of understanding.

VII. A Child Is Killed

> Insupportable est la mort de l'enfant: elle réalise le plus secret et le plus profond de nos vœux (. . .)
>
> Il est remarquable que, jusqu'à ce jour, on se soit plus volontiers arrêté (. . .) dans la constellation oedipienne, [sur les] fantasmes du meurtre du père, de prise ou de mise en pièces de la mère, laissant pour compte la tentative de meurtre d'Oedipe-enfant dont c'est l'échec qui a assuré et déterminé le destin tragique du héros.
>
> Serge Leclaire, *On tue un enfant*

What, indeed, is the cause of Miles's death? The final paragraph suggests that he is accidentally suffocated by the governess in the strength of her passionate embrace:

> The *grasp* with which I *recovered* him might have been that of catching him in his fall. I *caught* him, yes, I *held* him—it may be imagined with what a passion; but at the end of a minute I began to feel what it truly was that I *held*. We were alone with the quiet day, and his little heart, dispossessed, had stopped. (chap. 23, p. 88)

The word "grasp," which commands this *closing* paragraph, thus appears to account for Miles's death. Interestingly enough, this same word "grasp" also commands the *opening* paragraph of the last chapter. It is as though the beginning and end of the last chapter were both placed in the grasp of the word "grasp," as though that word had as its role at once to introduce and to bring to a conclusion the story's final act. Here is then the opening sentence of the last chapter:

> My *grasp* of how he received this suffered for a minute from something that I can only describe as a fierce split of my attention—a stroke that, at first, as I sprang straight up, reduced me to the mere blind movement of *getting hold of him, drawing him close* and, while I just fell for support against the nearest piece of furniture, instinctively keeping him with his back to the window. (chap. 24, pp. 84–85)

In spite of the apparent symmetry of its two occurrences, however, the word "grasp" does not have the same meaning in both cases: in the opening sentence ("my *grasp* of how he received this") the word is used in its *abstract* sense of "comprehension," "understanding"; in the closing sentence ("the *grasp* with which I recovered him"), it is used in its *concrete*, physical sense of "clasp," "hold." In repeating the word "grasp" in its two different senses in these two symmetrical, strategic points of the final chapter, James's text seems to *play* upon the two connotations, to play them off against each other in order to reveal their fundamental interaction and their complicity. The implicit question behind this semantic play which frames the novel's ending thus becomes: what does a "grasp" involve? What are the relation and the interaction between the act of understanding ("my grasp of how he received this") and the act of clasping in one's arms, to the point of suffocating ("the grasp with which I recovered him")? Curiously enough, in a very different context, it is precisely by a similar double image highlighting the interaction between the mental and physical act of grasping that Cicero chooses to reflect upon the very nature of understanding: "Except for the sage," he writes, "no one knows anything, and that fact was demonstrated by Zeno by means of a gesture. He held up his hand, its fingers extended. That's representation, *visum*, he said. Then he curled back his fingers a bit. That's assent, *assensus*. Next, he completely closed his hand and made a fist, and declared that that was comprehension, *comprehensio*. That's why he gave it the name *catalepsis*,[38] which had not been used before him. Finally, he brought his left hand toward his right hand and grasped his fist tightly; that, he said, was science, *scientia*, something none but the sage pos-

---

[38]Etymologically, "a seizing."

Henry James

sess."[39] It is thus the governess's very "science" which seems to kill the child. Just as Cicero illustrates the act of comprehension by the image of a closed fist, James seems to literalize and at the same time ironize the same act by the suffocating gesture of a tightly closed embrace.

> Mightn't one, to reach his mind, risk the stretch of a stiff arm across his character? (chap. 22, p. 111)

> . . . the grasp with which I recovered him (. . .), I caught him, yes, I held him. . . (chap. 23, p. 88)

The comprehension ("grasp," "reach his mind") of the meaning the Other is presumed to know, which constitutes the ultimate aim of any act of reading, is thus conceived as a violent gesture of appropriation, a gesture of domination of the Other. Reading, in other words, establishes itself as a relation not only to *knowledge* but equally to *power*; it consists not only of a search for meaning but also of a struggle to control it. Meaning itself thus unavoidably becomes the outcome of an act of violence:

> To do it in *any** way was an *act of violence,* for what did it consist of but the obtrusion of the idea of grossness and guilt on a small helpless creature who had been for me a revelation of the possibilities of beautiful intercourse? (. . .) I suppose I now *read into our situation a clearness* it couldn't have at the time. (chap. 23, p. 84; *James's italics; other italics mine)

But why is violence necessary in order for meaning to appear as "clearness" and as light? What is the obstacle to clearness that the violence of the act of reading must eliminate? What does comprehension ("my grasp of how he received this") suffer from before the physical pressure of its embrace ("the grasp with which I recovered him") insures its triumph? Let us take another look at the opening lines of the last chapter:

> My grasp of how he received this *suffered* for a minute from something that I can describe only as a *fierce split of my attention*—a

[39]Cicero, quoted by J.-A. Miller, "Théorie de lalangue (rudiment)," in *Ornicar,* no. 1 (January 1975), 22.

207

stroke that at first, as I sprang straight up, reduced me to the mere blind movement of getting hold of him, drawing him close and, while I just fell for support against the nearest piece of furniture, instinctively keeping him with his back to the window. (chap. 24, pp. 84–85)

Just before this passage, the governess has asked Miles the decisive question of whether he did steal her letter. But her ability to *grasp* the effect of her own question on Miles suffers, as she herself puts it, from a "fierce *split* of her attention": her attention is *divided* between Miles and the ghost at the window, between a conscious signifier and the unconscious signified upon which the latter turns, between a conscious perception and its fantasmatic double, its contradictory extension toward the prohibited unconscious desire that it stirs up. Thus divided, her attention fails to "grasp" the child's reaction. The failure of comprehension therefore springs from the "fierce split"—from the *Spaltung*—of the subject, from the *divided state* in which meaning seems to hold the subject who is seeking it.[40] But it is precisely this division, this castrating "split," which must be reduced or dominated, denied or overcome, by the violence of a suffocating hold.

> . . . something that I can describe only as a fierce split of my attention—a stroke that at first (. . .) reduced me to the mere blind movement of getting hold of him, drawing him close. . .

> . . . yet I believe that no woman so overwhelmed ever in so short a time recovered her command of the *act*. (chap. 24, pp. 84–85; James's italics)

[40]Like the ghost, Miles's language (which is responsible for his dismissal from school and is thus related to the missing content of the letter) equally *divides* the "attention" of the governess and her "grasping" mind, by manifesting a *contradiction*—a split within language itself—between the statement and the utterance of the child, between the speaker and his speech: " 'What did you do?' 'Well—I said things.' 'But to whom did you say them?' (. . .) '[To] those I liked.' Those he liked? I seemed to float not into clearness, but into a darker obscure (. . .) there had come to me out of my very pity the appalling alarm of his being perhaps innocent. (. . .) He turned to me again his little beautiful fevered eyes. 'Yes, it was too bad (. . .). What I suppose I sometimes said. To write home.' " "*I can't name*," comments the governess, "the exquisite pathos of the *contradiction* given to *such a speech by such a speaker*" (chap. 24, p. 87). "What the unconscious forces us to examine," writes Lacan, "is the law according to which no utterance can ever be reduced simply to its own statement" (*Ecrits*, p. 892).

James originally wrote "recovered her *grasp* of the act." It is in the revised New York edition that "grasp" is replaced by "command." But what *act* is it of which the governess regains her *understanding* ("grasp"), i.e., her *control* ("command")?

> It came to me in the very horror of the immediate presence that the *act* would be, seeing and facing what I saw and faced, *to keep the boy himself unaware.* (chap. 24, p. 85)

It should be remembered that in this final chapter the entire effort of the governess aims at *reading* the knowledge of the child, and thus at naming truth and meaning. But in this passage, paradoxically enough, the very act of *reading* the child's knowledge turns out to be an act of suppressing, or *repressing*, part of that knowledge: of "keeping the boy himself *unaware.*" As an object of suppression and of repression, the knowledge of the child itself becomes thereby the very emblem of the unconscious; of the unconscious that is always, in a sense, the knowledge of a child about to die and yet immortal, indestructible; the knowledge of a child dead and yet which one has always yet to kill. "The unconscious," says indeed Lacan, "is knowledge; but it is a knowledge one cannot know one knows, a knowledge that cannot tolerate knowing it knows"[41]—a knowledge, in other words, that cannot tolerate, and that escapes, in every sense, conscious *reflection.*

> What was prodigious was that at last, by my success, his sense was sealed and his communication stopped: *he knew that he was in presence, but knew not of what* (. . .). My eyes went back to the window only to see that the air was clear again (. . .). There was nothing there. I felt that the cause was mine and that I should surely get *all.** (chap. 24, pp. 85–86; *James's italics; other italics mine)

The act of reading, the attempt to grasp and hold the signified, goes thus hand in hand with the repression or obliteration of a signifier—a repression the purpose of which is to eliminate meaning's *division.* "The act would be, *seeing* and facing what I *saw* and faced, to keep the boy himself unaware (. . .). My eyes went back to the window only to *see* that the air was clear again. (. . .) There was nothing there." *To see* (and by the same token, *to read:* "to see

---

[41]"Les Non-dupes errent" (seminar), 1974 (unpublished).

letters," "to see ghosts") is therefore paradoxically not only *to perceive*, but also *not to perceive:* to *actively* determine an area as *invisible*, as *excluded* from perception, as external by definition to visibility. To see is to draw a *limit* beyond which vision becomes barred. The rigid *closure* of the violent embrace implied by the act (by the "grasp") of understanding is linked, indeed, to the violence required to impose a *limit*, beyond which one's eyes must *close*. For it is not the closing of one's eyes that determines the invisible as its empirical result; it is rather the invisible (the repressed) that predetermines the closing of one's eyes. The necessity of shutting one's eyes actively partakes, indeed, of the very act of seeing, knowing, reading:

> . . . my equilibrium depended on the success of my rigid will, the will *to shut my eyes as tight as possible* to the truth that what I had to deal with was, revoltingly, against nature. I could only get on at all by taking nature into my confidence and my account (. . .). No attempt, none the less, could well require more tact than just this attempt to supply, one's self, *all** the nature. How could I put even a little of that article into a *suppression of reference* to what had occurred? How, on the other hand, could I *make a reference* without a *new plunge into the* hideous *obscure?* (chap. 22, p. 80; *James's italics; other italics mine)

To grasp: to close one's arms, to stifle. To see: to close one's eyes, to suppress a reference, or else to make a reference and by that very act to take "a new plunge into the obscure," that is, into the invisible. Paradoxically enough, however, it is precisely the imposition of a limit beyond which vision is prohibited which dispels the "split of attention" and at the same time the split of meaning, and which hence makes possible the illusion of total *mastery* over meaning as a whole, as an unimpaired *totality*[42]:

[42]Totality as such is both *unique* (since it includes *everything*, nothing is left outside it) and *univocal* (continuous, *coherent*, undivided, homogeneous). Thus it is that the governess can say: "That can have *but one* meaning (. . .) to put the thing with some *coherence* . . . " (chap. 2, p. 11). "The principle of coherence," writes E. D. Hirsch, "is precisely the same as the principle of a boundary. Whatever is continuous with the visible part of an iceberg lies inside its boundaries, and whatever lies within these falls under the criterion of the continuity. The two concepts are codefining" (E. D. Hirsch, *Validity in Interpretation* [New Haven: Yale University Press, 1967], p. 54).

My eyes went back to the window only to see that the air was clear again. (. . .) There was nothing there. I felt that the cause was mine and that I should surely get *all*. (chap. 24, p. 86; James's italics)

I seemed to myself to have *mastered* it, to *see it all*. (chap. 21, p. 78)

The principle of totality being the very principle of a *boundary* and of the repression inherent in it, the text's irony here lies in the suggestion that the illusion of total *mastery*, of "seeing *all*," is in reality a counterpart to the act of "*shutting one's eyes* as tight as possible to the truth." Now, to *master*, to become a Master, is inevitably in this text also to become *like the Master*. As the reader will recall, the Master is indeed the incarnation of the very principle of *censorship* and of the imposition of a *limit*, as constitutive of authority as such: of the authority of *consciousness* itself as *mastery*. But his is a mastery that exerts its authority not as an imperative to *know*, but as an imperative *not* to know. To "master," therefore, to understand and "*see it all*," as the governess complacently puts it to herself, is in this text, ironically enough, to occupy the very place of *blindness:* of the blindness to which the Master voluntarily commits himself at the outset of the story, by ordering the suppression of all information,[43] by prohibiting the governess from informing him of anything at all. Through the governess's own action, the quest for mastery will thus repeat itself as a form of blindness:

. . . a stroke that reduced me to the mere *blind* movement of getting hold of him, drawing him close (. . .) instinctively keeping him with his back to the window.
(. . .)
He almost smiled at me in the desolation of his surrender. (. . .) I was *blind* with *victory*. (chap. 24, pp. 85, 87)

[43]This suppression of information is also the function of the *Masters* (the head-masters) of Miles's school, since their letter suppresses all mention of the grounds of the child's dismissal: "I turned it over. 'And these things came round—?' 'To the *masters?* Oh yes!' he answered very simply. 'But I didn't know they'd tell.' 'The *masters?* They didn't—*they've never told*. That's why I ask you.'" (chap. 24, p. 87.) The word "Master" thus comes to signify, in James's text, at once the principle of authority and the principle of repression—the very principle of the *authority to repress:* to repress at once mentally and physically, in a psychoanalytical but equally in a political sense (cf. Miles's dismissal from school and, ultimately, his murder).

To master, to "see *all*," is thus not only to be blind with victory, but also, and quite literally, to be triumphant *out of* blindness.

The violence of the blind grip through which the governess seizes Miles recalls the image of the quasi-compulsive clasping of a sinking boat's helm which the governess evokes so as metaphorically to justify in her own eyes her quest for mastery, her effort to control the situation: "It was in short just by clutching the helm that I avoided total wreck" (chap. 22, p. 79). This metaphor of the boat recurs several times in the text. Marking here the ending of the story, it is also found at the beginning, at the conclusion of the very first chapter:

> It was a big, ugly (. . .) house, (. . .) in which I had the fancy of our being almost as lost as a handful of passengers in a great drifting ship. Well, I was, strangely, at the helm! (chap. 1, p. 10)

The metaphor of the helm serves to bring out the underlying interdependence between meaning and power: to clutch the helm, to steer the ship, is in effect to guide it, to give it a *direction* and a *sense*, to *control* its direction or its sense. Indeed, throughout the story, the governess's very act of reading consists in her *imposing meaning*, in her imposing sense both as a *directive* and as a *direction* upon the others:

> This is why I had now given to Mrs. Grose's steps *so marked a direction*—a direction that made her, when she perceived it, oppose a resistance (. . .).
> "You're *going to the water*, Miss?—you think she's *in**?" (chap. 19, p. 68; *James's italics)

> I could only get on at all by taking "nature" into my confidence (. . .), by treating my monstrous ordeal as *a push in a direction unusual*. (chap. 22, p. 80)

> "Is she *here**?" Miles panted as he caught with his sealed eyes the *direction* of my words. (chap. 24, p. 88; *James's italics)

In "clutching the helm," in giving direction to the ship she steers, the governess, whose reading alone indeed commands the situation, clutches at power as sense, and at sense as power: she leads us to believe, along with those under her direction, that if her power is as such meaningful, it is because it is meaning itself that is in power; that it is her sense which commands, and that her command indeed *makes sense:* "She has 'authority'," writes James, "which is a good deal to have given her"; "It constitutes no little of a character indeed (. . .) that she is able to make her particular *credible* statement of such strange matters" (New York Preface, p. 121). Putting into effect the very title of her function, the "governess" does *govern:* she does indeed clutch at the helm of the boat with the same kind of violence and forceful determination with which she ultimately grips the body of little Miles. The textual repetition of the metaphor of the boat thus serves to illustrate, through the singular gesture of grasping the rudder-bar, the very enterprise of reading as a political project of sense-control, the taking over of the very power implied by meaning.

Curiously enough, the image of the boat recurs in yet another strategic, although apparently unrelated context in the story: in the incident beside the lake during which the governess comes upon Flora playing (under the influence, thinks the governess, of Miss Jessel) with two pieces of wood out of which she is trying to construct a toy boat:

> [Flora] had picked up a small flat piece of wood, which happened to have in it a *little hole* that had evidently suggested to her the *idea of sticking in another fragment* that might *figure as a mast* and *make the thing a boat.* This second morsel, as I watched her, she was very markedly and intently attempting to *tighten in its place.*
> (. . .)
> I got hold of Mrs. Grose as soon after this as I could (. . .)
> I still hear myself cry as I fairly threw myself into her arms: "*They know*—it's too monstrous: they know, they know!"
> "And what on earth—? (. . .)"
> "Why, all that *we** know—and heaven knows what else besides!"
> (chaps. 6–7, p. 30; *James's italics; other italics mine)

This incident is crucial, not only because it constitutes for the governess a decisive proof of the children's knowledge, but also because, implicitly but literally, it evokes an image related to the very *title* of the story: in attempting to fit the stick into the hole as a mast for her little boat, Flora "tightens it in its place" with a gesture very like that of *tightening a screw.*

But what precisely does this gesture mean? The screw—or the mast—is evidently, in this incident, at least to the governess's eyes, a phallic symbol, a metaphor connoting sexuality itself. This phallic connotation, the reader will recall, was pointed out and underlined, indeed, by Wilson. Wilson's exegesis, however, viewed the sexual reference as an *answer*, as the literal, proper meaning which it sufficed to *name* in order to understand and "see it all," in order to put an end to all textual questions and ambiguities. As an emblem of the sexual act, Flora's boat was for Wilson a simple indication of the literal object—the real organ—desired by the governess without her being able or willing to admit it. But it is precisely *not* as an unequivocal *answer* that the text here evokes the phallus, but on the contrary rather as a *question*, as a figure—itself ambiguous—produced by the enigma of the *double meaning* of the metaphorical equation: phallus = ship's mast. To say that the mast is in reality a phallus is no more illuminating or unambiguous than to say that the phallus is in reality a mast. The question arises not of what the mast "really is" but of what a phallus— *or* a mast—might be, if they can thus so easily be interchangeable, i.e., signify what they are not. What is the meaning of this movement of *relay* of meaning between the phallus and the mast? And since the mast, which is a figure of the phallus, is also a figure of the *screw*, it seems that the crucial question raised by the text and valorized by its title might be: what is, after all, a *screw* in *The Turn of the Screw*?

Let us take another look at Flora's boat. It is as a phallic symbol that the boat disturbs the governess and convinces her of the perversity of the children: "They know—it's too monstrous: they know, they know!" The screw, or the phallic mast, thus constitutes for the governess a *key to meaning*, a *master-signifier:* the very key to what the Other knows.

In such a context it is no longer possible to be insensitive to the remarkable phonetical resemblance between the word "mast" and the word "master," which it cannot but bring to mind: indeed, if the mast is a kind of "master," i.e., a dominant element determining both the structure and the movement of a boat, the Master is himself a kind of "mast" which at once determines and supports the structure and the movement of the entire story of *The Turn of the Screw*. As one of the principal elements in a ship, the mast is thus not unrelated to the helm that the governess clutches with the same convulsive grasp as that with which she seizes Miles (who is himself a little Master).[44]

Now, to suggest that all these metaphorical elements—*Miles* in the governess's arms, the tightly gripped *helm* in the uncanny drifting ship, the little *mast* in Flora's boat, and the *screw* in *The Turn of the Screw*—refer alternately to the phallus *and* to the Master (as well as to one another), is to set up a *signifying chain* in which the phallus (or the screw, or the mast, or the Master), far from incarnating the unambiguous literal meaning behind things, symbolizes rather the incessant *sliding* of signification, the very principle of movement and displacement which on the contrary *prevents* the chain (or the text) from ever stopping at a final, literal, fixed meaning. The phallus, far from being a real object, is in fact a *signifier*; a signifier that only appears to become a Master—a key to meaning and a key to the knowledge of the Other—by virtue of its incarnating, like the Master, the very function of the semiotic *bar*—the very principle of imposition of a limit, the principle of censorship and of repression which forever *bars* all access to the signified as such.[45]

> "The question is," said Alice, "whether you can make words mean so many different things."
> "The question is," said Humpty Dumpty, "which is to be master—that's all."[46]

In reaching out both for the master and for the mast, in aspiring to *be*, in fact, herself a master and a mast, in clasping Miles as she would clutch at the ship's helm, the governess becomes, indeed, the *Master* of the ship, the Master of the *meaning* of the story (a

[44]Cf.: "At this, with one of the quick *turns* of simple folk, she suddenly flamed up. '*Master* Miles!—him* an injury?'" (chap. 2, p. 11).

[45]Cf. J. Lacan, *The Meaning of the Phallus (La Signification du phallus)*: "In Freudian thought, the phallus is not a fantasy, if a fantasy is understood to be an imaginary effect. Nor is it as such an object (partial, internal, good, bad, etc.) if the term is used to designate the reality involved in a relationship. It is still less the organ, penis or clitoris, which it symbolizes. It is not without cause that Freud took his reference from the *simulacrum* it was for the ancients. For the phallus is a signifier (. . .). It can only play its role under a veil, that is, as itself the sign of the latency which strikes the signifiable as soon as it is raised to the function of a signifier (. . .). It then becomes that which (. . .) bars the signified." (*Ecrits*, pp. 690–692.)

[46]Lewis Carroll, *Through the Looking-Glass*, VI.

master-reader) in two different ways: in clutching the helm, she *directs* the ship and thus apparently determines and controls its sense, its meaning; but at the same time, in the very gesture of directing, steering, she also masters meaning in the sense that she represses and limits it, striking out its other senses; in manipulating the rudder bar, she also, paradoxically, *bars* the signified. While the governess thus believes herself to be in a position of command and mastery, her *grasp* of the ship's helm (or of "the little Master" or of the screw she tightens) is in reality the grasp but of a *fetish*, but of a *simulacrum* of a signified, like the simulacrum of the mast in Flora's toy boat, erected only as a filler, as a stop-gap, designed to fill a hole, to close a gap. The screw, however, by the very gesture of its tightening, while seemingly filling the hole, in reality only makes it deeper.

> I was blind with victory, though even then *the effect that was to have brought him so much nearer* was already that of an *added separation*. (chap. 24, p. 87)

> The grasp with which I recovered him might have been that of catching him in his fall. I caught him, yes, I held him—it may be imagined with what a passion; but at the end of a minute I began to feel *what it truly was that I held*. We were alone with the quiet day, and his little heart, dispossessed, had stopped. (chap. 24, p. 88)

Even though, within this ultimate blind grip of comprehension, the "name" had been "surrendered" and meaning at last *grasped*, the governess's very satisfaction at the successful ending of the reading process is comprised by the radical frustration of a tragic loss: the embrace of meaning turns out to be but the embrace of death; the grasp of the signified turns out to be the grasp but of a corpse. The very enterprise of appropriating meaning is thus revealed to be the strict appropriation of precisely *nothing*—nothing alive, at least: "le démontage impie de la fiction et conséquemment du mécanisme littéraire," writes Mallarmé, "pour étaler la piece principale ou rien (. . .) le conscient manque chez nous de ce qui là-haut éclate."[47]

[47] "The impious dismantling of fiction and consequently of the literary mechanism as such in an effort to display the principal part or nothing, (. . .) the conscious lack(s) within us of what, above, bursts out and splits": Mallarmé, *La Musique et les lettres*, in *Oeuvres complètes* (Paris: Pléiade, 1945), p. 647; my translation.

Literature, suggests thus Mallarmé, like the letters of *The Turn of the Screw*, contains precisely "nothing"; fiction's mainspring is but "nothing," because consciousness in us is lacking, and cannot account for, "that which bursts." But what, precisely, bursts or splits, if not consciousness itself through the very fact that, possessing *nothing* (as it does in the end of *The Turn of the Screw*), it is dispossessed of its own mastery? What is it that bursts and splits if not consciousness itself to the extent that it remains estranged from that which splits, estranged, in other words, from its own split? When Miles dies, what is once again radically and unredeemably *divided*, is at once the unity of meaning and the unity of its possessor: the governess. The attempt to *master* meaning, which ought to lead to its *unification*, to the *elimination* of its contradictions and its "splits," can reach its goal only at the cost, through the infliction of a new wound, of an added split or distance, of an irreversible "separation." The seizure of the signifier creates an unrecoverable *loss*, a fundamental and irreparable *castration:* the tightened screw, the governed helm, bring about "the supreme surrender of the name," *surrender* meaning only by *cleaving* the very *power* of their holder. Meaning's *possession* is itself ironically transformed into the radical *dispossession* of its possessor. At its final, climactic point, the attempt at *grasping* meaning and at *closing* the reading process with a *definitive* interpretation in effect discovers—and comprehends—only death.

The Turn of the Screw could thus be read not only as a remarkable *ghost* story, but also as a no less remarkable *detective* story: the story of the discovery of a *corpse* and of a singularly redoubtable crime: *the murder of a child*. As in all detective stories, the crime is not uncovered until the end. But in contrast to the classical mystery novel plot, *this* crime is also not *committed* until the end: paradoxically enough, the process of detection here *precedes* the committing of the crime. As a *reader*, the governess plays the role of the detective: from the outset she tries to *detect*, by means of logical inferences and decisive "proofs," both the *nature of the crime* and the *identity of the criminal*.

> I remember (. . .) my thrill of joy at having brought on a *proof.* (chap. 20, p. 71)

> I was so determined to have all my *proof*, that I flashed into ice to challenge him. (chap. 24, p. 88)

It didn't last as *suspense*—it was superseded by horrible *proofs.* (chap. 6, p. 28)

Ironically enough, however, not knowing what the crime really consists of, the governess-detective finally ends up *committing it herself.* This unexpected and uncanny turn given by James's story to the conventions of the mystery novel is also, as it happens, the constitutive narrative peripeteia of one of the best known detective stories of all time: *Oedipus Rex.* In James's text as well as in Sophocles', the self-proclaimed detective ends up discovering that he himself is the author of the crime he is investigating: that the crime is his, that he is, himself, the criminal he seeks. "The interest of crime," writes James, in a discussion of modern mystery dramas, "is in the fact that it compromises the criminal's personal safety":

> The play is a tragedy, not in virtue of an avenging deity, but in virtue of a preventive system of law; not through the presence of a company of fairies, but through that of an admirable organization of police detectives. Of course, *the nearer the criminal and the detective are brought home to the reader, the more lively his "sensation."*[48]

The Turn of the Screw appears indeed to have carried this ideal of proximity or "nearness" (of the criminal and the detective to the reader) to its ultimate limits, since the criminal himself is here as *close* as possible to the detective, and the detective is only a detective in his (her) function *as a reader.* Incarnated in the governess, the detective and the criminal both are but dramatizations of the *condition of the reader.* Indeed, the governess as at once detective, criminal, and reader is here so intimately "brought home" to the reader that it is henceforth *our own* search for the mysterious "evil" or the hidden meaning of *The Turn of the Screw* that becomes, in effect, itself nothing other than a repetition of the crime. The reader of *The Turn of the Screw* is also the detective of a crime that in reality is his, and that "returns upon himself." For if it is by the very act of forcing her suspect to confess that the governess ends up committing the crime she is investigating, it is nothing other than the very *process of detection* that *constitutes the crime.* The detection process, or reading process, turns out to be, in other

[48]From a review of "Aurora Floyd," by M. E. Braddon, in *Norton,* p. 98.

words, nothing less than a peculiarly and uncannily effective *murder weapon*. The story of meaning as such (or of consciousness) thus turns out to be the uncanny story of the crime of its own detection.

Just as, in the end, the *detective* is revealed to be the *criminal*, the doctor-therapist, the would-be *analyst*, herself turns out to be but an analysand. *The Turn of the Screw* in fact deconstructs all these traditional oppositions; the exorcist and the possessed, the doctor and the patient, the sickness and the cure, the symptom and the proposed interpretation of the symptom, become here interchangeable, or at the very least, undecidable. Since the governess's "remedy" is itself a symptom, since the patient's "cure" is in effect his murder, nothing could indeed look more like *madness* than the very self-assurance of the project (of the notion) of *therapy* itself. There can be no doubt, indeed, that the ship is really drifting, that the governess is in command but of a "drunken boat." Sailing confidently towards shipwreck, the helm that the governess violently "grasps" and "clutches" is indeed the helm of a phantom ship.

DU FOND DU NAUFRAGE

(. . .)

LE MAITRE

(. . .)

jadis il empoignait la barre

(. . .)

hésite
cadavre par le bras

écarté du secret qu'il détient

(. . .)

Fiançailles

dont

le voile d'illusion rejailli leur hantise
ainsi que le fantôme d'un geste

chancellera
s'affalera
folie[49]

---

[49]FROM THE BOTTOM OF A SHIPWRECK / THE MASTER / formerly he gripped the helm / hesitates / a corpse by the arm / distanced from the secret he holds / Betrothal of which / the spewed forth veil of illusion their obsession / as the ghost of a gesture / will collapse / madness (Mallarmé, *Un Coup de dés*, in *Oeuvres complètes*, pp. 459–464; translation mine).

VIII. Meaning and Madness: The Turn of the Screw

> Les hommes sont si nécessairement fous que ce serait être fou par
> un autre tour de folie de n'être pas fou.
>
> > Pascal

> But this is exactly what we mean by operative irony. It implies
> and projects the possible other case.
>
> > H. James, Preface to "The Lesson of the Master"

The fundamental metaphor of the title—*The Turn of the Screw*—
has thus itself been given an unexpected turn of the screw: on the
sexual level, the seizure of the phallic signifier as a *master*-signifier—as the very fetish of plenitude and potency—amounts
to a void, to a castrating *loss* of potency; on the *cognitive* level, the
grasp of the signifier as a key to meaning—as the final proof that
everything *makes sense*—amounts to a loss of common sense, to
the interpreter's loss of his senses, and to the ultimate nonsense of
death. By the turn of the screw given to "the turn of the screw," the
delusory, self-evident metaphor of control (over the screw) turns out
to be an essential metaphor of loss—the loss, precisely, of control
over the *mechanical* functioning of a machine. The manipulator of
the screw, who believes himself to be in control of its successive
turns, in control of an enterprise of fixity and closure, discovers that,
in reality, he himself is nothing but a screw, a cog in the wheel of a
machine that runs by itself, automatically and repetitively.

> We had, all three, with *repetition*, got into such splendid training that
> we went, each time, *almost automatically*, to *mark the close* of the
> incident, *through the very same movements*. (chap. 13, p. 53)

The "incident," however, is never "closed," since the movement
of the screw constitutes in fact not a circle, but a spiral that never
closes: as a perfect illustration of the Freudian concept of the repetition compulsion, the spiral consists of a series of repeated cir-
clings in which what turns is indeed bound to *re-turn*,[50] but in

[50]Cf. chap. 13, p. 51: "All roads lead to Rome, and there were times when it might
have struck us that almost every (. . .) subject of conversation skirted forbidden

which what circularly thus returns only returns so as to *miss* anew its point of departure, to miss the closing point, the completion (or perfection) of the circle. The successive turns and returns of the spiral *never meet*, never touch or cross one another; hence, what the spiral actually *repeats* is a missed meeting with itself, a *missed encounter with what returns.* The screw, in order to precisely function properly, be operative, can by no means *close* the circle; it can but repeat it; it can but repeat the turn and repeat its own returns, and its own repetition of its turns, "through the very same movements."

No longer a *substantial* metaphor, the figure of a *substance* (which, like the phallic mast on Flora's boat, is designed to fill a hole, to be the central plenitude supporting and securing an enterprise of fixity), the turning screw turns out to be a *functional* metaphor, the figure of a dynamic *functioning:* it is not so much the screw itself that counts, as the very turning *movement* of its twists and whirls, and the very turns it at the same time marks and misses. It is, indeed, quite striking that the ghosts' appearances so very often have to do—in all senses of the word—with *turns:*

> . . . I could take a *turn into the grounds* and enjoy, almost with a sense of property (. . .), the beauty and dignity of the place. (. . .) One of the thoughts that (. . .) used to be with me (. . .) was that it would be(. . .) charming (. . .) suddenly to meet someone. Someone would appear there at the *turn of a path* (. . .). What arrested me on the spot (. . .) was the sense that my imagination had, in a flash, *turned real.* He did stand there (. . .) at the very top of the tower . . . (chap. 3, pp. 13–16)

> I sat reading (. . .). I found myself, at the *turn of a page* (. . .) looking (. . .) hard at the door of my room. (. . .) I went straight along the lobby (. . .) till I came within sight of the tall window that presided over the great *turn of the staircase.* (. . .) I require no lapse of seconds to stiffen myself for a third encounter with Quint. (chap. 9, pp. 40–41)

But what, in fact, is the significance of a *turn*, if not that of a *change*, precisely, of *direction*, the modification of an orientation,

---

ground. Forbidden ground was the question of the *return* of the dead. . ." Cf. also The New York Preface: "To bring the bad dead back to life for a *second round* of badness is to warrant them as indeed prodigious" (p. 122).

that is, both a *displacement* and a *choice of sense,* of meaning? And if indeed what is at stake in *The Turn of the Screw* is the question of *sense* in *all* its senses (meaning, sanity, direction), it is not surprising to discover that the text is organized as a veritable *topography of turns.* The screw, however, *turns in place:* the topography of turns and of circular returns is in reality but the tight enclosure of a labyrinth: "It was a *tighter place* still than I had yet *turned round in*" (chap. 22, p. 79). The labyrinth thus annihilates the value, or the meaning, of its turns: while a turn as such indicates *direction, sense,* the topographical economy of a labyrinth on the contrary implies the *loss* of all *sense of direction.* And the loss of the sense of direction is, or can be, indeed fatal: it is just such a state of disorientation that brings about, in fact, the very death of Peter Quint:

> Peter Quint was found (. . .) stone dead on the road from the village: a catastrophe explained (. . .) by a visible wound to his head; such a wound as might have been produced—and as, on the final evidence, *had** been—by a *fatal slip,* in the dark and after leaving the public house, on the steepish icy slope, *a wrong path altogether,* at the bottom of which he lay. The icy slope, *the turn mistaken* at night and in liquor, *accounted for much—practically, in the end* and after the inquest and boundless chatter, *for everything.* (chap. 6, p. 28; **James's italics; other italics mine)

If the "wrong path" or "the turn mistaken" can "account for much," or even, "in the end (. . .) for everything"—notably for the *accident of death*—could they not account equally "in the end" for the novel's *end,* for that other *accident of death of little Miles,* doubled as it is by a "second death" of Peter Quint, by the disappearance of the ghost? The parallel, in any case, is striking. The hypothetical, possible *madness* of the governess could then itself be accounted for "in the end" by a "turn mistaken," by a misguided choice of sense or of direction, indeed by nothing other than a fatal, deadly *reading mistake.* The semantic charge of the word "turn" itself in fact connotes the possible resonance of "an attack of madness" (cf. "turns of hysteria"), upon which the text occasionally seems to play. At the crucial moment when the governess is furiously accusing Flora of *seeing* Miss Jessel and of refusing to admit it, Mrs. Grose, who, like the girl, sees nothing, protests against the governess's accusation:

"What a dreadful turn, to be sure, Miss! Where on earth do you see anything?" (chap. 20, p. 72)

Does the word "turn" here mean "a turning point," "a change of meaning," "a turn of events," or "a turn of hysteria," "an attack of nervousness," "a fit," "a spell"? And if it means a turning point (a change of meaning), does it designate a simple *reorientation* or a radical *disorientation*, i.e., a delirious twist and *deviation?* Or does the "turn" name, precisely, the textual ironic figure of its own rhetorical capacity to *reverse itself,* to turn meaning into madness, to "project the possible other case" or other turn? Whatever the case, the metaphor of the "turn of the screw," in referring to a *turn*—or a twist—of sense, establishes an ironical equivalence between direction and deviation, between a turn of sense and a turn of madness, between the turn of an interpretation and the turning point beyond which interpretation becomes delirious. The governess herself is in fact quite aware of the possibility of madness, of her own madness, as the very risk involved in reading, as the other turn—the other side of the very coin of meaning:

> I began to watch them in a stifled suspense, a disguised excitement that might well, had it continued too long, have *turned to* something like *madness*. What saved me, as I now see, was that it *turned to* something else altogether (. . .) it was superseded by horrible proofs. Proofs, I say, yes—from the moment I really *took hold*. (chap. 6, p. 28)

To "take hold"—to seize the screw and tighten it once more so as to gain control of sense, of meaning—is thus conceived as a means of preserving and securing lucidity and sanity, as a gesture of protection against the threat of madness. The question of "taking hold" is often, in effect, associated with the very question of *equilibrium:*

> I had felt it again and again—how *my equilibrium depended on the success of my rigid will* (. . .). I could only get on at all (. . .) by treating my monstrous ordeal as a push in a direction unusual, of course, and unpleasant, but demanding, after all (. . .) only *another turn of the screw* of ordinary human virtue. (chap. 22, p. 80)[51]

---

[51]Cf. chap. 24, p. 88: "The grasp with which I recovered him might have been that of *catching him in his fall.* I caught him, yes, *I held him. . ."* and chap. 24, p. 85: ". . . the mere blind movement of *getting hold* of him (. . .) while I just *fell for support* against the nearest piece of furniture. . ."

The expression "turn of the screw" is, indeed, itself twice used explicitly in the text, in two entirely different contexts. The question thus arises whether, within their very differences, these two textual uses of the expression are nonetheless linked to each other in a revealing way. In the context just quoted, we have seen that the "turn of the screw" is directly linked to the question of *equilibrium*, of balance, and therefore also to the question of the loss of balance, of the loss of equilibrium, to the very possibility of *madness*; in the other context—that of the prologue—the expression "turn of the screw" is, on the other hand, used in relation to the question of the reception of the story, of the narrative's impact on its listeners (readers), of the tale's *reading-effect*. From one context to the other, from the story to its "frame," it is once again *reading* and *madness* that interact and confront each other through the differential repetition of the expression, "turn of the screw." But their interaction, this time, also implicates *us* as the story's readers, places *us* in the same boat as the governess, since the prologue's use of the expression "turn of the screw" names the "effect" produced precisely on its readers by the very story of *The Turn of the Screw*. Douglas, in this manner, introduces the story he is about to tell:

> "I quite agree—in regard to Griffin's ghost (. . .)—that its appearing first to the little boy, at so tender an age, adds a particular touch. But it's not the first occurrence of its charming kind that I know to have involved a child. If the child *gives the effect another turn of the screw*, what do you say to *two** children?"
>
> "We say, of course," somebody exclaimed, "that they give *two turns!*[52] Also that we want to hear about them." (Prologue, p. 1; *James's italics; other italics mine)

[52]If the presence of a child in a ghost story gives a "turn of the screw" to the effect of horror produced upon the reader, the presence of *two* children obviously does not, however, give that effect "*two* turns." The listener's response does not correspond to Douglas's intention in asking the question. The expression "to give a turn of the screw" is a cliché which as such produces meaning only as a reified *unit*, but cannot be divided into its component parts, is not susceptible to modification; it is thus impossible to say "to give two turns of the screw"—or at any rate to say it is to disrupt the cliché's ordinary meaning. As a stereotype signifying "a strengthening (of the effect)," the expression "to give a turn of the screw" is not mathematizable: like the act of turning the screw itself, the cliché lends itself not to *addition*, but to *repetition*; in order to indicate an *added strengthening*, it is only possible to *repeat* the *same* cliché: not "give *two* turns," but, as the governess and Douglas both put

In what way, however, does the turn of the screw given by the children to the story's reading-effect more specifically refer to the turn of the screw given by the governess to "ordinary human virtue"? Like the story's reader, dramatized in the frame by the listener who replies "two turns!" the governess is herself essentially a *reader*, engaged in an interpretative enterprise. Now, what the governess precisely tells us of the "turn of the screw of ordinary human virtue" is that this turn of the screw is designed to insure her very *equilibrium*. Her equilibrium indeed depends on the strength of her "rigid will," on her capacity to withstand "a push in a direction unusual" by tightening the screw, on her mastery of the screw's direction and of its meaning, on the strength and rigidity of her "hold": "ordinary human virtue," in other words, is nothing other than an enterprise of mastery, a *system of control over meaning*. But in what way does the governess's reading strategy relate to the position of the reader in the story's frame? How is this *hold* on meaning at the very heart of the story linked with the

---

it, "give *another* turn of the screw." The answer to Douglas's question can only *repeat* the terms of its formulation: "two children would indeed give the effect *another* turn of the screw." In this sense, Douglas's question is a *rhetorical* one—an *affirmation* which in truth does not ask nor call for an answer. In addition, if the effect of horror is linked to the presence of a child, the relation of effect to cause (of horror to child) is not *quantitative*, but *qualitative:* what produces the effect is not the *number* of children, but *childhood* as such. The number "two" used by Douglas is not meant as an enumeration, as a *quantitative* measure, but as a superlative, as a *qualitative* measure. Douglas's proposal to outdo the previous narrative constitutes not an *arithmetical* but a *rhetorical* outbidding. Douglas is tantalizing the hushed little circle with a better, more thrilling version of the *same* type of ghost story: the *two* children, in this sense, amount to the *same*.

The listener's interpretation (2 children = 2 turns) is thus a reading-mistake, an error of interpretation. The error lies in taking rhetoric as such (the rhetorical question as well as the rhetorical outbidding) *literally*.

In answering "two turns!" the reader thus produces a difference, or a split, in the text's very relation (or identity) to itself. Curiously enough, however, this *misreading*, this misguided suggestion that the story will have "two turns"—two different senses or directions—rejoins in fact precisely the fundamental *reality* of the text, the very *truth* of its duplicity and of its ambiguity. The text itself could thus say of its readers as the governess says of Miles: "horrible as it was, his lies made up my truth" (chap. 2, p. 84).

In including at its very outset its own misreading, in dramatizing its own rhetoricity as a potentiality for error which, however, effectively deconstructs the decidable polarity between truth and error, the very metaphor of "the turn of the screw," through the turn of the screw given to its meaning by its own enunciation, thus refers at once to a reading-effect and to a reading-mistake.

turn of the screw of its reading-effect? Does the turn of the screw of the reading-effect itself involve some kind of a *hold?*

Indeed, while the ending of the story recounts the way in which the governess-reader takes *hold* at once of meaning and of the child ("I caught him, yes, I *held* him"), the beginning of the story, in a strikingly parallel way, introduces in its very first sentence another type of hold implied by reading: *"The story had held us, round the fire, sufficiently breathless . . ."* (Prologue, p. 1). With respect to the hold defining the reading-enterprise ("another turn of the screw of ordinary human virtue"), the hold defining the reading-effect is thus reversed: while the governess as a reader strives to *get hold of the story*, the reading-effect is such that it is rather the story itself which *takes hold of its readers.* The reading-enterprise and the reading-effect turn out to be diametrically opposed: to *hold* the signifier (or the story's meaning) is in reality but to *be held* by it. This, then, is the final turn of the screw of the metaphor of the turn of the screw: the reader who tries to take hold of the text can but find himself taken in *by* it. As a performative (and not a cognitive) figure of the ironic textual force of reversal and of chiasmus, of the subversion of the subject by the very irony of language, the "turn of the screw"—or *The Turn of the Screw*— *acts out*, indeed, the very narrative—or tale—of reading, as precisely *the story of the subversion of the reader.* While the reader thus believes he holds and comprehends the story, it is in effect the story that holds and comprehends the reader. But what, precisely, is the story's hold on us? In what way are we at once held and comprehended by the story?

IX. The Madness of Interpretation: Literature and Psychoanalysis

> "Do you know what I think?"
> "It's exactly what I'm pressing you to make intelligible."
> "Well," said Mrs. Briss, "I think you are crazy."
> It naturally struck me. "Crazy?"
> "Crazy."
> I turned it over. "But do you call that intelligible?"
> She did it justice. "No; I don't suppose it *can* be so for you if you *are insane.*"

I risked the long laugh which might have seemed that of madness. " 'If I am' is lovely." And whether or not is was the special sound, in my ear, of my hilarity, I remember just wondering if perhaps I mightn't be.

H. James, The Sacred Fount

The indication that *The Turn of the Screw* is constructed as a *trap* designed to close upon the reader is in fact, as we saw earlier, explicitly stated by James himself:

> It is an excursion into chaos while remaining, like Blue-Beard and Cinderella, but an anecdote—though an anecdote amplified and highly emphasized and *returning upon itself*; as, for that matter, Cinderella and Blue-Beard return. I need scarcely add after this that it is a piece of ingenuity pure and simple, of cold artistic calculation, an *amusette** to catch those not easily caught (the "fun" of the *capture* of the merely witless being ever but small), the jaded, the disillusioned, the fastidious. (The New York Preface, *Norton*, p. 120; *James's italics; other italics mine)

What is interesting about this trap is that, while it points to the possibility of two alternative types of reading, it sets out, in capturing *both* types of readers, to eliminate the very demarcation it proposes.[53] The alternative type of reading which the trap at once elicits and suspends can be described as the *naïve* ("the capture of the merely witless") and the *sophisticated* ("to catch those not easily caught . . . the jaded, the disillusioned, the fastidious"). The trap, however, is specifically laid not for naïveté but for *intelligence* itself. But in what, indeed, does intelligence consist, if not in the determination to *avoid the trap?* "Those not easily caught" are precisely those who are *suspicious*, those who sniff out and detect a trap, those who refuse to be *duped:* "the disillusioned, the

---

[53]These two types of reading thus recall the illusory "two turns" which the mistaken reader in the frame attributes to the screw of the text's effect. (Cf. Prologue, p. 1, and, above, note 52.) But we have seen that the "two turns" in fact amount to the same: based on the symmetry implied by the "*two children*," the apparent *difference* between the "two turns" is purely *specular*. This is the final irony of the figure of the turn of the screw: while appearing to double and to multiply itself, the turn of the screw only *repeats* itself; while appearing to "turn," to *change* direction, sense, or meaning, the turning sense in fact does not change, since the screw *returns upon itself*. And it is precisely through such a "return upon itself" that the trap set by the text, says James, catches the reader.

jaded, the fastidious." In this sense the "naïve reading" would be one that would *lend credence* to the testimony and account of the governess, whereas the "disillusioned" reading would on the contrary be one that would suspect, demystify, "see through" the governess, one that, in fact, would function very much like the reading carried out by Wilson, who in effect opens his discussion by *warning* us precisely against a *trap* set by the text, a "trick of James's":

> A discussion of Henry James's ambiguity may appropriately begin with *The Turn of the Screw*. This story (. . .) perhaps *conceals another horror behind the ostensible one*. (. . .) It is a not infrequent *trick of James's* to introduce sinister characters with descriptions that at first sound flattering, so *this need not throw us off*. (*Wilson*, p. 102)

Since the trap set by James's text is meant precisely for "those not easily caught"—those who, in other words, watch out for, and seek to avoid, all traps—it can be said that *The Turn of the Screw*, which is designed to snare *all* readers, is a text particularly apt to catch the *psychoanalytic* reader, since the psychoanalytic reader is, *par excellence*, the reader who *would not be caught*, who would not be made a *dupe*. Would it be possible then to maintain that *literature*, in *The Turn of the Screw*, constitutes *a trap for psychoanalytical interpretation*?

Let us return, one last time, to Wilson's reading, which will be considered here not as a model "Freudian reading," but as the illustration of a prevalent tendency as well as an inherent temptation of psychoanalytical interpretation as it undertakes to provide an "explanation," or an "explication" of a literary text. In this regard, Wilson's later semi-retraction of his thesis is itself instructive: convinced by his detractors that for James the ghosts were real, that James's *conscious* project or intention was to write a simple ghost story and not a madness story, Wilson does not, however, give up his theory that the ghosts consist of the neurotic hallucinations of the governess, but concedes in a note:

> One is led to conclude that, in *The Turn of the Screw*, not merely is the governess self-deceived, but that James is self-deceived about her. (*Wilson*, note added 1948, p. 143)

This sentence can be seen as the epitome, and as the verbal formulation, of the desire underlying psychoanalytical interpretation:

the desire to be a *non-dupe*, to interpret, i.e., at once uncover and avoid, the very traps of the unconscious. James's text, however, is made of traps and dupery: in the first place, from an analytical perspective, the governess is *self-deceived;* duping us, she is equally herself a *dupe* of her own unconscious; in the second place, in Wilson's view, James himself is self-deceived: the author also is at once our duper and the dupe of his unconscious; the reader, in the third place, is in turn duped, deceived, by the very rhetoric of the text, by the author's "trick," by the ruse of his narrative technique that consists in presenting "cases of self-deception" "from their own point of view" (*Wilson*, p. 142). Following Wilson's suggestions, there seems to be only one exception to this circle of universal dupery and deception: the so-called Freudian literary critic himself. By avoiding the double trap set at once by the unconscious and by rhetoric, by remaining himself *exterior* to the reading-errors that delude and blind both characters and author, the critic thus becomes the sole agent and the exclusive mouthpiece of the *truth* of literature.

This way of thinking and this state of mind, however, strikingly resemble those of the governess herself, who is equally preoccupied by the desire, above all, not to be made a dupe, by the determination to avoid, detect, demystify, the cleverest of traps set for her credulity. Just as Wilson is distrustful of James's narrative technique, suspecting that its rhetoric involves a "trick," i.e., a strategy, a ruse, a wily game, the governess in turn is suspicious of the children's rhetoric: "'It's a game,' I went on, 'it's a policy and a fraud'" (chap. 12, p. 48). And just as Wilson, struck by the *ambiguity* of the text, concludes that the governess, in saying *less* than the truth, actually says *more* than she means—the governess herself, struck by the ambiguity of Mrs. Grose's speech, concludes in a parallel fashion that Mrs. Grose, in saying less than *all*, nonetheless says *more* than she intends to say:

. . . my impression of her having accidentally said more than she meant. . .

I don't know what there was in this brevity of Mrs. Grose's that struck me as ambiguous. (chap. 2, pp. 12–13)

I was (. . .) still haunted with the shadow of something she had not told me. (chap. 6, p. 27)

Like Wilson, the governess is *suspicious* of the ambiguity of signs and of their rhetorical reversibility; like Wilson, she thus proceeds to *read* the world around her, to *interpret* it, not by looking *at* it but by seeing *through* it, by demystifying and *reversing* the values of its outward signs. In each case, then, it is *suspicion* that gives rise as such to *interpretation*.

But isn't James's reader-trap, in fact, a *trap set for suspicion?*

> . . . an *amusette** to catch those not easily caught (. . .). Otherwise expressed, the study is of a conceived "tone," the tone of *suspected* and felt *trouble*, of an inordinate and incalculable sore—the tone of tragic, yet of exquisite, mystification. (New York Preface, *Norton*, p. 120; *James's italics; other italics mine)

The Turn of the Screw thus constitutes a trap for psychoanalytical interpretation to the extent that it constructs a trap, precisely, for suspicion. It has indeed been said of psychoanalysis itself that it is a veritable "school of suspicion."[54] But what, exactly, is suspicion? "Oran," reads the opening line of Camus' *The Plague*, "was a city without suspicion." Brought by "the Plague," suspicion will then signify, in this case, the awakening of consciousness itself through its mêlées with death, with fear, with suffering—the acquisition of a keen awareness of the imminence of a catastrophe of unknown origin, which has to be prevented, fought against, defeated. If it is thus the plague that brings about suspicion, it is well known, indeed, that Freud himself, at the historic moment of his arrival in the United States, said precisely that he had brought with him, ironically enough, "the plague" . . . Psychoanalysis, therefore, could very accurately be described as a "school of suspicion," a school that teaches an awareness of the Plague. What, however, is the alternative to suspicion? James's text can perhaps provide an answer. In the New York Preface, to begin with, the alternative to the suspicious reader was incarnated in the so-called "witless" reader ("the 'fun' of the capture of the merely witless being ever but small"); suspicion would thus seem to be equivalent to "wit," to the *intelligence* of the reader. In the text of *The Turn of the Screw* itself, moreover, the alternative to the suspicion of the governess is, symmetrically, the naïve *belief* of Mrs. Grose, who un-

---

[54]The formula is Paul Ricoeur's.

suspectingly lends credence to whatever the governess may choose
to tell her. And, as if the very name of Mrs. Grose were not a
sufficient clue to James's view of the attitude of *faith* that he thus
opposes to suspicion, the fact that Mrs. Grose *does not know how
to read* ("my counselor couldn't read!" chap. 2, p. 10) clearly suggests a parallel with the "witless" reader that the New York Preface in its turn opposes to the suspicious, unbelieving reader, the
one who is precisely difficult to catch. Psychoanalysis, therefore, is
strictly speaking a "school of suspicion" to the extent that it is, in
effect, a *school of reading*. Practiced by Wilson as well as by the
governess, but quite unknown to Mrs. Grose, "suspicion" is directed, first and foremost, toward the non-transparent, arbitrary
nature of the sign: it feeds on the discrepancy and distance that
separate the signifier from its signified. While suspicion constitutes, thereby, the very motive of the process of interpretation,
the very moving force behind the "wit" of the discriminating reader, we should not forget, however, that readers are here "caught" or
trapped, not *in spite of* but *by virtue of, because of* their intelligence and their sophistication. Suspicion is itself here part of the
mystification ("the tone of *suspected* and felt trouble . . . the tone
of tragic, yet of exquisite, *mystification*"): the alert, suspicious,
unduped reader is here just as "caught," as mystified, as the naïve
believer. Like faith (naïve or "witless" reading), suspicion (the intelligence of reading) is here a *trap*.

The trap, indeed, resides precisely in the way in which these two
opposing types of reading are themselves inscribed and comprehended in the text. The reader of *The Turn of the Screw* can
choose either to *believe* the governess, and thus to behave like
Mrs. Grose, or *not to believe the governess*, and thus to behave
precisely *like the governess*. Since it is the governess who, within
the text, plays the role of the suspicious reader, occupies the *place*
of the interpreter, to *suspect* that place and that position is, thereby, *to take it*. To demystify the governess is only possible on one
condition: the condition of *repeating* the governess's very gesture.
The text thus constitutes a reading of its two possible readings,
both of which, in the course of that reading, it deconstructs.
James's trap is then the simplest and the most sophisticated in the
world: the trap is but a text, that is, an invitation to the reader, a
simple invitation to undertake its reading. But in the case of *The
Turn of the Screw*, the invitation to undertake a reading of the text

is perforce an invitation to *repeat* the text, to enter into its labyrinth of mirrors, from which it is henceforth impossible to escape.

It is in just the same manner as the governess that Wilson, in his
reading, seeks to avoid above all being duped: to avoid, precisely,
being the governess's dupe. Blind to his own resemblance to the
governess, he repeats, indeed, one after the other, the procedures
and delusions of her reading strategy. "Observe," writes Wilson,
"from a Freudian point of view, the significance of the governess's
interest in the little girl's piece of wood" (*Wilson*, p. 104). But to
"observe" the *signified* behind the wooden *signifier*, to observe the
meaning, or the significance, of the very *interest* shown for that
signifier, is precisely what the governess herself does, and invites
others to do, when she runs crying for Mrs. Grose, "They know—
it's too monstrous: they know, they know!" (chap. 7, p. 30). In just
the same manner as the governess, Wilson equally *fetishizes* the
phallic simulacrum, delusively raises the mast in Flora's boat to
the status of Master-Signifier. Far from following the incessant
slippage, the unfixable movement of the signifying chain from link
to link, from signifier to signifier, the critic, like the governess,
seeks to *stop* the meaning, to *arrest* signification, by a grasp, precisely, of the Screw (or of the "clue"), by a firm hold on the Master-
Signifier:

> What if the hidden theme (. . .) is *simply sex* again? . . . the *clue of
> experience* . . . (*Wilson*, p. 115)
> When one has once *got hold of the clue to this meaning* of The Turn
> of the Screw, one wonders how one could ever have missed it.
> (*Wilson*, p. 108)

Sharing with the governess the illusion of having understood *all*, of
having *mastered* meaning by clutching at its clue, at its master-
signifier, Wilson could have said, *with* the governess and *like* her,
but *against* her: "I seemed to myself to have mastered it, to see it
all" (chap. 21, p. 78). In Wilson's case as in the governess's, the
move toward mastery, however, is an aggressive move, an "act of
violence," which involves a gesture of repression and of *exclusion*.
"Our manner of excluding," writes Maurice Blanchot, "is at work
precisely at the very moment we are priding ourselves on our gift
of universal comprehension." In their attempt to elaborate a
speech of mastery, a discourse of *totalitarian* power, what Wilson

and the governess both *exclude* is nothing other than the threatening power of rhetoric itself—of sexuality as *division* and as meaning's *flight*, as contradiction and as ambivalence; the very threat, in other words, of the unmastery, of the impotence, and of the unavoidable castration that inhere in *language*. From his very *grasp* of meaning and from the grasp of his interpretation, Wilson thus excludes, *represses*, the very thing that led to his analysis, the very subject of his study: the role of language in the text, "the ambiguity of Henry James":

> Henry James never seems aware of the amount of space he is wasting through the long abstract formulations that do duty for concrete details, the unnecessary circumlocutions and the gratuitous meaningless verbiage—the *as it were's* and *as we may say's* and all the rest—all the words with which he pads out his sentences and which themselves are probably symptomatic of a tendency to stave off his main problems. (*Wilson*, p. 129; Wilson's italics)

As Jean Starobinski puts it elsewhere, "The psychoanalyst, the expert on the rhetoric of the unconscious, does not himself wish to be a rhetorician. He plays the role that Jean Paulhan assigns to the terrorist as such: he demands that one speak in clear language."[55] In demanding that the text "speak in clear language," Wilson thus reveals the *terroristic status* of his psychoanalytic exegesis. But the governess as well demands "clear language": she terrorizes in effect the child into "surrendering the name," into giving, that is, to the ghost its *proper name*. Wilson's treatment of the text indeed corresponds point for point to the governess's treatment of the child: Wilson, too, forces as it were, the text to a *confession*. And what, in fact, is the main effort of the analytical interpreter as such, if not, at all events, to extort the *secret* of the text, to compel the language of the text—like that of the child—to confess or to avow: to avow its *meaning* as well as its *pleasure*; to avow its pleasure and its meaning to the precise extent that they are *unavowable*.

It is thus not insignificant for the text's subtle entrapment of its psychoanalytical interpretation that the governess ends up *killing the child*. Neither is it indifferent to the textual scene that the

[55]Jean Starobinski, *La Relation critique* (Paris: Gallimard, 1970), p. 271; my translation.

Latin word for child, *infans*, signifies precisely, "one incapable of speaking." For would it not be possible to maintain that Wilson, in pressing the text to confess, in forcing it to "surrender" its *proper name*, its explicit, literal meaning, himself in fact commits a *murder* (which once more brings up the question of *tact*), by suppressing within language the very silence that supports and underlies it, the silence *out of which* the text precisely speaks?

> . . . a stillness, a pause of all life, that had nothing to do with the more or less noise we at the moment might be engaged in making . . .
> (chap. 13, p. 53)

As the figure of a *knowledge which cannot know itself*, which cannot reflect upon nor name itself, the child in the story incarnates, as we have seen, *unconscious* knowledge. To "grasp" the child, therefore, as both the governess and Wilson do, to press him to the point of suffocating him, of killing or of stifling the silence within him, is to do nothing other than to submit, once more, the silent speech of the unconscious to the very gesture of its *repression*.

Here, then, is the crowning aberration that psychoanalysis sometimes unwittingly commits in its mêlées with literature. In seeking to "explain" and *master* literature, in refusing, that is, to become a *dupe* of literature, in killing within literature that which makes it literature—its reserve of silence, that which, within speech, is incapable of speaking, the literary silence of a discourse *ignorant of what it knows*—the psychoanalytic reading, ironically enough, turns out to be a reading that *represses the unconscious*, that represses, paradoxically, the unconscious it purports to be "explaining." To *master*, then (to become the Master), is, here as elsewhere, to *refuse to read* the letters; here as elsewhere, to "see it all" is in effect to "shut one's eyes as tight as possible to the truth"; once more, "to see it all" is in reality to *exclude*; and to exclude, specifically, the unconscious.

Thus repeated on all levels of the literary scene, by the governess as well as by her critics, in the story as well as in its reading, this basic gesture of repression, of exclusion, is often carried out under the auspices of a label which while naming that which is cast out, excluded, also at the same time sanctions the exclusion. That subtle label is the term "madness" used by the interpreter to mark what is repressed as indeed *foreclosed*, external to, shut out from, meaning. Wilson thus suggests that the governess is *mad*, i.e., that her point of view *excludes* her, and hence should be excluded, from the "truth" and from the meaning of her story. But the governess herself in her own reading, indeed, refers no less insistently to the question of insanity, of madness. She is preoccupied, as we have seen, by the alternative of madness and of sense as mutually exclusive; she is quite aware, in fact, that the possibility of her own madness is but the converse—the other side, the other turn—of her seizure and *control* of sense, of her "grasp" of and her firm "hold"[56] on meaning, a hold involving the *repression* of otherness as such, an exclusion of the Other. To "grasp," "get hold" of sense will therefore also be to *situate* madness—*outside*, to shut it out, to *locate* it—in the Other: to cast madness as such onto the other insofar as the Other in effect *eludes one's grasp.* The governess indeed maintains that the children are no less than *mad*;[57] when Mrs. Grose urges her to write to the Master about the children's strange behavior, the governess demurs:

> "By writing to him that his house is poisoned and his little nephew and niece *mad?*"
> "But if they *are*, Miss?"
> "And if I am myself, you mean? That's charming news to be sent him by a person (. . .) whose prime undertaking was to give him no worry." (chap. 12, pp. 49–50)

It is thus *either* the governess *or* the children who are mad: if the children are *not* mad, the governess could well be; if the children *are* mad, then the governess is truly in the right, as well as in her right mind. Hence, to *prove* that the children *are* mad (that they are *possessed* by the Other—by the ghosts) is to prove that the governess is *not* mad: to point to the madness of the Other is to

[56]Cf. chap. 6, p. 28: ". . . a suspense (. . .) that might well (. . .) have *turned* into *something like madness.* (. . .) It *turned* to *something else altogether* (. . .) from the moment I really *took hold.*" Cf. also chap. 12, p. 48: "I go on, I know, as if I am *crazy*, and it's a wonder I'm not. What I've seen would have made *you* so; but it only made me more lucid, made me *get hold* of still other things. . ."

[57]To begin with, she claims they are "possessed," that is, *unseizable*, possessed precisely *by the Other*: "Yes, *mad* as it seems! (. . .) They haven't been good—they've only been absent. (. . .) They're simply leading a life of their own. They're not mine—they're not ours. They're his and they're hers!" (chap. 12, pp. 48–49).

deny and to negate the very madness that might be lurking in the self. The Other's madness thus becomes a decisive proof and guarantee of one's own sanity:

> Miss Jessel stood before us (. . .). I remember (. . .) my thrill of joy at having brought on a *proof.* She was there, and I was justified; *she was there, so I was neither cruel nor mad.* (chap. 20, p. 71)

Thus, for the governess to be in *possession* of her *senses,* the *children* must be *possessed* and *mad.* The governess's very *sense,* in other words, is founded on the children's *madness.* Similarly but conversely, the story's very *sense,* as outlined by Wilson, by the *logic* of his reading, is also, paradoxically, *based on madness*—but this time on the madness of the *governess.* Wilson, in other words, treats the governess in exactly the same manner as the governess treats the children. It is the governess's madness, that is, the exclusion of her point of view, which enables Wilson's reading to function as a *whole,* as a system at once *integral* and *coherent*—just as it is the *children's* madness, the exclusion of *their* point of view, which permits the governess's reading, and its functioning as a *totalitarian* system.[58]

"It is not by locking up one's neighbor," as Dostoevsky once said, "that one can convince oneself of one's own soundness of mind." This, however, is what Wilson seems precisely to be doing, insofar as he is duplicating and *repeating* the governess's gesture. This, then, is what psychoanalytical interpretation might be doing, and indeed is doing whenever it gives in to the temptation of *diagnosing* literature, of indicating and of *situating madness* in a literary text. For in shutting madness up in literature, in attempting not just to explain the literary symptom, but to explain away the very symptom of literature itself, psychoanalysis, like the governess, only diagnoses literature so as to *justify itself,* to insure its own *control* of meaning, to deny or to negate the lurking possibility of its own madness, to convince itself of its own incontrovertible soundness of mind.

The paradoxical trap set by *The Turn of the Screw* is therefore such that it is precisely by proclaiming that the governess is mad

---

[58]Cf.: " 'It's a game,' I went on—'it's a policy and a fraud!' (. . .) 'Yes, *mad* as it seems!' The very act of bringing it out really helped me to trace it—follow it up and *piece it all together"* (chap. 12, pp. 48–49).

that Wilson inadvertently *imitates* the very madness he denounces, unwittingly *participates in it.* Whereas the diagnostic
gesture aims to situate the madness in the other and to disassoci-
ate oneself from it, to exclude the diagnosis from the diagnosed,
here, on the contrary, it is the very gesture of exclusion that includes: to exclude the governess—as mad—from the place of
meaning and of truth is precisely to repeat her very gesture of
exclusion, to *include oneself,* in other words, within her very madness. Unsuspectingly, Wilson himself indeed says as much when
he writes of another Jamesian tale: "The book is not merely mystifying, but maddening" (*Wilson,* p. 112).

Thus it is that *The Turn of the Screw* succeeds in *trapping* the
very analytical interpretation it in effect *invites* but whose authority it at the same time *deconstructs.* In inviting, in *seducing* the
psychoanalyst, in tempting him into the quicksand of its rhetoric,
literature, in truth, only invites him to *subvert himself,* only lures
psychoanalysis into its necessary self-subversion.

In the textual mechanism through which the roles of the governess and of the children become reversible, and in the text's tactical
action on its reader, through which the roles of the governess and
of her critic (her demystifier) become symmetrical and interchangeable—the textual dynamic, the rhetorical operation at work
consists precisely in the *subversion* of the *polarity* or the *alternative* that opposes as such analyst to patient, symptom to interpretation, delirium to its theory, psychoanalysis itself to madness. That psychoanalytical theory itself occupies precisely a
symmetrical, and hence a specular, position with respect to the
madness it observes and faces, is in fact a fundamental given of
psychoanalysis, acknowledged both by Freud and by Lacan. Lacan
as well as Freud recognize indeed that the very value—but equally
the risk—inherent in psychoanalysis, its insightfulness but equally its blindness, its truth but also its error, reside precisely in this
turn of the screw: "The discourse of the hysteric," writes Lacan,
"taught [Freud] this other substance which entirely consists in the
fact that such a thing as a signifier exists. In taking in the effect of
this signifier, within the hysteric's discourse, [Freud] was able to
give it that *quarter-turn* which was to turn it into analytical discourse" (*Encore,* p. 41). Freud, in turn, acknowledges a "striking
similarity" between his own psychoanalytical theory and the delirious ravings of President Schreber: "It remains for the future to

decide," writes Freud, "whether there is more delusion in my theory than I should like to admit, or whether there is more truth in Schreber's delusion than other people are as yet prepared to believe."[59]

It is doubtless no coincidence, therefore, that the myth of Oedipus—the psychoanalytical myth *par excellence*—should happen to recount not only the *drama of the symptom* but equally the very *drama of interpretation*. The tragedy of Oedipus is, after all, the story no less of the analyst than of the analysand: it is specifically, in fact, the story of the deconstruction, of the subversion of the polarity itself that distinguishes and opposes these two functions. The very *murder* that Oedipus commits is indeed constitutive in the story, just as much of the impasse of the interpreter as of the tragedy of the interpreted. For it is the murder which founds the rhetorical movement of substitution as a *blind* movement, leading blindly to the commutation, or to the switch between interpreter and interpreted: it is by murdering that the interpreter takes the place, precisely, of the symptom to be interpreted. Through the blind substitution in which Oedipus unwittingly takes the place of his victim, of the man he killed, he also, as interpreter (as the detective attempting to solve the crime), and equally unwittingly, comes to occupy the place and the position of the very *target* of the blow that he *addresses to the Other*. But Wilson also is precisely doing this, unknowingly assuming the position of the target, when he inadvertently repeats the gesture of the governess at whom he aims his blow, thereby taking her *place* in the textual structure.

It is through *murder* that Oedipus comes to be *master*. It is by *killing literary silence*, by stifling the very silence that inhabits literary language as such, that psychoanalysis *masters* literature, and that Wilson claims to *master* James's text. But Oedipus becomes master only to end up *blinding himself*. To blind oneself: the final gesture of a master, so as to delude himself with the impression that he still is in control, if only of his self-destruction, that he still can master his own blindness (whereas his blind condition in reality preexisted his self-inflicted blindness), that he still can master his own loss of mastery, his own castration (whereas he

[59]S. Freud, *Three Case Histories*, ed. Philip Rieff (New York: Collier Books, 1963), p. 182.

in reality *undergoes* it, everywhere, from without); to blind oneself, perhaps, then, less so as to punish, to humiliate oneself that so as to persist, precisely, in *not seeing*, so as to deny, once more, the very truth of one's castration, a castration existing outside Oedipus's gesture, by virtue of the fact that his conscious mastery, the mastery supported by his consciousness, finds itself subverted, by virtue of the fact that the person taken in by the trap of his detection is not the Other, but he himself—by virtue of the fact that he *is* the Other. And isn't this insistence on not seeing, on not knowing, precisely what describes as well the function of the Master in *The Turn of the Screw?* In its efforts to master literature, psychoanalysis—like Oedipus and like the Master—can thus but blind itself: blind itself in order to deny its own castration, in order not to see, and not to read, literature's subversion of the very possibility of psychoanalytical mastery. The irony is that, in the very act of judging literature from the height of its masterly position, psychoanalysis—like Wilson—in effect rejoins within the structure of the text the masterly position, the specific place of the Master of *The Turn of the Screw:* the place, precisely, of the textual *blind spot.*

Now, to occupy a blind spot is not only to be blind, but in particular, to be blind to one's own blindness; it is to be unaware of the fact that one occupies a spot *within* the very blindness one seeks to demystify, that one is *in* the madness, that one is always, necessarily, *in* literature; it is to believe that one is on the *outside*, that one *can* be outside: outside the traps of literature, of the unconscious, or of madness. James's reader-trap thus functions by precisely luring the reader into attempting to avoid the trap, into believing that there *is* an outside to the trap. This belief, of course, is itself one of the trap's most subtle mechanisms: the very act of trying to escape the trap is the proof that one is caught in it. "The unconscious," writes Lacan, "is most effectively misleading when it is caught in the act."[60] This, precisely, is what James suggests in *The Turn of the Screw.* And what James in effect *does* in *The Turn of the Screw*, what he undertakes through the performative action of his text, is precisely to mislead us, and to catch us, by on the contrary inviting us to *catch the unconscious in the act.* In attempting to escape the reading-error constitutive of rhetoric, in

---

[60]*Scilicet*, no. 1 (1968), 31 ("La Méprise du sujet supposé savoir").

attempting to escape the rhetorical error constitutive of literature, in attempting to master literature in order *not to be its dupe*, psychoanalysis, in reality, is *doubly duped:* unaware of its own inescapable participation *in* literature and *in* the errors and the traps of rhetoric, it is blind to the fact that it itself exemplifies no less than the *blind spot* of rhetoricity, the spot where any affirmation of mastery in effect amounts to a self-subversion and to a self-castration. *"Les non-dupes errent"* [non-dupes err], says Lacan. If James's text does not explicitly make such a statement, it enacts it, and acts it out, while also dramatizing at the same time the suggestion that this very sentence—which entraps us in the same way as does the "turn of the screw"—this very statement, which cannot be affirmed without thereby being negated, whose very diction is in fact its own contradiction, constitutes, precisely, the position *par excellence* of *meaning* in the *literary utterance:* a rhetorical position, implying a relation of mutual subversion and of radical, dynamic contradiction between utterance and statement.

The fact that literature has no outside, that there is no safe spot assuredly outside of madness, from which one might demystify and judge it, locate it in the Other without oneself participating in it, was indeed ceaselessly affirmed by Freud in the most revealing moments of his text (and in spite of the constant opposite temptation—the mastery temptation—to which he at other times inevitably succumbed). Speaking of *The Sandman* and of Nathanael's uncanny madness—a madness textually marked, in Hoffmann's rhetoric, by the metaphor of Nathanael's distorted vision, due to the glasses bought from the Sandman (from the optician Coppola) and through which Nathanael at times chooses to behold the world which surrounds him; glasses through which he looks, at any rate, before each of his attacks of madness and of his attempts at murder—Freud emphasizes the fact that the reader is rhetorically placed *within* the madness, that there is no place from which that madness can be judged *from the outside:*

> . . . We perceive that he [Hoffmann] means to *make us, too, look through the fell Coppola's glasses* (. . .)
> We know now that we are not supposed to be looking on at the products of a madman's imagination behind which we, with the superiority of rational minds, are able to detect the sober truth . . .[61]

[61]S. Freud, "The Uncanny," trans. Alix Strachey, in *Freud on Creativity and the Unconscious* (New York: Harper Torchbooks, 1958), p. 137.

In a parallel manner, *The Turn of the Screw* imposes the governess's distorted point of view upon us as the rhetorical *condition* of our perception of the story. In James's tale as in Hoffmann's, madness is uncanny, *unheimlich*, to the precise extent that it *cannot be situated*, coinciding, as it does, with the very space of reading. Wilson's error is to try to *situate* madness and thereby situate *himself outside it*—as though it were possible, *in* language, to *separate* oneself from language; as though readers, looking through the governess's madness and comprehended by it, could situate *themselves* within it or outside it with respect to it; as though readers could indeed know *where* they are, what their place is and what their position is with respect to the literary language which itself, as such, does not know what it knows. Thus it is that when, in another of James's novels, *The Sacred Fount*, the label "madness" is ironically applied to the narrator as the last word—the last judgment in the book, "You *are* crazy, and I bid you good night"[62]—the narrator, indeed, experiences this last word as the loss of his capacity to situate himself: "Such a last word," he remarks, "(. . .) put me altogether nowhere."[63]

"It's a game," says the governess of the behavior of the children that in her turn she claims to be "mad"—"It's a *game*, it's a *policy* and a *fraud*" (chap. 12, p. 48)— "It's all a mere mistake and a worry and a joke" (chap. 20, p. 72), answers, indirectly, Mrs. Grose, when she realizes that it is the governess who is mad, and that the children are but the victims of her delirium. The "mistake," the "worry" and the "joke," in Mrs. Grose's mouth, refer to, and affirm, the non-existence of the ghosts; they thus describe, accuse, excuse, the governess's madness. This ambiguous description of the error at the heart of *The Turn of the Screw* as at once tragic and comic, as both a "worry" and a "joke," is also implicit in James's statement in the New York Preface:

> The study is of a conceived "tone," the tone of suspected and felt trouble, of an inordinate and incalculable sore—*the tone of tragic, yet of exquisite, mystification.* (p. 120)

The mystification is indeed exquisitely sophisticated, since it *comprehends* its very *de-mystification*. Since Wilson's gesture re-

---

[62]H. James, *The Sacred Fount* (New York: Charles Scribner's Sons, 1901), p. 318.
[63]*Ibid.*, p. 319.

peats the governess's, since the critic here participates in the madness he denounces, the psychoanalytical (or critical) *demystification*, paradoxically enough, ends up reproducing the literary *mystification*. The very thrust of the mystification was, then, to make us believe that there is a radical difference and opposition between the turn of the screw of mystification and the turn of the screw of demystification. But here it is precisely literature's mystification that demystifies and catches the "demystifier," by actively, in turn, *mystifying him*. Thus, paradoxically enough, it is mystification that is here demystifying, while demystification itself turns out to be but mystifying. The demystifier can only err within his own mystification.

"We could well wonder," writes Lacan of Poe's *Purloined Letter* but in terms applicable equally to *The Turn of the Screw*, "whether it is not precisely the fact that *everyone is fooled* that constitutes here the source of our pleasure."[64] If the literary mystification is, in James's term, "exquisite," it is indeed because it constitutes a source of pleasure. The mystification is a game, a joke; to play is to be played; to comprehend mystification is to be comprehended *in* it; entering into the game, we ourselves become fair game for the very "joke" of *meaning*. The joke is that, by meaning, everyone is fooled. If the "joke" is nonetheless also a "worry," if, "exquisite" as it may be, mystification is also "tragic," it is because the "error" (the madness of the interpreter) is the error of life itself. "Life is the condition of knowledge," writes Nietzsche; "Error is the condition of life—I mean, ineradicable and fundamental error. The knowledge that one errs does not eliminate the error."[65]

X. A Ghost of a Master

> The whole point about the puzzle is its ultimate insolubility. How skillfully he managed it (. . .). The Master indeed.
>
> Louis D. Rubin, Jr., *One More Turn of the Screw*

> Note how masterly the telling is (. . .) still we must own that something remains unaccounted for.
>
> Virginia Woolf, *Henry James's Ghosts*

[64] J. Lacan, "Séminaire sur *La Lettre volée*," *Ecrits*, p. 17.
[65] F. Nietzsche, *The Will to Power*.

The postbag (. . .) contained a letter for me, which, however, in the hand of my employer, I found to be composed but of a few words enclosing another, addressed to himself, with a seal still unbroken. "This, I recognize, is from the head-master, and the head-master's an awful bore. Read him, please; deal with him; but mind you, don't report. Not a word. I'm off!"

H. James, *The Turn of the Screw*

Thus it is that within the space of a joke that is also a worry, within the space of a pleasure that is also a horror, Henry James, Master of ceremonies, himself takes pleasure in turning the screw, in tightening the spring of our interest:

That was my problem, so to speak, and my *gageure*—(. . .) to work my (. . .) *particular degree of pressure on the spring of interest.* (Preface to "The Golden Bowl," *AN*, p. 331)

—"You almost *killed* me,"

protests, in Mozart's opera *Don Giovanni*, the valet of Don Giovanni, Leporello;

—"Go on,—You are mad,
It was only a *joke*,"

replies his Master with a laugh. If the joke in *The Turn of the Screw* is equally a deadly, or a ghostly one, it is because the author—the master-craftsman who masters the "turns" of the game—has chosen indeed to *joke with death* itself. It is in his capacity as master of letters that James turns out to be a master of ghosts. Both ghosts and letters are, however, only "operative terms": the operative terms of the very movement of death within the signifier, of the capacity of *substitution* that founds literature as a paradoxical space of pleasure and of frustration, of disappointment and of elation:

What would the operative terms, in the given case, prove, under criticism, to have been—a series of *waiting satisfactions* or an array of *waiting misfits*? The misfits had but to be positive and concordant, in the special intenser light, to represent together (*as the two sides of a coin show different legends*) just so many *effective felicities* and *substitutes*. (. . .) Criticism after the fact was to find in them arrests

243

and surprises, emotions alike of disappointment and of elation: all of which means, obviously, that the whole thing was a *living** affair. (Preface to "The Golden Bowl," *AN*, pp. 341–342; *James's italics; other italics mine)

If death is but a joke, it is because death is, in a sense, as Georges Bataille has put it, "an imposture." Like the ghosts, death is precisely what cannot die: it is therefore of death, of ghosts, that one can literally say that they are "a *living* affair," an affair of the living, the affair, indeed, of living.

Master of letters and of ghosts alike, James, in contrast to his interpreters, lets himself become as much as possible a *dupe*, precisely, of their literality. It is as the dupe of the very letter of his text that James remains the Master, that he deflects all our critical assaults and baffles all our efforts to master him. He proclaims to know nothing at all about the content—or the meaning—of his own letter. Like the letters in the very story of *The Turn of the Screw*, his own letter, James insists, contains precisely *nothing*. His text, he claims, can, to the letter, be taken as

a poor pot-boiling *study of nothing* at all, *qui ne tire pas à consé-quence.** It is but a monument to my fatal technical passion, which prevents my ever giving up anything I have begun. So that when *something that I have supposed to be a subject turns out on trial to be none, je m'y acharne d'autant plus.** (Letter to Paul Bourget, August 19, 1898; *Norton*, p. 109; *James's italics; other italics mine)

As regards a presentation of things so fantastic as in that wanton little tale, I can only blush to see real substance read into them. (Letter to Dr. Waldstein, October 21, 1898; *Norton*, p. 110)

My values are positively all blanks save so far as an excited horror, a promoted pity, a created expertness (. . .) proceed to read into them more or less fantastic figures. (New York Preface, *Norton*, p. 123)

Master of his own fiction insofar as he, precisely, *is* its dupe, James, like the Master in *The Turn of the Screw*, doesn't want to *know* anything about it. In his turn, he refuses to read our letters, sending them back to us unopened:

I'm afraid I don't quite *understand* the principle question you put to me about "The Turn of the Screw." However, that scantily matters;

for in truth I am afraid (. . .) that I somehow can't pretend to give any coherent account of my small inventions "after the fact." (Letter to F. W. Myers, December 19, 1898, *Norton*, p. 112)

Thus it is that James's very mastery consists in the denial and in the deconstruction of his own mastery. Like the Master in his story with respect to the children and to Bly, James assumes the role of Master only through the act of claiming, with respect to his literary "property," the "license," as he puts it, "of disconnexion and disavowal" (Preface to "The Golden Bowl," *AN*, p. 348). Here as elsewhere, "mastery" turns out to be self-dispossession. Dispossessing himself of his own story, James, more subtly still, at the same time dispossessed his own story of its master. But isn't this precisely what the Master does in *The Turn of the Screw*, when, dispossessing the governess of her Master (himself), he gives her nothing less than "supreme authority"? Is it with "supreme authority" indeed that James, in deconstructing his own mastery, vests his reader. But isn't this gift of supreme authority bestowed upon the reader as upon the governess the very thing that will precisely *drive them mad?*

That one should, as an author, *reduce one's reader* (. . .) *to such a state of hallucination* by the images one has evoked (. . .)—nothing could better consort than that (. . .) with the desire or the pretension to cast a literary spell. (Preface to "The Golden Bowl," *AN*, p. 332)

It is because James's mastery consists in knowing that mastery as such is but a *fiction*, that James's law as master, like that of the Master of *The Turn of the Screw*, is a law of flight and of *escape*.[66] It is, however, through his escape, through his *disappearance* from the scene, that the Master in *The Turn of the Screw*, in effect, *becomes a ghost*. And indeed it could be said that James himself becomes a phantom master, a Master-Ghost *par excellence* in terms of his own definition of a ghost:

Very little appears to be [done]—by the persons appearing; (. . .) *This negative quantity is large—*(. . .). Recorded and attested "ghosts" are

---

[66]Cf. "Our noted behaviour at large may show for ragged, because it perpetually *escapes our control*; we have again and again to consent to its appearing in undress—that is, in no state to brook criticism." "It rests altogether with himself [the artist] not to (. . .) 'give away' his importances." (*AN*, p. 348.)

in other words (. . .), above all, *as little continuous and conscious and responsive,* as is consistent with their taking the trouble—and an immense trouble they find it, we gather—to appear at all. (The New York Preface, *Norton,* p. 121)

Now, to state that the Master has become himself a ghost is once again to repeat the very statement of *The Turn of the Screw:* there are *letters* from the moment there is no Master to receive them— or to *read* them: letters exist because a Master ceases to exist. We could indeed advance this statement as a definition of literature itself, a definition implicated and promoted by the practice of Henry James: literature (the very literality of letters) is nothing other than the Master's death, the Master's transformation into a ghost, insofar as that death and that transformation define and constitute, precisely, *literality* as such; literality as that which is essentially impermeable to analysis and to interpretation, that which necessarily remains unaccounted for, that which, with respect to what interpretation does account for, constitutes no less than *all the rest:* "All the rest is literature," writes Verlaine.[67] "The rest," says the dying artist in James's novel *The Middle Years,* "the rest is the madness of art": the *rest,* or literality, that which will forever make us *dupes* insofar as the very knowledge it conveys but cannot know, the knowledge which *our* knowledge cannot integrate, *dispossesses* us both of our mastery and of our Master. "That all texts see their literality increase," writes Lacan, "in proportion to what they properly imply of an actual confrontation with truth, is that for which Freud's discovery demonstrates the structural reason" (*Ecrits,* p. 364). To quote James again:

It's not that the muffled majesty of authorship doesn't here *ostensibly** reign; but I catch myself again shaking it off and disavowing the pretence of it while I get down into the arena and do my best to live and breathe and rub shoulders and converse with the persons engaged in the struggle that provides for the others in the circling tiers the entertainment of the great game. There is no other participant, of course, than each of the real, the deeply involved and immersed and more or less bleeding participants. (Preface to "The Golden Bowl," *AN,* p. 328; *James's italics)

[67]"Il faut aussi que tu n'ailles point / Choisir tes mots sans quelque méprise / Rien de plus cher que la chanson grise / Où l'Indécis au Précis se joint / (. . .) Et tout le reste est littérature." (P. Verlaine, *Art poétique.*)

The deeply involved and immersed and more or less bleeding participants are here indeed none other than the members of the "circle round the fire" which we ourselves have joined. As the fire within the letter is reflected on our faces, we see the very madness of our own art staring back at us. In thus mystifying us so as to demystify our errors and our madness, it is we ourselves that James makes laugh—and bleed. The joke is indeed on us; the worry, ours.

AFTERTHOUGHTS

8

Madness and the Literary: Toward the Question of the Book

In what way does madness account for the thing called literature? Why madness? Could I not just as well have said the "reason" of the text? What, finally, was at issue here, *texts about madness* or *the very madness of the text?*

This book has attempted precisely to examine the *relation* between the two: to think about what "speaking about madness" means by exploring the relationship between the texts of madness and the madness of texts. I have tried to show some of the ways in which the rhetoric of madness and the madness of rhetoric in effect do meet and act upon each other, and not simply through a play on words.

What we find in these texts on a first reading is the thematization of a certain discourse about madness, which, mobilizing all the linguistic resonances of eloquence, asserts madness as the meaning, the *statement* of the text. This is what is called in this book the "rhetoric of madness." Now, whether this discourse about madness is a way of saying "I"—the cry of the subject who, considering himself as "mad," thereby claims to be exceptional (the narrator of *Memoirs of a Madman*)—or a way of saying "(s)he," of acting out a diagnosis which, projecting madness outside, *locates* it in *the Other* (Wilson explaining the madness of the governess, the governess asserting the madness of the children), the rhetoric of madness always turns out to be mystified and mystifying. *To talk about madness* is always, in fact, *to deny it*. However one represents madness to oneself or others, to represent madness is always, consciously or unconsciously, to play out the *scene* of the denial of *one's own* madness.

But even though the discourse *on* madness is not a discourse *of* madness (is not strictly speaking a mad discourse), nevertheless there still exists in these texts a *madness that speaks*, a madness that is acted out in language, but whose role no speaking subject can assume. It is this movement of non-totalizable, ungovernable linguistic play, through which meaning misfires and the text's *statement* is estranged from its *performance*, that I call in this book the "madness of rhetoric."

Paradoxically, then, the madness of rhetoric is precisely what *subverts* the rhetoric of madness. It is at the very point where the mystified pathos of the subject and the false scientific neutrality of the exclusion of the Other are both subverted, at the very point where the rhetoric of madness is undermined, that the madness (rhetoricity) of the text is situated. If the rhetoric of madness is a rhetoric of denial, denial is itself inhabited by the madness it denies.

Madness, in other words, is what a speaking subject can neither simply deny nor simply affirm or assume.

It is somewhere *between* their affirmation and their denial of madness that these texts about madness *act*, and that they act themselves out as madness, i.e., as *unrepresentable*. It is somewhere between their literary rhetoric of madness and the madness of their literary rhetoric that these texts, in *speaking about* madness, in effect *enact* their madness, enact the *encounter* between "speaking about madness" and the "madness that speaks." If the texts about madness are not conscious (are not *present to*) their own madness, it is because they are, paradoxically, the very madness they are speaking about.

*   *   *

But, madness in what sense? one might ask. What, in the end, does madness really mean in this book? What is the rhetorical status of the term "madness" in my own critical and theoretical discourse? Is madness used here in its literal sense or is it simply a metaphor?

23086000051856

' 1996

15 NOV 1996

CE ***
ed by another member of the
due date.   Thank you.
****

:ion; a history   001631696   01 MAY 97
rate is $1.00 a day.

Carlota Caulfield
FOREIGN LANGUAGES DPT.
MILLS COLLEGE
Oakland, CA 94613

14

*** RECALL N

The following item(s) have been rec
Mills Community. Please return by
****

BNF 616.89 F762m Madness and civil
New duedate is 21 NOV 96, Recall fi

The texts studied in this book do not permit a simple, unambiguous answer to that question. Whether they discuss psychosis, neurosis, or simply the stereotypical, stylistic usage of the term "madness," the texts about madness baffle our preconceived notions about the rhetorical status of the madness they both express and put in question. As this book draws to a close, I would like to open up the following question: Might it not be possible to define the very specificity of literature as that which *suspends the answer* to the question of knowing whether the madness literature speaks of is literal or figurative? The specific property of the thing called literature is such, in other words, that the rhetorical status of its madness can no longer be determined.

* * *

To put it differently, I would like to suggest that literature's particular way of speaking about madness consists in its unsettling the boundary, not only between *symptom* and *metaphor*, between "the madness that gets locked up" and "the hallucination of words," but, more specifically and more strangely, *between psychosis and stereotype,* between the madness of *Aurélia* and the madness of *Memoirs of a Madman.* The uncanny quality of what literature conveys resides in the uncanniness of this encounter, this linking effected by the signifier "madness" between the functioning of cliché and the functioning of psychosis.

It is doubtless no coincidence that Jacques Lacan, studying the writings of psychotics that at first appeared to be "inspired," identifies as their salient feature what he calls their "stereotypy," their "automatism": "Nothing is in fact less inspired," he writes, "than these writings experienced as inspired." In this strictly clinical study, Lacan brings to light the central role of rhythm in psychotic writing: "Conceptual formulations (. . .) have no more importance than do the interchangeable words in a rhyming song. Far from motivating the melody, the words are rather sustained by it (. . .). In these writings, only the rhythmic formula is given, a formula which remains to be filled in by ideational content."[1]

Now literature also, through the very topos of madness, points toward a complicity between the signs of inspiration and the signs

[1]Annales médico-psychologiques, 1931.

of automatism. It seems to me that, if only we knew how to listen, literature might have something entirely new to say about *rhythm* and about *the enigma of the very meaning of automatism.* The unsuspected knowledge underlying literature's uncanny linkage of psychosis and of stereotype constitutes, perhaps, the question of the future: the question that literature, from its unique position, invites us to ask and that, from its unique position, it addresses *to* psychiatry, psychoanalysis, biology, and linguistics.

*   *   *

If literature, from its unique position, has something to teach us about madness, can madness in turn teach us something about literature? It seems to me that if something like literature exists, only madness can explain it. But if, as in my view, it is madness that accounts for the thing called literature, this is not, as some have thought, by virtue of a "sublimation" or a properly therapeutic function of writing, but rather by virtue of the dynamic *resistance to interpretation* inherent in the literary thing. In the end, madness in this book can be defined as nothing other than an irreducible resistance to interpretation.

Madness, in other words (like literature), consists neither in *sense* nor in *non-sense:* it is not a final *signified*—however missing or disseminated—nor an ultimate *signifier* that resists exhaustive deciphering; it is rather, I would suggest, a kind of *rhythm;* a rhythm that is unpredictable, incalculable, unsayable, but that is nonetheless fundamentally narratable as the story of the slippage of a reading *between* the excessive fullness and the excessive emptiness of meaning.

Every reading is a narration whose rhythm is determined by the rhetoric of what it fails to say about its relation to the text and to the madness of the text.

The final theoretical proposition to emerge from this book's analysis is thus the following:

The more a text is "mad"—the more, in other words, it resists interpretation—the more the specific modes of its resistance to reading constitute its "subject" and its literariness. What literature recounts in each text is precisely *the specificity of its resistance to our reading.*

That, at any rate, is the way I view today the relation between literature and madness. Such is, at the very least, the story of my reading, the narrative that, in its rhythm and its rhetoric, its theories and its resistances, I would like to offer as a question—as a *sign*—to an interpretant to come.